Praise for *The Good Ancestor*

'A great antidote to the short-term thinking that comes easily
to us all. If you want to be a good ancestor, start by reading this book'
Nigel Warburton, author of *A Little History of Philosophy*

'I judge a book's usefulness by how many pages I'm compelled
to dog-ear and underline. This book on the pragmatics of
long-term thinking earned 50-plus dog-ears'
Stewart Brand, creator of the *Whole Earth Catalog* and
co-founder of the Long Now Foundation

'An important and fascinating book that asks whether we've got
what it takes to become citizens rather than consumers and create
an ecological civilisation. *The Good Ancestor* is a triumph'
Sir Tim Smit, co-founder of the Eden Project

'How timely can a book be? Roman Krznaric fizzes with
ideas about how we tackle that cuckoo in the nest, short-term
thinking. We need to think today for tomorrow, to give
future generations their rightful seat at the table'
Lord John Bird MBE, founder of *The Big Issue*

'Krznaric's seamless and magical prose delights on every
page. Let's engrave his "six ways to think long" across the
gateway to every Parliament in the world'
Professor Tim Jackson, author of *Prosperity Without Growth*

'There could be few more urgent tasks for any thinking person alive
today than encountering this book. Read it: with slow deliberate care . . .'
Professor Rupert Read, UEA, author of *This Civilisation Is Finished*
and Extinction Rebellion Political Liaison and Spokesperson

'From the seventh-generation thinking of Native American tribes to
legally empowered guardians of the future and citizens' assemblies,
Krznaric explores a wealth of ways we can become good ancestors.
For anyone who is interested in how we can get today's society to
leave the world better than they found it – this is your guide'
Sophie Howe, Future Generations Commissioner for Wales

'Krznaric asks the defining moral question for our age: how will future generations look back on our legacy? A superb intellectual history and razor-sharp analysis of contemporary politics, this book will change how you think about the world and is a call to action. Read it. You owe it to your children's children'
Kevin Watkins, Chief Executive of Save the Children

'In this persuasive book, one of our leading thinkers Roman Krznaric expands his ground-breaking work on empathy to argue that our only hope of survival is to develop deep empathy for future generations across time and space'
Professor Morten Kringelbach, neuroscientist, Universities of Oxford and Aarhus, Denmark

'With a dazzling range of sources, zinging with ideas, stories and jaw-dropping graphics, *The Good Ancestor* is packed with information and insight. Every school should have a copy, with its maps and plans on every classroom wall'
Michael Wood, historian, broadcaster and author of *The Story of China*

'A fascinating and inspiring exploration of one of the great relationship questions of the 21st century: how can we extend our circle of care to future generations?'
John Gray, *New York Times* bestselling author of *Men Are from Mars, Women Are from Venus*

'Roman Krznaric passionately argues that thinking long term would bring untold benefits and may very well be vital to our survival as a species. Lose yourself in these pages, expand your time horizons, and reimagine your relationship to time, to the future, to activism'
Rob Hopkins, founder of the Transition Town movement and author of *From What Is to What If*

The Good Ancestor

HOW TO THINK LONG TERM IN A SHORT-TERM WORLD

Roman Krznaric

WH
ALLEN

1 3 5 7 9 10 8 6 4 2

Published in 2020 by WH Allen, an imprint of Ebury Publishing,
20 Vauxhall Bridge Road,
London SW1V 2SA

WH Allen is part of the Penguin Random House group of companies
whose addresses can be found at global.penguinrandomhouse.com

Extract from 'Hieroglyphic Stairway' by Drew Dellinger, reprinted by
permission of the author. Quote attributed to Jonas Salk used with permission of
the Jonas Salk Legacy Foundation and the family of Jonas Salk.

First published by WH Allen in 2020

www.penguin.co.uk

A CIP catalogue record for this book is available from the British Library

Hardback ISBN 9780753554494
Trade Paperback ISBN 9780753554500

Typeset in 11.25/16 pt Sabon Next LT Pro by Jouve UK, Milton Keynes
Printed and bound in Great Britain by Clays Ltd, Elcograf S.p.A.

Penguin Random House is committed to a sustainable future
for our business, our readers and our planet. This book is made
from Forest Stewardship Council® certified paper.

The most important question we must ask ourselves is,
'Are we being good ancestors?'

Jonas Salk

it's 3:23 in the morning
and I can't sleep
because my great great grandchildren
ask me in dreams
what did you do while the earth was unravelling?

Drew Dellinger

Contents

11

Cultural Evolution

12

The Path of the Good Ancestor

Appendix

The Intergenerational Solidarity Index

Preface

Coronavirus (COVID-19) spread worldwide just as this book was going to press. The pandemic has understandably focused our attention on the here and now, with families, communities, businesses and governments acting to confront the fierce urgency of the crisis. In the midst of such an immediate threat, what insights does long-term thinking offer?

Most obviously, those countries that had already made long-term preparations for possible pandemics have so far been able to deal with the virus most effectively: while Taiwan had virus testing and tracing mechanisms in place following its experience of the 2003 SARS outbreak, the US response was hampered by having disbanded the National Security Council's pandemic unit in 2018. At the same time, the catastrophic impacts of coronavirus are a stark reminder that we should be thinking, planning and budgeting for multiple risks that lie on the horizon – not only the threat of further pandemics, but the climate crisis and unchecked technological developments.

Humanity's response to the virus will clearly have long-term consequences that ripple into the decades ahead. Many governments may try to cling on to the emergency powers they have granted themselves – such as heightened citizen surveillance – leaving an authoritarian residue that undermines new democratic possibilities. On the other hand, the rupture that the pandemic has caused may open space for a fundamental rethink of our politics, economies and lifestyles. Just as pioneering long-term institutions such as welfare states and the World Health Organization emerged from the ashes of the Second World War, so too could coronavirus trigger the long-term thinking now needed to challenge the dangers of short-termism, and build resilience in the face of a very uncertain future.

By making wise – and long – choices at this time of crisis, we could well become the good ancestors that future generations deserve.

Oxford, March 2020

PART ONE

THE TUG OF WAR FOR TIME

1

How Can We Be Good Ancestors?

We are the inheritors of gifts from the past. Consider the immense legacy left by our ancestors: those who sowed the first seeds in Mesopotamia 10,000 years ago, who cleared the land, built the waterways and founded the cities where we now live, who made the scientific discoveries, won the political struggles and created the great works of art that have been passed down to us. We seldom stop to think about how they have transformed our lives. Most of their names have been forgotten by history, but among those who are remembered is the medical researcher Jonas Salk.

In 1955, after nearly a decade of painstaking experiments, Salk and his team developed the first successful and safe polio vaccine. It was an extraordinary breakthrough; at the time, polio paralysed or killed over half a million people worldwide each year. Salk was immediately hailed as a miracle worker. But he was not interested in fame and fortune – he never sought to have the vaccine patented. His ambition was to 'be of some help to humankind' and to leave a positive legacy for future generations. There's no doubt he succeeded.

In later years, Salk expressed his philosophy of life in a single question: 'Are we being good ancestors?'[1] He believed that just as we have inherited so many riches from the past, we must also pass them on to our descendants. He was convinced that in order to do so – and to confront global crises such as humanity's destruction of the natural world and the threat of nuclear war – we needed a radical shift in our temporal perspective towards one far more focused on long-term thinking and the consequences of our actions beyond our own lifetimes. Rather than thinking on a scale of seconds, days and months, we should extend our time horizons to encompass decades, centuries and millennia. Only then would we be able to truly respect and honour the generations to come.

Salk's question may turn out to be his greatest contribution to history. Rendered in a more active form – 'How can we be good ancestors?' – I consider it the most important question of our time, and one that offers hope for the evolution of human civilisation. The challenge of answering it has inspired this book, but also haunts its pages. It calls on us to consider how we will be judged by future generations, and whether we will leave a legacy that benefits or cripples them. The old biblical aspiration to be a Good Samaritan is no longer enough. It's time for a twenty-first-century update: to be a Good Ancestor.

The Future Has Been Colonised

Becoming a good ancestor is a formidable task. Our chances of doing so will be determined by the outcome of a struggle for the human mind currently taking place on a global scale between the opposing forces of short-term and long-term thinking.

At this moment in history the dominant force is clear: we live in an age of pathological short-termism. Politicians can barely see beyond the next election or the latest opinion poll or tweet. Businesses are slaves to the next quarterly report and the constant demand to ratchet up shareholder value. Markets spike then crash in speculative bubbles driven by millisecond-speed algorithms. Nations bicker around international conference tables, focused on their near-term interests, while the planet burns and species disappear. Our culture of instant gratification makes us overdose on fast food, rapid-fire texting and the 'Buy Now' button. 'The great irony of our time,' writes the anthropologist Mary Catherine Bateson, 'is that even as we are living longer, we are thinking shorter.'[2] This is the age of the tyranny of the now.

Short-term thinking is hardly a new phenomenon. History is littered with examples, from Japan's reckless destruction of its old-growth forests in the seventeenth century to the runaway speculation that led to the Wall Street Crash in 1929. Nor is it always a bad thing: just as a parent might suddenly need to rush an injured child to hospital, a government needs to respond rapidly and with agility to crises like an earthquake or epidemic. But scan the daily news and you will see multiple instances of harmful short-termism.[3] Governments preferring the quick fix of putting more criminals behind bars rather than dealing with the deeper social and economic causes of crime. Or continuing to subsidise the coal industry instead of supporting the transition to renewable energy. Or bailing out insolvent banks after a crash rather than restructuring the financial system. Or failing to invest in preventative health care, child poverty and public housing. Or – the list goes on and on.

The dangers of short-termism go far beyond these areas of public policy and have now brought us to a crisis point. This is due, firstly, to the growing prospect of what is known as 'existential risk', which typically refers to low-probability but high-impact events that could be caused by new technologies. High on the list are threats from artificial intelligence systems, such as lethal autonomous weapons that cannot be controlled by their human makers. Other possibilities include genetically engineered pandemics or a nuclear war triggered by a rogue state in an era of increasing geopolitical instability. Risk scholar Nick Bostrom is particularly concerned about the future impact of molecular nanotechnology and worries that terrorists might get hold of self-replicating, bacterium-scale nanobots that get out of control and poison the atmosphere. In the face of these threats, many existential risk experts believe that there is around a one-in-six chance that humanity will not make it to the end of the century without catastrophic loss of life.[4]

Just as serious is the possibility of civilisational breakdown due to our relentless destruction of the ecological systems on which our well-being – and life itself – depends. As we keep thoughtlessly pumping out fossil fuels, poisoning our oceans and destroying species at a rate that amounts to a 'sixth extinction', the prospect of devastating impacts gets ever closer. In our hyper-networked age, this threat now exists on a worldwide scale: we have no Planet B to run to. According to environmental historian Jared Diamond, such ecological destruction has been at the root of civilisational collapse throughout human history. Its major underlying cause, he argues, is an overdose of 'short-term decision-making' coupled with an absence of 'courageous long-term thinking'.[5] We have been warned.

These challenges confront us with the inescapable paradox that the need for long-term thinking is a matter of utmost urgency, requiring immediate action in the present. 'Right now we are facing a man-made disaster of global scale, our greatest threat in thousands of years: climate change,' David Attenborough told world leaders at UN climate talks in 2018. 'If we don't take action, the collapse of our civilisations and the extinction of much of the natural world is on the horizon.' According to the naturalist, 'What happens now, and in these next few years, will profoundly affect the next few thousand years.'[6]

Such statements should put us on red alert. But they often fail to convey who exactly will bear the consequences of our temporal myopia. The answer is not just our own children and grandchildren, but the billions of human beings who will be born in the centuries ahead, and who far outnumber everyone alive today.

The moment has come, especially for those living in wealthy nations, to recognise a disturbing truth: that we have colonised the future. We treat the future like a distant colonial outpost devoid of

people, where we can freely dump ecological degradation, technological risk and nuclear waste, and which we can plunder as we
please. When Britain colonised Australia in the eighteenth and nineteenth centuries, it drew on a legal doctrine now known as *terra
nullius* – 'nobody's land' – to justify its conquest and treat the indigenous population as if they didn't exist or have any claims on the
land.[7] Today our societal attitude is one of *tempus nullius*: the future
is seen as 'nobody's time', an unclaimed territory that is similarly
devoid of inhabitants. Like the distant realms of empire, it is ours for
the taking. Just as indigenous Australians still struggle against the
legacy of *terra nullius*, so too there is a struggle to be had against the
doctrine of *tempus nullius*.

The tragedy is that the unborn generations of tomorrow can do
nothing about this colonialist pillaging of their futures. They cannot
throw themselves in front of the king's horse like a suffragette, block
an Alabama bridge like a civil rights activist or go on a Salt March to
defy their colonial oppressors like Mahatma Gandhi. They are granted
no political rights or representation, they have no influence at the ballot box or in the market. The great silent majority of future generations
is rendered powerless and airbrushed out of our minds.

The Conceptual Emergency of Long-Term Thinking

This is not the end of the human story. We are at a potential pivot
point in history, with multiple forces beginning to coalesce into a
global movement intent on liberating us from our addiction to the
present tense and forging a new era of long-term thinking.

Its advocates include urban designers and climate scientists, hospital doctors and tech CEOs, who are starting to recognise that a
blinkered short-termism lies at the root of many of today's crises – the
threat of ecosystem collapse, the risks of automation, the rise of mass

global migration, widening wealth inequality – and that the obvious antidote is more long-term thinking. Al Gore argues that 'governing institutions have been suborned by vested interests obsessed with short-term gain rather than long-term sustainability.' Astrophysicist Martin Rees is concerned that there is 'too little planning, too little horizon-scanning, too little awareness of long-term risks' and suggests that we should learn from China about long-range policymaking.[8] The former Facebook executive Chamath Palihapitiya has admitted that 'the short-term, dopamine-driven feedback loops that we have created are destroying how society works', while the chief economist of the Bank of England has openly criticised the 'rising tide of myopia' in capital markets and corporate behaviour.[9] At the same time, there is an emerging international consensus that the lives of future people should not be side-lined in today's moral deliberations and policy decisions. Over the past 25 years, more than 200 UN resolutions have explicitly mentioned the welfare of 'future generations', while Pope Francis has proclaimed that 'intergenerational solidarity is not optional, but a basic question of justice'.[10]

This growing public belief in the importance of long-term thinking as a civilisational priority is unprecedented. Yet far more impressive than such an abundance of fine words has been an explosion of practical projects and initiatives dedicated to turning it into a reality. The Svalbard Global Seed Vault, built inside a rock bunker in the remote Arctic, aims to keep over a million seeds from 6,000 species secure for at least a thousand years. There are novel political structures, such as the Future Generations Commissioner in Wales and the UAE's Ministry of Cabinet Affairs and the Future. These have been accompanied by youth activism, including the Plant-for-the-Planet campaign started in 2007 by a nine-year-old German boy, Felix Finkbeiner, which has resulted in tens of millions of trees being planted in 130 countries. In the creative arts, musician Jem Finer's composition 'Longplayer' began playing in a London lighthouse at midnight on 31 December 1999, and will play without repetition for a millennium.

Long-term thinking appears to be gaining traction, but there is a problem. Although it can be found in pockets of the science and arts communities, and among some far-sighted businesses and political activists, it still exists on the margins, not only in Europe and North America, but also in the world's emerging powerhouse economies. It has failed – so far – to penetrate deep into the mental structures of the modern mind, which continues to be trapped by the straitjacket of short-termism.

Moreover, as a concept long-term thinking is strikingly undeveloped. I have found myself in countless conversations where it is offered as a solution to our planetary ills but nobody can really explain what it is. The phrase might yield nearly a million hits in an online search, but it is rarely accompanied by a clear sense of what it means, how it works, what time horizons are involved and what steps we must take to make it the norm. While public figures like Al Gore might champion its virtues, it remains abstract, formless, a panacea without principles or a programme. This intellectual vacuum amounts to nothing less than a conceptual emergency.[11]

If we aspire to be good ancestors then our first task is to fill this vacuum. This book attempts to do so by offering a set of six visionary and practical ways to cultivate long-term thinking. Together they provide an essential mental toolkit for challenging our obsession with the here and now.

My focus on these six ways is based on a deep conviction that ideas matter. I agree with H.G. Wells – perhaps the most influential of all futures thinkers – that 'human history is, in essence, a history of ideas.' It is the prevailing culture of ideas that shapes the direction of a society, that determines what is thinkable and unthinkable, what is possible and impossible. Yes, factors like economic structures, political systems and technology all play vital roles, but never underestimate the power of ideas. Consider just a few that have been highly influential: that the earth is the centre of the universe; that we are primarily driven by self-interest; that humans are separate from nature; that men are superior to women; that the path to salvation is God or capitalism or communism. Call them worldviews, mental frames, paradigms or mindsets: all of them have determined the course of civilisations.[12] And at this moment in history, short-term thinking – a belief in the primacy of the now – is one of the ideas that reigns supreme and urgently needs to be challenged.

The musician and cultural thinker Brian Eno had already recognised the importance of this issue back in the 1970s when he coined the concept of the 'long now'. Eno had begun to notice just how many people were immersed in a 'short now' mentality, where 'now' meant seconds, minutes or maybe a few days. A result of this high-velocity, short-term culture was a lack of concern for future generations who were facing myriad threats, from environmental collapse to the proliferation of weapons. 'Our empathy doesn't extend far forward in time,' he wrote. The antidote was a longer sense of now, where our idea of what constitutes 'now' extends backwards and forwards by hundreds, if not thousands of years, and our moral vision extends with it.[13] This book offers foundations for creating a 'long now civilisation', a civilisation that has overcome its colonial mentality of enslaving future generations to the present.

For over a decade, my own research and writing on empathy has focused on how we can step into the shoes of people from different social backgrounds in today's world and understand their feelings and perspectives (what is technically known as 'cognitive empathy' or 'perspective-taking' empathy). But I have long wrestled with an even greater challenge: how do we make a personal, empathic connection with future generations whom we can never meet and whose lives we can barely imagine? In other words, how do we empathise not just across space but across time? This book explores how we might do so. In the three years I have spent writing it, I have come to recognise that empathy is not the only bridge we need to extend our moral vision forward in time and that other related concepts, such as intergenerational justice and indigenous perspectives of planetary stewardship, can also play a key role. The result is a book that takes an interdisciplinary journey through realms ranging from moral philosophy and anthropology to the latest neuroscience research, conceptual art and political science. While attempting to take into account a broad range of social, economic and cultural perspectives, the analysis is inevitably limited by my own social positioning, so the 'we' that appears in this book usually refers to the economically secure inhabitants of Western industrialised nations, sometimes known as the Global North.

The Tug of War for Time

The national liberation struggles of the twentieth century were fought with guns. The intergenerational liberation struggle of the twenty-first century is a battle of ideas, taking the form of a titanic tug of war for time (see below). On one side, six drivers of short-termism threaten to drag us over the edge of civilisational breakdown. On the other, six ways to think long are drawing us towards a culture of longer time horizons and responsibility for the future of humankind.

The six ways to think long, explored in Part Two, are the core cognitive skills for becoming a good ancestor: a set of fundamental attitudes, beliefs and ideals. They fall into three clusters. *Imagining* the future is grounded in Deep-Time Humility and developing a Transcendent Goal for humanity. *Caring* about the future requires a Legacy Mindset and a sense of Intergenerational Justice. *Planning* for the future beyond our own lifetimes is a skill emerging from Cathedral Thinking and Holistic Forecasting. None of them alone will be

The tug of war for time

Six drivers of short-termism

Six ways to think long

Tyranny of the Clock
the acceleration of time
since the Middle Ages

Deep-Time Humility
grasp we are an eyeblink
in cosmic time

Digital Distraction
the hijacking of attention
by technology

Legacy Mindset
be remembered
well by posterity

Political Presentism
myopic focus
on the next election

Intergenerational Justice
consider the seventh
generation ahead

Speculative Capitalism
volatile boom-bust
financial markets

Cathedral Thinking
plan projects beyond
a human lifetime

Networked Uncertainty
the rise of global risk
and contagion

Holistic Forecasting
envision multiple pathways
for civilisation

Perpetual Progress
the pursuit of
endless economic growth

Graphic: Nigel Hawtin

Transcendent Goal
strive for
one-planet thriving

enough to create a long-term revolution of the human mind. But together – and when practised by a critical mass of people and organisations – a new age of long-term thinking could arise out of their synergy.

Although the drivers of short-termism, which appear throughout the book, are a formidable force, their victory in the tug of war for time is by no means guaranteed. Contrary to popular opinion, long-term thinking may be one of the greatest unsung talents of our species. We don't just think fast and slow, as Daniel Kahneman has taught us – we also think short and long. The capacity to think and plan over long timespans is wired into our brains and has enabled monumental feats, such as the construction of London's sewers after the Great Stink of 1858, the public investment of Roosevelt's New Deal and the dedicated struggles of anti-slavery campaigners and advocates for women's rights. As we will discover, it is the secret evolutionary ingredient that gives the six ways to think long their potential and power.

How can the imaginative leap to long-term thinking be transformed into actions that reshape the contours of history? This question is the focus of Part Three, which tells the stories of a pioneering band of 'time rebels' who are struggling against the rampant short-termism of the modern world and attempting to put the six ways into practice. They include the global climate strike movement led by Swedish teenager Greta Thunberg, as well as organisations such as Extinction Rebellion in the UK and Our Children's Trust in the US. Other rebels can be found in the radical regenerative economics movement and among advocates for citizens' assemblies, from Spain to Japan.

They are up against some formidable opponents, including those trying to hijack long-term thinking for self-serving ends, especially in the financial sector: as the former head of investment bank Goldman Sachs Gus Levy once proudly declared, 'We're greedy, but long-term greedy, not short-term greedy.'[14] Moreover, the time rebels must confront the stark reality that some of the fundamental ways we organise society, from nation states and representative democracy to consumer culture and capitalism itself, are no longer appropriate for the age we live in. They were invented centuries ago in the Holocene – the 10,000-year geological era of stable climate during which human civilisation thrived – at a time when our planet could largely absorb the ecological impact of material progress, the costs and risks of new technologies and the strains of population growth. That epoch has now passed as we move into the Anthropocene, the new era in which humans have created an unstable earth system threatened by ecological breakdown.[15]

This is the classic QWERTY problem writ large: just as the layout of our inefficient QWERTY keyboards was actually designed in the 1860s to prevent mechanical typewriter keys jamming by placing commonly used letters far apart, so we are lumbered with institutions that were designed for the challenges of a different age. It is virtually impossible to escape the conclusion that if we want to create a world fit for both current and future generations, we will need to profoundly rethink and redesign core aspects of society – how our economies function, how our politics works, what our cities look like – and ensure they are underpinned by new values and goals to secure the long-term thriving of humankind. And we have precious little time in which to do it.

Is there an ideal time horizon to which we should aspire in the tug of war against short-termism? This book proposes a hundred years as a minimum threshold for long-term thinking. This is the current length of a long human lifespan, taking us beyond the ego boundary of our own mortality so we begin to imagine futures that we can influence yet not participate in ourselves.[16] It extends much further than the maximum five or ten-year outlook found in corporations, towards the time horizon of actions like planting an oak tree, which will mature long after we have gone. We can also learn from those with a longer vision. The seventh-generation decision-making of many indigenous peoples encompasses a timespan of nearly two centuries. The Long Now Foundation in California is even more ambitious and sets the time horizon at 10,000 years, on the grounds that the first human civilisations emerged ten millennia ago at the end of the last Ice Age, so we should develop an equal perspective into the future.[17] We need to be adventurous with our temporal imaginations. At the very least, when you aim to think 'long-term', take a deep breath and think 'a hundred years and more'.

The Prospect of Radical Hope

Can we really make this seismic paradigm shift, so that long-term thinking permeates not just our personal decision-making but the very fabric of our public institutions, economic systems and cultural life? The literary critic Terry Eagleton makes a helpful distinction between optimism and hope.[18] Optimism can be thought of as a cheery disposition to always look on the bright side of life, even despite the evidence. It is an attitude that can easily breed complacency and in-action. Hope, on the other hand, is a more active and radical ideal that recognises the real possibility of failure, yet at the same time holds on to the prospect of success despite the odds, driven by a deep commitment to an outcome we value.

This is a book about hope rather than optimism. There is a real possibility that humankind will not wake from its short-termist slumber until an extreme cataclysm takes place – and by then it may be too late to alter our course from the same self-destructive fate as the Roman Empire and the Mayans. But the prospect of civilisational breakdown is far from inevitable, especially if we harness the power of collective action to forge radical change. The first lesson history teaches is that nothing is inevitable until it happens. We should feel hope when remembering that colonialism and slavery came to an end. We should feel hope in the transformative potential of the six ways to think long and in the emerging time rebellion dedicated to winning the tug of war against short-termism. We should acknowledge too that future generations would never forgive us if we gave up while there was still the possibility of change, no matter the odds. We must hear their voices in our dreams and heed them in our decisions.

The path of the good ancestor lies before us. It is our choice whether or not to take it.

2

The Marshmallow and the Acorn

Inside Our Time-Torn Brains

C lose your eyes and imagine holding in the palm of each hand a small object that encapsulates the everyday dilemmas we face in our fraught relationship with time. In your left hand you'll find a squishy pink marshmallow. And in your right hand there is a shiny green acorn.

Together they symbolise the fascinating tension that exists within the time horizons of the human mind. Our brains are wired for both short- and long-term thinking, and there is a constant tug of war between them. From the personal to the political, from our private lives to public life, this tension is ever-present. Should you splash out on a beach holiday or save for your retirement? Will politicians enact policies fit for the century ahead or focus on quick wins for the next election? Are you more likely to post a selfie on Instagram for popularity, or plant a seed in the ground for posterity?

Each one of us has what I think of as a 'marshmallow brain', which can become fixated on short-term desires and rewards. But we each also possess an 'acorn brain', which allows us to envision distant futures and work towards long-term goals. The interplay between these two time zones in our minds is a good part of what makes us distinctively human.

The acorn brain makes an almost literal appearance in Jean Giono's *The Man Who Planted Trees*, the story of a shepherd who pops acorns into the ground each day as he tends his sheep and after several decades has grown a vast oak forest – and we find that story compelling. Despite this, and our evident long-term capabilities, the dominant narrative in society constantly emphasises our inherent short-termism. In my research for this book, whether talking to psychologists or economists, futurologists or civil servants, I repeatedly encountered the belief that we are predominantly driven by immediate rewards and instant gratification, and that there is consequently little hope that we can rise to the long-term challenges of our age. An essay by Nathaniel Rich about our failure to act on the climate crisis illustrates this view. 'Human beings,' he writes, 'whether in global organisations, democracies, industries, political parties or as individuals, are incapable of sacrificing present convenience to forestall a penalty imposed on future generations.'[1]

If we hope to be good ancestors, it is essential to challenge this assumption and fully recognise that our minds are indeed capable of long-term thinking. Doing so is a starting point for building a society that overcomes its current myopic focus on the present. The various forms of long-term thinking explored in this book – such as cathedral thinking, holistic forecasting, and aspiring to a transcendent goal – are founded on our in-built ability to envision and plan for the future. Without it, we would never have invented agriculture, built the cathedrals of medieval Europe, created public health care systems or voyaged into space. And today we need it more than ever.

This chapter shows that we are capable of such long-term feats by exploring how the acorn brain works and how it developed over two million years of evolutionary history. But we must begin by revealing the inner workings of its great rival: the marshmallow brain.

How the Marshmallow Brain Drives Human Behaviour

I am sitting in an Oxford coffee shop with neuroscientist Morten Kringelbach, a world-renowned expert on pleasure and the brain, eager to discuss the human capacity for long-term thinking. He orders a chocolate brownie and, when it arrives, slides the plate in front of me. I decline the offer, telling him that I'm on a health drive. I look down at the brownie. It looks back. We continue to exchange glances. After a few minutes I can no longer resist my chocolate addiction and I take a bite.

Human beings, Morten tells me, have a pleasure system in our brains that drives us to seek short-term pleasures and rewards, while also prompting us to avoid immediate pain. Many of these pleasures play a positive role in our lives, such as the warm feeling of sun on our skin, the comfort of an embrace or the pleasures we get from sharing and conversation. Sometimes, however, the pleasure system goes awry and becomes dominated by short-term desires and impulses that can easily transform into addictions: we crave the sugar rush of a fizzy drink or can't tear ourselves away from a video game. It is this 'addictive brain', he says, that we really have to watch out for and that drives harmful short-term behaviours (including being hooked on chocolate). These short-term addictive and impulsive traits are what I describe as the marshmallow brain, for reasons that will become clear below.

An early insight into its functioning was revealed in a groundbreaking 1954 study, in which electrodes were implanted into the hypothalamus of rats, and the electrodes then connected to a lever that the rats could press to receive an electric brain stimulus. It turned out that the rats repeatedly pressed the lever – up to 2,000 times per hour – and gave up normal activities like feeding, drinking and sex in order to do so. This research, and subsequent replications, suggests that there are specific brain regions associated with addictive desires, and that the chemical dopamine plays a key role in aiding neural signalling in such areas.[2] Like it or not, we share a common ancestry with rats (going back around 80 million years), so it is not surprising that later research showed that humans possess similar brain regions.[3]

Evolutionary biologists suggest that our focus on short-term pleasures, desires and rewards developed as a survival mechanism in conditions where food might be scarce or safety at risk. Long before the invention of chocolate brownies, our brains developed short-term processing systems directing us to eat all we could when we could, and to make a run for it when we encountered predators. That's why we automatically lean over to smell a newly baked cake without a pause for thought and equally why we immediately turn on our heels if there's a Rottweiler racing towards us.[4]

So when we find it hard to resist the lure of food or drugs, we know that our ancient addictive brain is most probably at work. When we swipe our phones to check for new messages, we're like those rats obsessively pressing the lever, seeking the instant thrill of a dopamine rush that has been intentionally designed into the technology. And when we can't resist a drag on a cigarette after a few drinks at a party, we're obeying the deep call of our palaeomammalian ancestry. How's that for an excuse?

In fact, much of the everyday short-termism of consumer culture – from bingeing on junk food to the customer stampede at a clearance sale – can be traced back to the here-and-now instincts that are part of our evolutionary heritage. 'The propensity for overconsumption,' argues neuroscientist Peter Whybrow, 'is the relic of a time when individual survival depended upon fierce competition for resources . . . The ancient brain that drives us – evolved in scarcity, habit-driven and focused on short-term survival – is poorly matched to the frenzied affluence of contemporary material culture.'[5]

Human beings will even favour satisfying short-term desires over long-term personal interests. Smoking is an obvious example, but we may also eat fatty foods knowing full well that they could give us heart disease further down the line, or choose to spend our savings on a blowout Caribbean holiday rather than put the money away for a rainy day. When it comes to our personal time horizons, our future selves often come second place to the immediate pleasures of the present. We typically prefer a smaller, sooner reward rather than a larger, later one – a phenomenon known as 'hyperbolic discounting'.[6]

One of the best-known examples of our short-term impulsiveness and desire for instant rewards is the marshmallow test. In the 1960s, Stanford psychologist Walter Mischel placed a single marshmallow or similar treat in front of children aged between four and six. If they could resist eating it for 15 minutes when left alone in a room, he told them, they would be rewarded with a second marshmallow. The fact that two-thirds of the children couldn't resist eating the marshmallow in front of them is often taken as evidence of our inherent short-term natures.

Yet the marshmallow test, for all its fame, is only part of the story of who we are. For a start, it's worth recognising that fully one-third of the children in Mischel's experiment resisted the temptation. Moreover, replication of the test has shown that the ability to delay gratification is highly dependent on context. If the children don't trust that the researcher will return, they are more likely to grab the marshmallow, and those from wealthier backgrounds find it easier to resist the treat; a lack of trust and fear of scarcity can push us towards short-termism.[7]

More importantly, as neuroscientists such as Morten Kringelbach acknowledge, we are far more than rats pressing levers or snatchers of sugary snacks; the ancient marshmallow brain exists alongside much newer parts of our neuroanatomy that give us the ability to think and plan for the long term. It's time to discover the acorn brain.

Meet Your Acorn Brain

Around 12,000 years ago, in the early Neolithic period, one of our ancestors did something extraordinary: instead of eating a seed, she decided to save it to plant the next season. This moment – the beginning of the agricultural revolution – marks a turning point in the evolution of the human mind and is the symbolic birth of long-term thinking.

Having the foresight to save seeds for growing crops and the restraint to resist eating them during the long, hungry months of winter, demonstrates the remarkable capacity of *Homo sapiens* to catapult their minds from the present into the distant future, and to embark on projects and ventures with long time horizons. This aspect of our neurological wiring deserves a name: the acorn brain. And we've all got one. But how exactly does it work, where does it come from and how powerful is it?

The functioning of the acorn brain is the subject of a new field of research known as prospective psychology, which argues that what makes humans unique is our ability to think about, or 'prospect', the future. To borrow a term from psychologist Martin Seligman, we are *Homo prospectus*, a species 'guided by imagining alternatives stretching into the future'.[8] While Freud may have encouraged us to journey into our pasts, our minds are naturally drawn to look in the opposite direction. We are constantly imagining possibilities, making plans and wandering over the contours of both the near and long-term future. As the psychologist Daniel Gilbert puts it, we are 'the ape that looks forward'.[9]

The evidence is compelling. No other animal appears to consciously think about and plan for the future as much as human beings. Squirrels might bury their nuts for the winter, but they do so instinctively when the duration of daylight begins to shorten, not because they have consciously decided to make a survival plan. Studies of animal behaviour reveal that other species such as rats have excellent memories, but they can only think around half an hour ahead in time. Although chimpanzees will strip the leaves off a branch to make a tool for poking into a termite hole, there is no evidence that they will prepare a dozen of these tools to be set aside so they can be used next week.[10]

But this is exactly the kind of thing a human will do. We are planners *extraordinaire*. We plan holidays for next summer, design gardens that will only look beautiful in a decade, save up for our children's college education and even compile song lists for our own funerals. That's the acorn brain in action. This ability to prospect is what enables us to survive and thrive. 'Our singular foresight created civilisation and sustains society,' argues Martin Seligman. 'The power of prospection is what makes us wise. Looking into the future, consciously and unconsciously, is a central function of our large brain.'[11]

It all starts in early childhood. By the age of around five, children are able to imagine the future, predict future events and distinguish them from the past and present – which is why at around that age my twins started giving me little lists of what they wanted for their birthday several months in advance. By the time they reach their teens, they will have developed a sophisticated capacity for mental time travel that enables anticipation and planning over long time frames, an understanding of historical time stretching across centuries and an ability to contemplate their own death.[12]

How much future thinking and planning do we engage in on a daily basis? Far more than traditional psychology typically assumes. One study of 500 Chicago residents, which asked them what they were thinking about at random moments during the day via a mobile phone app, showed that they spent around 14 per cent of the day thinking about the future and only 4 per cent thinking about the past (the rest of their thoughts were either about the present or not time-specific). Of the time spent dwelling on the future, around three-quarters of it involved making plans.[13] So we think about the future around three times as much as the past, and for every seven hours of thinking we do, roughly one hour of it concerns things that have yet to happen.

Most of this neural processing about the future takes place in an area of the brain called the frontal lobe, which sits at the front of the head above the eyes. People who sustain damage to it can often appear perfectly normal, being able to chat away happily about the weather, drink a cup of tea and do a memory test. But they may fail utterly at anything involving planning, like saying what they will do in the afternoon or completing a puzzle that requires thinking ahead. The frontal lobe (and especially the part of it known as the dorsolateral prefrontal cortex) is the operations centre of the acorn brain, a time machine that enables us to envision situations that are weeks or even decades in the future, and to map out complex plans and processes over long timespans.

The curious thing about the frontal lobe is that it is a relatively new addition to the brain, having only developed in the last two million years (the first brains appeared on earth around 500 million years ago). During this period, our cranial matter more than doubled in mass, from the 1.25-pound brain of *Homo habilis* to the nearly three pounds of *Homo sapiens*. Yet this sudden growth spurt was not evenly distributed; it appeared disproportionately at the front, so the low, sloping foreheads of our earliest ancestors were gradually pushed forward until they reached the almost vertical position they have today. And this is the very part of our cerebral apparatus that is mainly responsible for forward planning and other so-called 'executive functions', such as abstract reasoning and problem solving.[14]

Despite this evolutionary advance in our capacity to think long, most of our prospecting focuses on the very near future. The Chicago study showed that around 80 per cent of thoughts relating to the future referred to the same or next day, with only 14 per cent concerning over a year ahead and just 6 per cent looking more than ten years into the future.[15] So while the acorn brain certainly exists as part of our functional neuroanatomy, it is clearly dominated by our short-term marshmallow brain and struggles to escape its influence.

The implications are profound. According to Daniel Gilbert, one of the founders of prospective psychology, if alien scientists wanted to destroy our species, they wouldn't send down little green men to blast us into oblivion – that would quickly trigger our well-honed defence mechanisms. Instead, they would invent something like global warming, which would slip under the radar of the human brain because we simply aren't very good at acting on long-term threats. Although we will swiftly get out of the way of a baseball speeding towards our head, we are far less adept at dealing with a danger coming several years or decades down the line. Yet the fact that we can do any long-term thinking at all 'is one of the brain's most stunning innovations', argues Gilbert; we just need to understand that it's at an early stage of development.[16]

> We're very good at clear and present danger, like every mammal is. But we've learned a new trick in the last couple of million years – at least we've kind of learned it. Our brains, unlike the brains of almost every other species, are prepared to treat the future as if it were the present. We can look ahead to our retirements or to a dental appointment, and we can take action today to save for our retirement or to floss so that we don't get bad news six months down the line. But we're just learning this trick. It's a very new adaptation in the animal kingdom and we don't do it all that well.[17]

It's not as if we are unable to think about the long-term future – that would be a genuinely disastrous neurological handicap that would inhibit any response to the ecological, social and technological threats on the horizon, from conflict over water resources to the risk of cyber-attacks on a country's defence system. The problem is just that *we don't do it all that well*. Unsurprisingly, some people have already learned to do it well, from indigenous communities who use seventh-generation decision-making to engineers who design bridges that last a century and cosmologists steeped in the mysteries of deep time. Most of us, however, are like old dogs struggling to learn the new trick.

Humanity's acorn brain clearly has enormous potential, and if we hope to become good ancestors we must learn to tap into its power. Simply realising that we have one is a crucial first step. But the very existence of the acorn brain begs a critical question: how did it even develop in the first place?

The Cognitive Leap to Long-Term Thinking

Over a period of two million years, our ancestors performed an incredible feat: they grew brains that allowed them to escape the present moment and become part-time residents of the future. Evolutionary psychologists and archaeologists suggest that the capacity to think and plan for the long term must have conferred an evolutionary advantage. Being able to consider what lies ahead, to anticipate change and make plans emerged as survival mechanisms that made up for what our species might have lacked in strength, speed or agility.[18] Four main factors have enabled this seismic cognitive leap: wayfinding, the 'grandmother effect', social cooperation and tool innovation (see below). Each of them represents an essential scene in the slow-time psychodrama of human evolution.

'Our nature lies in movement; complete calm is death,' wrote the seventeenth-century thinker Blaise Pascal. It was an apt observation, because our protohuman ancestors roved across the landscape from the earliest times – foraging, hunting, searching for water, migrating with the seasons and adapting to new environments. Over multiple millennia they developed a survival skill known as 'wayfinding', a capacity to orient themselves in physical space and navigate from place to place. Part of this skill involved generating 'cognitive maps' in their minds that helped them record key landmarks, follow familiar routes and return safely home. But this mental cartography required not just mapping *place* but also mapping *time*. Hunters could save

How humans grew long brains

A two-million-year story

Wayfinding

Human survival depended on an ability to plan hunting and foraging trips and develop time-specific 'cognitive maps'

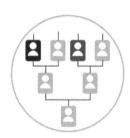

Grandmother effect

Grandmothers provided essential care for children, extending intergenerational time horizons

Social cooperation

Cooperative relationships of trust, reciprocity and empathy were based on creating bonds that persisted through time

Tool innovation

Advances in stone tool technology required a capacity to plan complex sequenced processes and identify future goals

Graphic: Nigel Hawtin

precious energy and even lives if they not only planned the route but could plan out the time needed to travel from place to place. As the ecologist Thomas Princen explains, this was how early humans began developing an ability to plan for the future: 'the cognitive capacity to image those places and imagine the time required to get to them, were thus both geographic (where the stream is in relation to the forest) and temporal (how many days and nights it will take to go to both the stream and the forest).'[19]

Over the last century, anthropologists have studied wayfinding among indigenous peoples, from the stick maps of canoeists in the Marshall Islands that depict dangerous reefs and complex tidal movements, to the songlines or dreaming tracks of Aboriginal peoples in Australia that enable them to literally sing a trail of landmarks that appear across vast territories.[20] We are the inheritors of such traditions, which have bequeathed us the cognitive talent to plan not just our journeys across the landscape but our travels through the timescapes of the future, guided by a temporal GPS of the human mind.

A second long-brain enabler, sometimes called the 'grandmother effect', derives from a biological peculiarity of our species: the extended period of dependence of a human child. Most mammals can walk within a matter of hours and reproduce within a year after they are born. Not so humans. We are pretty much helpless and vulnerable for our first few years, and do not become fully independent and capable of reproduction until our teens. Yet it is not just parents who help rear children so they can eventually pass on their genes: studies show that the presence of grandparents – especially maternal grandmothers – is important for reducing infant and child mortality. Just as, in a herd of deer, the presence of older post-reproductive females increases the survival chances of the young because the elders know where to find food or water in times of scarcity, so a human grandmother provides care, knowledge and other valuable forms of support.[21]

The fact that we have grandmothers who live long past their reproductive age is likely a result of Darwinian selection: their presence enabled everyone to survive. It was through the grandmother effect that our ancestors became embedded in multigenerational kinship groups that helped them develop time horizons – and an ethic of care and responsibility – encompassing some five generations, stretching at least forwards by two and backwards by two from their own.[22]

The grandmother effect was reinforced and extended by a third factor: our deep instinct for social cooperation. For at least three centuries – going back to the writings of figures such as Thomas Hobbes and John Locke – we have been told that human beings are a naturally selfish and individualistic species.[23] But in one of the greatest U-turns in the history of science, evolutionary biologists now recognise that we rank as one of the most social of all mammals. Darwin had known it all along: 'An advancement in the standard of morality will certainly give an immense advantage to one tribe over another,' he wrote in *The Descent of Man* (1871), and he believed that a tribe's success would be enhanced if its members 'were always ready to aid one another, and to sacrifice themselves for the common good'.[24] That is, natural selection works at the level of the group, not just the individual: when food is scarce or predators are on the prowl, working together is the best way to ensure survival. This explains how we developed cooperative traits such as mutual aid, empathy, altruism and trust. As the primatologist Frans de Waal pointed out to me, 'Empathy and solidarity are bred into us.'[25]

But what has this got to do with long-term thinking? Social cooperation requires an imaginative capacity to see into the future. Relationships of trust and reciprocity work best when people know that the help they give to someone in the present will likely be returned at a future date, when they are in need themselves: time is written into the social contract, it is woven into the very fabric of mutual aid. Similarly, empathy is based on an ability to anticipate the needs, feelings and goals of others. When a friend loses her job, we may try to imagine what her emotional state might be and the best support we could give. In doing so, we are prospecting the future by simulating an array of possibilities. In fact, most aspects of social life require an ability to catapult our minds forward in time: social emotions such as guilt and shame function by anticipating our own future feelings; making a promise to someone builds in a timeline of obligation and responsibility; and the simple act of gauging someone's intentions is based on identifying different possible futures. As Martin Seligman argues, 'How would we coordinate and cooperate if we could not form reliable expectations of what others would do in a range of situations? Or have reliable expectations of what we ourselves will be able to do or be sufficiently motivated to do?'[26] The conclusion is clear: our social nature evolved in tandem with a talent for mental time travel.

A final driver, which rapidly accelerated the evolutionary development of long-term thinking and planning, switches our attention from the relational to the technological: the unrivalled human genius for toolmaking.

I have to admit that I always used to glaze over in museums when looking at cabinets of stone tools filled with rows of roughly hewn flints. Yet that all changed when I discovered the research of archaeologist Sander van der Leeuw, a world authority on Stone Age tool technology. It turns out that flaked stone tools are an indicator of the cognitive evolution of the human brain and provide the best-known evidence of our growing capacity for complex multi-stage planning. According to Van der Leeuw, stone tool development passed through a number of stages over a two-million-year period. The simplest tools were those with natural points and edges. But then our Palaeolithic ancestors learned to create a sharp edge by flaking off part of the stone by hitting it against another surface. They then jumped to creating tools with two flaked edges meeting to form a line, something that other primates never learned to do. Following this, by around

20,000 years ago they had mastered making tools and weapons in three dimensions, removing multiple flakes at specific angles to create sharpened points based on the intersection of three planes.

What insights do such technological advances offer about the human brain? Making these tools was not simply a matter of randomly bashing off bits of stone with no predetermined plan. As tools became more sophisticated, they required an ever-clearer conception of the finished product, along with the ability to work backwards mentally to plan the multiple stages of stone knapping required to create it. In what is known as the Levallois technique, for instance, the removal of one flake was at the same time preparation for the removal of the next one. This could only be done by developing an ability to invert causal sequences in the mind ('A causes B, so if I want B to happen, I have to do A').[27] Such complex planning resembles that of a sculptor who chisels away superfluous material to reveal a form they have already envisioned within the stone.

The advances in knapping techniques, argues Van der Leeuw, reflect a step change in the human mind:

> In the process of acquiring the capability to conceive of and to make stone tools in three dimensions, our ancestors had also acquired a number of other conceptual tools. One of these is the capacity to plan and execute complex sequences of actions . . . A threshold is thus crossed, which, from this time onwards, allows for a major acceleration in the development of human control over matter.[28]

In his view, the very birth of agricultural societies more than ten millennia ago could never have happened without this leap in cognitive dexterity. The ability to make complex plans involving multiple sequential processes, and to devise strategies directed towards future goals, enabled Neolithic humans to engage in activities that required long time horizons, such as practising crop rotation, domesticating wild grains, breeding animals and eventually constructing the first cities. In effect, there was no fundamental conceptual difference between making stone tools in discrete steps over several hours, and planning crops over several months or constructing a pyramid over several decades. As Van der Leeuw writes, 'We thus see the same mechanisms at work as in artifact manufacture: stretching of temporal sequences and temporal separation between different parts of a "manufacturing" sequence.'[29] So all those stone tools gathering dust in museums reveal the greatest of all human achievements: the emergence of civilisation itself.

The Gift of the Temporal Pirouette

The marshmallow brain and the acorn brain may be in constant struggle with each other, but at the same time they have bequeathed us an astonishing evolutionary gift: agile imaginations that can shift in an instant from thinking on a scale of seconds to a scale of years. Our minds dance across multiple time horizons on a day-to-day basis, rapidly swivelling our attention from one perspective to another. We are experts at the temporal pirouette. Whether we are fully making use of this gift, however, is another matter.

The graphic below reveals how this capacity to range across time is expressed in both personal and public life. In personal life we sometimes think, plan and operate on a scale of minutes or seconds, such as when responding to a text message. But our minds can instantly switch to a scale of hours (thinking about when our phone battery will die) or days (looking forward to a weekly exercise class), or months (planning a three-month diet), or years (deciding to do a college degree), and occasionally a scale of decades (taking out a mortgage). Yet we rarely think far beyond the threshold of our own

PUBLIC LIFE		PERSONAL LIFE
Cathedral building Seventh-gen thinking Seed banks	**Centuries**	Planting an oak tree Time capsules Belief in the afterlife
Space programmes Energy transitions Chinese planning	**Decades**	Mortgage Pension saving Making a will
Trade negotiations Olympic Games Election cycles	**Years**	College degree Career plans Raising children
Quarterly reporting Fashion fads Software updates	**Months**	School term Pregnancy Diet
Daily newspapers Discount sales Music festivals	**Days**	Postage Weekly shop Exercise classes
Opening hours Parking meters Public meetings	**Hours**	Work shift Sunday lunch Phone battery
Traffic lights 24/7 news 999 response	**Minutes**	Emailing Taking a shower Coffee break
Quiz shows Stock markets Public auctions	**Seconds**	Texting 1-click buying Cycle of breath

PUBLIC LIFE   PERSONAL LIFE

HUMAN TIME HORIZONS

Graphic: Nigel Hawtin

lifetimes: death is the common cut-off point for our imaginings. Survey data shows that for most people, even from different cultures and religious backgrounds, the future goes dark after 15 to 20 years.[30] We simply find it difficult to picture more than a few decades ahead, which is why it can be so hard to save for old age.

A range of time horizons similarly operates in public life. High-frequency share trading works in milliseconds, fashion fads and quarterly business reporting in months, and election cycles in years. Temporal vision seldom extends further than a decade, although there are exceptions, such as NASA's 30-year space exploration programme, the Chinese government's 35-year National Plans and long-term seed banks. In general, the public future goes dark after around three decades. In 2020, it is difficult to find any governments, corporations or international organisations that are making substantive plans beyond 2050.

In both public and private life, then, we are operating within a relatively narrow temporal bandwidth and failing to draw on the imaginative capacity of our acorn brains to think into the long future. Moreover, forces such as digital technology are driving us towards even shorter horizons than in the past, so more and more of our activity is being concentrated in the bands closest to the present. The future is rapidly closing in on us.

Yet we must extend our vision if we hope to have a chance of meeting the challenges of existential risk and civilisational breakdown that our species will be confronting not just in the decades ahead, but in the centuries and millennia to come. The future needs to stay illuminated far beyond 20 or 30 years.

We now know that we are more than capable of stretching our minds into those distant horizons. Thanks to the wayfinders, the grandmothers, the social cooperators and the toolmakers of the past, we have a profound new story about human nature, one telling us that we are not merely prisoners of our marshmallow brains but that we also have acorn brains wired into us. This readies us to leap into the different forms of long-term thinking that appear in the coming chapters: our minds are prepped for forging long-term legacies, for the strategic planning of cathedral thinking, for forecasting the pathways of civilisation, and for identifying distant goals and striving for them.

Changing the story about who we are makes a difference. If we keep telling ourselves that we are primarily driven by short-termism and instant gratification, it is likely we will exacerbate such traits; we will create expectations, offer incentives and design a world that feeds our marshmallow brain. This, of course, is already happening. Think about that ubiquitous symbol of instant consumer culture: the Buy Now button. Perhaps no other technology has been so perfectly designed to tap into our short-term impulsiveness. But imagine if, just when you were about to click, a box opened offering alternative options, like 'Buy in a Week', 'Buy in a Month', 'Buy in a Year' or even 'Borrow from a Friend', and that you were sent a reminder after the selected time had lapsed to see if you still really wanted the item. And now imagine if equivalent long-term designs were built into our political institutions, legal frameworks, energy systems, financial regulations, economic organisations and school curriculums. The world would look very different.

That is the kind of world we need to create. The challenge we face is to amplify our acorn brains and release their dormant power. That way, they can compete on at least equal terms with our ancient marshmallow brains, which are constantly pulling us towards shorter time horizons. We must switch them on, fire them up and send them into a longer now. It is time to put our acorn brains into action.

PART TWO

SIX WAYS TO THINK LONG

The following chapters describe the six ways to cultivate long-term thinking, which together comprise a mental toolkit for becoming a good ancestor. Their purpose is to help us imagine, care about and plan for the many possible futures that await humankind. Some of them touch us personally, helping us rethink our relationships with death, family and community. Others are about our collective plans and goals as a species, stretching into the centuries ahead. All of them, in their different ways, concern our interdependence with the living world and the need for a reconciliation with the fragile and finely balanced oasis known as planet Earth.

3

Deep-Time Humility

Humankind as an Eyeblink in Cosmic History

Our species, at this moment in history, is suffering from an acute crisis of perspective. Our time horizons are rapidly shrinking towards a narrow window of seconds, hours and days, just when our survival depends on broadening our temporal vision. As we busily check our phones, existential threats ranging from bioterrorism to drone warfare may be lurking just over the horizon, while sea levels rise slowly and imperceptibly, threatening to engulf our coastal cities. How can we extend our minds and gain a visceral sense of a longer now that helps divert our civilisational path from the perils of short-termism?

An essential starting point is to develop a sense of deep-time humility, where we grasp the insignificance of our own transitory existence in relation to the vast time frame of cosmic history, freeing our minds to look both far into the past and beyond our lifetimes into a distant future. We must accept the reality that our personal stories from birth to death, and all the achievements and tragedies of human civilisation, will barely register in the annals of cosmological time.

Diverting our gaze from a funnelled focus on the present to embrace deep time requires an immense imaginative leap. This chapter explores the different ways, over the past two centuries, that humankind has risen to this challenge. Yet first we need to confront the major barrier standing in the way, which has been fuelling our culture of short-termism for more than half a millennium: the tyrannical rule of the clock since the Middle Ages.

The Tyranny of the Clock

For most of human history, our ancestors had a cyclical view of time. They lived in tune with the rhythmic circles of life embedded in everything from their daily sleeping patterns to the regular revolutions of the moon, stars and the planet itself. In the 1930s, the Oglala Sioux leader Hehaka Sapa, or Black Elk, spoke of his circular conception of time and the cosmos:

> Everything an Indian does is in a circle, and that is because the Power of the World always works in circles . . . The wind, in its greatest power, whirls. Birds make their nests in circles, for theirs is the same religion as ours. The sun comes forth and goes down again in a circle. The moon does the same and both are round. Even the seasons form a great circle in their changing, and always come back again to where they were. The life of a man is a circle from childhood to childhood and so it is in everything where power moves.[1]

One of the great tragedies of human civilisation is that most societies, especially in the West, have lost touch with cyclical time and its inherently long-term perspective of eternal return, where time is forever recommencing. The ancient idea of time as a circle has been replaced by the notion of linear time, the arrow of time that runs in a straight line from the past, through the present and into the future. Why does it matter whether we conceive of time as a circle or a line? Because a line, unlike a circle, can be shortened.

Cyclical time began to unravel with the invention of the mechanical clock in Europe in the fourteenth century. These clocks did not simply allow the passing hours to be measured more accurately than with old instruments like sundials or water clocks. They also became instruments of power that could regiment, commodify and accelerate time itself. 'Who controls time?' appeared as a new question in human history.

The tyranny of the clock surfaced in the struggle between the Christian concept of time and what the historian Jacques Le Goff has termed 'merchant time'. According to official Church doctrine, time was a 'gift of God, and therefore cannot be sold'. The upshot was its opposition to the practice of usury – lending money with interest – as this effectively involved using time to make profit. That was bad news for merchants, who depended on lines of credit to run their businesses. More broadly, their commercial success was to a great extent based on their ability to use time to their advantage: knowing when to buy cheap and sell dear, how long shipments would take to arrive, predicting the timing of currency fluctuations and the likely price of next season's harvest, and how to get more work out of the labourers they employed in as short a time as possible. The dominant ideology among the growing merchant class in medieval Europe was that 'time is money' rather than a divine gift.

Gradually, with the help of the clock, merchant time came to overpower church time. In 1355, a new clock in the French town of Aire-sur-la-Lys chimed to demark the hours when trade could take place and the labouring hours of textile workers, all for the benefit of the merchants who ran the commune. In 1374, just four years after a public clock appeared in the German city of Cologne, the first law regulating the amount of time workers were allowed for lunch appeared – a prescient sign of things to come. 'The communal clock,' writes Le Goff, 'was an instrument of economic, social and political domination' that enabled the rise of commercial capitalism.[2]

While these early clocks marked only the hour or quarter-hour, by 1700 most clocks had acquired minute hands, and by 1800 second hands were standard.[3] This unprecedented ability to measure time precisely found its most authoritarian expression in the factory clock, which became a prime weapon of the Industrial Revolution. As the historian of technology Lewis Mumford argued, 'the clock, not the steam engine, is the key-machine of the modern industrial age.'[4] Soon workers were clocking in, filling out timesheets and being punished for lateness. With time sliced into smaller and smaller periods, business owners could measure the speed of their workers down to the second, and ratchet up the pace of the production line. Workers who tried to reject this regimentation by 'going slow' were swiftly sacked. The tyranny of the clock fed the growing culture of utilitarian efficiency, so brilliantly depicted by Charles Dickens in his 1854 novel *Hard Times*, where the office of Mr Gradgrind contained 'a deadly statistical clock in it, which measured every second with a beat like a rap upon a coffin-lid'.

The greed for speed embodied in the factory clock signalled the triumph of linear time. Now it was the artificial construct of minutes

Time becomes money: Workers line up at the clocking-in machine at the Rowntree chocolate factory, Yorkshire, 1933.

and seconds that mattered rather than the natural cycles of the moon or seasons. The long-term future began to fade away as the present loomed ever larger.

The future vanished further still into the distance with the transport and communications revolutions of the nineteenth century. The arrival of steam trains in the 1830s upped the tempo of daily life from the unhurried era of the horse and cart, while the telegraph and telephone annihilated both space and time (no more waiting weeks or months for letters to arrive). Today the internet and instant messaging have fully globalised the present tense by accelerating the speed of information flows on a worldwide scale. Yet they have also given rise to a new instrument of short-termism that threatens to trap us permanently in the here and now: digital distraction.

Digital technology has an unmatched power to hijack our immediate attention. While we would never put up with a GPS that kept taking us to the wrong destination, this is exactly what happens with the technologies that direct us through informational space.[5] We go online to do something useful like book a doctor's appointment and somehow get lured into watching movie spoofs on YouTube, buying a new yoga mat or checking our email (again). Social media apps and websites are designed to achieve 'engagement goals': they aim to keep us clicking, scrolling and swiping, while showing us as many ads or pages as possible. Tech firms are in the business of immersing us in a digital present that distracts us from pursuing goals of our own choosing, and against which long-term thinking can hardly compete. Sean Parker, founding president of Facebook, has admitted that hijacking our attention was an intentional objective of the company. 'The thought process was this,' he said. 'How do we consume as much of your time and conscious attention as possible?'[6]

The phones in our pockets have become the new factory clocks, capturing time that was once our own and offering in exchange a continuous electronic now full of infotainment, advertising and fake news.

The distraction industry works by cleverly tapping into our ancient mammalian brains: our ears prick up at the ping of an arriving message, or our attention switches to a video suddenly flickering on the edge of the screen, generating a sense of anticipation that triggers our dopamine system into action. Facebook is Pavlov, and we're the dogs.

This 500-year story reveals an essential truth: that time has transformed into a source of power. Formidable forces have sought to bring the control of time under their dominion, from the industrialists of the nineteenth century to today's social media companies which aim to capture and sell our attention spans. They are responsible for instigating what the social theorist Jeremy Rifkin has described as 'temporal warfare', seeking to dominate, speed up and foreshorten time for their own advantage.[7]

The war for time has also severed our links with the ecological choreography of the planet, formed by natural cycles of eternal return. We have broken the circle and put a line in its place: the forward thrust of the arrow of time. Its direction of travel has been propelled by artificial cycles of our own making. What seems to matter now is the tax year not the solar year, the quarterly report not the four seasons, the electoral cycle not the carbon cycle. Indeed, we are now altering nature's cycles with global heating that plays havoc with the seasons and biodiversity loss that sends ecosystems out of kilter.

But is there a way to shake off this historical inheritance and escape our myopic focus on the present? An answer lies in one of the most mind-altering discoveries of the modern scientific era: deep time.

The Discovery of Deep Time in Victorian England

The eighteenth century was an age of revolutions. But apart from the political upheavals in France and America, there was another revolution at that time, less bloody and convulsive but perhaps of greater significance. It began on 7 March 1785, when the medical doctor James Hutton delivered a turgid lecture at the Royal Society in Edinburgh about the formation of land masses and rock strata. Buried in it was a geological theory of seismic proportions, refuting the conventional Christian belief that the earth had been created by God in six days around 6,000 years earlier (one Cambridge professor, tracing back the biblical records, claimed that it all began at 9am on 26 October in 4004 BCE). Hutton argued that puzzling phenomena, such as the appearance of ancient clam fossils on mountaintops and rock strata juxtaposed at radically different angles, could only be explained by repeated cycles of deposition and uplift that had taken place over vast periods of time, perhaps millions of years or longer.[8] Hutton later took his friend John Playfair to visit some exposed rock layers demonstrating his theory, which prompted Playfair to declaim that 'the mind seemed to grow giddy by looking so far into the abyss of time.'[9]

While Hutton was not the first to question the age of the planet, his work was among the most influential and signalled a radical turning point in the history of the Western psyche (many non-Western cultures, it should be noted, were much more in tune with the true age of the earth).[10] Genesis was debunked (or so it seemed), and in its place was the extraordinary idea that earth was immeasurably old and that humankind had existed for only a miniscule portion of its history. But revolutions usually take longer than we think, and it was at least half a century before Hutton's ideas became conventional wisdom. They were gradually spread by pioneering scientists of the nineteenth century, who performed a slow-time pincer movement on the Victorian mind. From one side came geologists such as Charles Lyell, who further substantiated and developed Hutton's thesis. From another side came the evolutionary thinkers led by Charles Darwin, who insisted that processes like reptiles evolving wings and feathers, or the development of apes into humans, could never have happened in just the few thousand years of biblical time.

The discovery of what is now known as 'deep time' contributed to the Victorian craze for geology and archaeology. It also excited some of the greatest minds of the age, among them the writer H.G. Wells. 'We have become possessed of a new and once unsuspected history of the world,' he exclaimed. And if we could now look so far back into the past, he argued, why shouldn't we be able to look forward just as far? For Wells, the perspective of geological time called for 'the discovery of the future'. This would require a new science, a kind of temporal mirror image of geology 'to throw a searchlight of inference forward instead of backward', which would help predict the future by 'seeking for operating causes instead of for fossils'.[11]

Such statements have gained Wells his reputation as the inventor of the discipline of futurology (today called 'futures studies'), but his greatest impact may have been on the human imagination. Through novels such as *The Time Machine* (1895), in which a Victorian gentleman scientist sends himself forward to the year 802701 – Wells opened Western culture to long-term thinking, or what he referred to as 'an ever-expanding Now'.[12] Until then, few writers had thought of setting their stories far into the future; most utopian fiction was situated in a distant place – often some exotic undiscovered island – rather than a distant time. Wells did more than almost any writer to change this, and in the process helped give birth to the genre of science fiction, which soon became a popular creative outlet for exploring long-range futures.[13] Among its earliest and most brilliant exponents was the philosopher Olaf Stapledon, whose 1930 novel *Last and First Men: A Story of the Near and Far Future* – a major influence on visionary writers such as Arthur C. Clarke – chronicles the evolutionary history of humanity over the next two billion years and through 18 major biological and cultural revolutions. The timescale is so vast that all human history up to the author's present day is covered in the first two pages.

The challenge with deep time is that it is so difficult to transform from an abstract concept into a tangible one that profoundly enters and alters our being. John Playfair may have grown giddy when looking at rock strata on the east coast of Scotland in 1788, but I suspect that few people are similarly roused when gazing at layers of sedimentary rock. Or at least I'm not. And no matter how much I've studied those textbook geological tables listing periods like the Cambrian, the Devonian and the Cretaceous, they have never catapulted my mind back (or forwards) millions of years into deep-time ecstasy. It might be different for a geologist whose knowledge and love of their subject brings it to life, or for a kid obsessed with dinosaurs, but I find that such technical information leaves me stone cold.

The good news is that for more than a century, an imaginative band of scientists, writers and other creative thinkers have been doing their very best to convey the wonder and immensity of deep time in the face of stiff competition from the ticking clocks of industrial civilisation. Their efforts fall into three main areas: art, metaphor and experience. Never has their work been more relevant to us than now.

Deep-Time Art and the 10,000 Year Clock

Over the past decades, there has been a flowering of deep-time artistic endeavours that have used creative means to stretch our temporal imaginations. In 1977, two Golden Records designed to last a billion years were sent into space on the two Voyager spacecraft, each containing 'the sounds of earth' as a message of peace to the first aliens to find them. Now travelling beyond our solar system, the Records include recordings ranging from Mozart and Chuck Berry to birdsong and human laughter (critics point out that it would have been more realistic to also include sounds of war, violence, hunger and depression). Closer to home, Rachel Sussman, in a project titled The Oldest Living Things in World, has photographed lichens in Greenland that are over 2,000 years old and grow only one centimetre every hundred years. In 2015, Jonathon Keats installed a deep-time camera in Tempe, Arizona, which is taking a 1,000-year-long exposure of the city's skyline that will finally be exhibited in 3015. The artist Martin Kunze's Memory of Mankind project, which aims to preserve 'endangered memories', is depositing 1,000 of the most important books of humankind in an Austrian salt mine, to be stored on ceramic microfilm tablets for a million years.

Perhaps the most thought-provoking deep-time artwork of them all is The Clock of the Long Now, also known as the 10,000 Year Clock. A project of the Long Now Foundation, its purpose is to create a new mythology of time that challenges the pathologically short attention span of the modern world. As one of its inventors, Stewart Brand, puts it, 'How do we make long-term thinking automatic and common instead of difficult and rare? How do we make the taking of long-term responsibility inevitable? The device is a Clock, very big and very slow.'[14] The clock, which is designed to stay accurate for ten millennia, will be 200 feet tall, and is currently being built inside a remote limestone mountain in the Texas desert, although its complex engineering means it still may be more than a decade until it is completed. Visitors will have to endure a tough full-day hike to reach its inner workings. Once there, they will be greeted by the chime of ten bells, created by the musician Brian Eno, which will ring in a unique sequence each day for the 10,000 years – 3,652,500 days – of the clock's lifetime.[15]

The project has not, however, been without its critics. Some question whether a mechanical device, so resonant of the factory clocks that sped up time in the Industrial Revolution, is really the most appropriate way of reconnecting us with the cyclical biorhythms of the natural world. Others point out the inescapable irony that its major funder is Amazon founder Jeff Bezos, someone whose greatest legacy to humanity may be the Buy Now button. Bezos is known for championing the virtues of thinking long: 'every company,' he says, 'requires a long-term view.' At the same time, he has created a business that thrives on the short-term mentality of instant consumer gratification.[16] Despite such tensions, the 10,000 Year Clock remains striking for its cultural and temporal ambition, and may eventually become a site of pilgrimage for good ancestors, a potent symbol of the long mind of humanity.

The Power of Metaphor

Deep time lies at the heart of creation stories around the world, from the Australian Aboriginal Dreamtime, which goes back to the very beginning of time when ancestral spirits first created the land and its people, to the *kalpa* or 'day of Brahma', a 4.32-billion-year cycle in Hindu cosmology that measures the period between the creation and recreation of the universe. Storytelling, however, is about more than the narratives we use to make sense of the world and our place in it. It is also about the very forms of language we draw upon. When it comes to conveying the story of deep time, one of the most crucial tools at our disposal is metaphor, which can enable us to comprehend the vast numbers involved that so easily numb the mind. Perhaps the most powerful I have ever encountered is a simple and elegant metaphor from the writer John McPhee, who first coined the term 'deep time' in 1980:

> Consider the earth's history as the old measure of the English yard, the distance from the king's nose to the tip of his outstretched hand. One stroke of a nail file on his middle finger erases human history.[17]

I still tingle when I read those words. Some people, though, prefer to express our cosmic insignificance in relation to time periods like the calendar year rather than the length of a regal arm. In one popular example, the Precambrian period runs from New Year's Day until around Halloween, dinosaurs come and go between mid-December and Boxing Day, the last ice sheet melts a minute before midnight on 31 December and the Roman Empire exists for just five seconds.

Most depictions of deep time are historical: they begin in the distant past and bring us up to the present and the age of *Homo sapiens*. In doing so, there is a danger that humankind comes across almost as the zenith of the evolutionary process – an idea that may do little to encourage a sense of humility among our species. That is why we also need visions of deep time that explicitly look forwards as well as back, focusing just as much on the epochs to come. This is an approach often found among cosmologists, such as the British astrophysicist Martin Rees:

I'd like to widen people's awareness of the tremendous times-pan lying ahead – for our planet, and for life itself. Most educated people are aware that we're the outcome of nearly four billion years of Darwinian selection, but many tend to think that humans are somehow the culmination. Our sun, however, is less than halfway through its lifespan. It will not be humans who watch the sun's demise, six billion years from now. Any creatures that then exist will be as different from us as we are from bacteria or amoebae. Our concern with Earth's future is, understandably, focused upon the next 100 years at most – the lifetimes of our children and grandchildren. But awareness of this longer time horizon, and the immense potential that human actions this century could foreclose, offers an extra motive for proper stewardship of this planet.[18]

This message goes to the heart of the deep-time perspective. On the one hand, it serves to extend our imaginations from a short now to a longer now, where *Homo sapiens* are here for little more than an eye-blink of cosmic time. We are merely bit players appearing on stage for the briefest moment in a story stretching over aeons. On the other hand, it is a warning about our destructive potential: in an incredibly short period of time we have endangered a world that took billions of years to evolve. We are just a tiny link in the great chain of living organisms, so who are we to put it all in jeopardy with our ecological blindness and deadly technologies? Don't we have an obligation, a responsibility, to our planetary future and the generations of humans and other species to come?

Experiential Journeys and the Wisdom of Tree Time

If we hope to grasp the mysteries of deep time, it might not be metaphors or artworks that best help us comprehend its wonders, but lived experiences that become etched onto our mental land-scapes.

One way to start is to take a physical journey with an app called Deep Time Walk, in which you follow a 4.6-kilometre self-guided walk that represents the 4.6-billion-year history of the earth. Along the way the narrators describe the various stages of the birth of the planet and all its teeming lifeforms, with the final 20 centimetres covering the amount of time humans have been in existence. Then there is the Cosmic Pathway at the American Museum of Natural History in New York City. Visitors walk 360 feet around the history of the universe in an ascending spiral, where they finally come to a single strand of human hair, stretched taut, whose width represents the 30,000 years from the earliest known cave painting in Europe to the building of the pathway itself.

You don't need to travel to North America to experience this for yourself: tangible reminders of deep time are all around us. I recall once stargazing through a telescope and for the first time realising that it was a time machine enabling me to look deep into the past, since the light hitting my eye had been travelling for years or possibly centuries to reach the earth, and could even be coming from stars that no longer existed or from a time before humans had evolved.

Last summer I found myself hunting for fossils with my kids on the beach at the seaside town of Lyme Regis. Unlike the famous nineteenth-century fossil hunter Mary Anning 200 years earlier, I didn't find a spectacular ichthyosaur skeleton, but I did manage to spot a perfectly formed belemnite – an ancient squid-like creature – that had been dislodged from the cliff face by the crashing waves. Just a few centimetres long, I held it delicately in my hand. No human being had ever seen it or touched it before me. I was holding a piece of planetary history, 195 million years old. I was filled with wonder, and my mind went giddy staring into the abyss of time.

Ancient trees offer another profound way to commune with deep time. For over a century, visitors to the American Museum of Natural History have stood before a cross section of a giant sequoia tree and marvelled. When it was felled in California in 1891, it stood 331 feet high with a base measuring 90 feet. The 1,342 rings reveal that the tree dates back to the middle of the sixth century. Labels along its radius mark significant moments in history, from the crowning of Charlemagne in 800 and the conquest of Jerusalem during the First Crusade in around 1100, to the rise of Napoleon in 1800 and the end of the tree's life in the year that Arthur Conan Doyle published *The Adventures of Sherlock Holmes*. 'With these historic contrasts before us,' declared the *New York Times* in 1908, 'we can begin to picture in our imagination the span of life that has been enjoyed by this hardy forest Methuselah.'

But the labels don't tell the whole story. They don't tell us who stood beneath the tree's branches for shelter or hid behind its trunk

The giant sequoia in the American Museum of
Natural History in New York City.

in fear. They don't tell us about the Kings River Lumber Company, which took possession of 30,000 acres of sequoia forest in 1888 and by 1905 had felled over 8,000 rare trees, including the one in the museum, most of which were more than 2,000 years old. 'I never saw a Big Tree that had died a natural death,' wrote the conservationist John Muir. Still, for all the tragedies, when I gazed upon another cross section of the very same tree in the Natural History Museum in London, I felt an awe, a reverence and an expanding sense of now.

Such experiential encounters with ancient trees have the power to connect us with the wonders of deep time. Although no single tree can directly embody the millions and billions of years of cosmic history – periods that can seem almost unfathomable – they act as a bridge to such colossal expanses of time by having lifespans that can extend far longer than our own. They help us step outside the narrow confines of decades to a vision of centuries and even millennia. In California's White Mountains there are bristlecone pines that are almost 5,000 years old, and on Crete there is an olive tree that may be 3,000 years old and still bears fruit.[19] Such trees appear in fiction too, like Treebeard in J.R.R. Tolkien's *The Lord of the Rings*, a giant talking tree, or Ent, who is the oldest creature in Middle Earth. Anyone walking through an ancient woodland can feel time slow down and stretch out, and sense a longer now in the gnarled roots and dank air.

This capacity of trees to act as a conduit to deep time struck me many years ago when I was working as a gardener at an Oxford college. My colleagues and I planted dozens and dozens of trees that we knew we would never see fully mature within our own lifetimes – oaks and limes and copper beeches. Many of them would be casting their shade well into the twenty-second century, and beyond. Knowing that the trees could easily outlive me gave birth to a feeling of humility and respect for the living world as something so much larger than my own flicker of existence.

Trees embody our symbiotic relationship with the natural world. They act as our external lungs: a large tree can provide a day's supply of oxygen for four people, while the 3.1 trillion trees worldwide absorb around a third of the carbon dioxide we humans produce each year.[20] Yet apart from their life-giving qualities, we can also think of trees as slow-time clocks, not only marking the years with their gradually expanding growth rings but also marking the cyclical rhythms of nature by changing with the seasons. In the words of novelist Richard Powers, trees teach us about 'life at the speed of wood'.[21] The art of long-term thinking may lie in the capacity to think in 'tree time', a scale of hundreds and thousands of years that can open our minds to the depths of time.

There is, of course, no simple formula for experiencing deep time. It cannot be bought off-the-shelf or ordered on demand. But we can do our best, through simple actions like making a monthly pilgrimage to visit an ancient tree (preferably alive rather than dead). It might be wise to leave your phone locked away for the day, so you can sit in tranquillity beneath its branches without being tempted to take a selfie. As the Zen monk Thich Nhat Hanh playfully advised, 'Don't just do something; sit there.'[22] In our stillness, in our rapture, the aeons may begin to flow through us.

Return of the Whirling Circle

History has not been kind to deep time. Its discovery coincided with the growing dominance of short-term thinking in the Industrial Revolution, and it has since then faced relentless competition from the accelerating speed of digital culture. Over the past two centuries, the factory clock and the iPhone have been largely victorious over the geologist's hammer and the stargazer's telescope. The stock market takes little notice of scientists or artists who promote the virtues of thinking on a cosmological scale of millions of years, while most politicians would consider planning even three or four decades ahead to be wildly utopian.

Yet just as our moral imaginations have expanded over the centuries – from concern for our immediate family and tribe to ideals such as universal human rights and animal rights – so too our temporal imaginations have the potential to extend far further than the here and now. With the help of art, metaphor and experience, we can begin to make sense of deep time.

Some people question the value of such an endeavour, arguing that grasping deep time could be a recipe for apathy: why bother with the problems of the world when human existence is such a fleeting moment in relation to the vastness of cosmic history and we will all end up as little more than stardust scattered throughout the universe?

An encounter with deep time takes us in a different direction: towards purpose rather than futility. It offers a vital perspective on the compulsive short-termism of the modern world, taking our minds off the last tweet and the next deadline and allowing us to see a bigger picture. It helps us think about the consequences of our actions in the distant future, such as where artificial intelligence technologies or synthetic biology may eventually take our species. It puts us back in touch with cyclical time, enabling us to appreciate natural phenomena such as the carbon cycle, which operates on the scale of millennia and shapes the fate of life on earth. It helps position us in the grand pageant of life on our planet, part of a chain of existence that we have no right to break through reckless destruction of the ecosystems in which all living things exist.

We might begin our journeys towards deep time with a practice inspired by the Long Now Foundation that is powerful in its simplicity: placing a zero in front of the year every time we write the date. I am writing these words in 02019. With just a single extra digit – echoing one of Black Elk's whirling circles – we can start to imagine tens of thousands of years into the future.

4

Legacy Mindset

How Can We Be Remembered Well?

'Will future generations speak of the wisdom of their
ancestors as we are inclined to speak of ours?
If we want to be good ancestors, we should show
future generations how we coped with an age
of great change and great crises.'

– Jonas Salk[1]

How will the people of the future remember us? It is a question that goes to the heart of the human condition, tapping into the powerful desire to defy our own mortality by leaving a legacy for posterity. More than half a century of psychology research reveals that this near-universal drive tends to emerge as we enter the middle stages of life.[2] Most of us hope that our actions and influence will somehow ripple into the years ahead, ensuring that the fire of our own life keeps burning beyond the inevitability of death. Few people truly wish to be forgotten forever.

But we choose to express our legacy in very different ways. Some pursue an egocentric form of legacy, hoping to be remembered and glorified for their personal achievements. That was the approach of Alexander the Great, who had statues of himself built throughout his empire, including at the sacred Greek site of Olympia. The legacy he sought was to be venerated in perpetuity for his heroic actions and brilliant conquests, and to be memorialised like a god – unsurprising for someone who claimed to be a direct descendant of Zeus. Today's corporate oligarchs who use their philanthropic largesse to have buildings, football stadiums and museum wings named after themselves have similar ambitions.

A more common aspiration is to leave a familial legacy, typically in the form of an inheritance written into a will for children, grandchildren or extended family and ranging from money and property to precious family heirlooms. It is the kind of legacy valued by aristocrats who want to keep their landed estate within the family bloodline, but also by immigrants – like my father, a refugee from Poland to Australia after the Second World War – who work long hours in the hope of leaving enough money for their children to have more opportunities in life than they did. For many people, it is less important to leave material possessions than to pass down their values and culture, whether in the form of religious beliefs, native languages or family traditions.

Yet if we truly wish to become good ancestors, we need to expand our conception of legacy and think of it not just as a route to personal glory or as a bequest for our offspring, but as a practice of everyday life that benefits all future people. We can think of this as a transcendent 'legacy mindset', where we aim to be remembered by the generations who we will never know, the universal strangers of the future. We can cultivate this form of long-term thinking through three approaches: the death nudge, intergenerational gifts and the wisdom of *whakapapa*.

The Death Nudge

What do we know about the human desire and willingness to leave a transcendent legacy for complete strangers? One place to look for answers is to track 'legacy giving', where people leave money in their wills to charitable causes. At first sight the data look impressive; in the US, such charitable bequests amounted to over $40 billion in

2018, while in the UK legacy giving generates $3.2 billion annually, with organisations such as Cancer Research UK and the British Heart Foundation receiving over one-third of their income from such bequests. But look closer and the figures lose their shine. While 35 per cent of British people say that would like to leave a charitable gift in their wills, only 6.3 per cent actually do so.[3] We tend to see inheritance largely as a family affair rather than an opportunity to help causes that may benefit those outside our kin.

Yet there is fascinating new research emerging from behavioural psychology showing just how little it takes to channel more of our giving towards future generations. All it requires is a 'death nudge' – a well-placed reminder of our mortality.

In an experiment led by Kimberly Wade-Benzoni, one of the world's leading scholars of intergenerational decision-making, participants were split into two groups. The first group were asked to read an article about someone who had been killed in an aeroplane accident, while the second group read about a Russian mathematical whizz. They were then told that they were being entered into a lottery draw for $1,000, and were given the option of committing a portion of the prize to one of two charities: one that helped people in need in the present, or one that worked to help people in the future. The result? Those who read about the maths genius gave two and half times more to the present-focused charity than the future-oriented one. In contrast, those given the death nudge by the plane article allocated more than five times as much to the future charity than the present one.[4]

Another pathbreaking study demonstrated that people who were encouraged to think about their personal legacy by writing a short essay about how they wanted to be remembered by future generations after they had died, were willing to donate 45 per cent more money to an environmental charity than those who did not write an essay.[5]

A third powerful piece of research explored ways to encourage people in the UK to leave larger bequests to charities in their wills. If a lawyer did not ask their client if they wanted to leave money to charity, around 6 per cent freely chose to do so anyway, but if the lawyer explicitly asked, 'Would you like to leave a charitable gift in your will?' the figure jumped to 12 per cent. And if the lawyer went even further and said, 'Many of our customers like to leave a gift to charity in their will. Are there any charitable causes that you're passionate about?' 17 per cent of those asked chose to leave a charity bequest.[6] So even a small change in wording can significantly influence legacy giving.

These findings offer an important takeaway. Economists typically assume that people heavily 'discount the future', placing relatively little value on the interests of future generations. But with just a few well-directed prompts, all that can change. It's as if there is a 'legacy switch' in our brains that simply needs to be flicked on. Get people to directly focus their minds on legacy giving and they will be more disposed to do so.

Moreover, the studies show that thinking about death and how we want to be remembered when we are gone can have enormous social benefits by helping to forge a sense of intergenerational care and responsibility. This is very much counter to the culture of death denial that pervades Western society. We expend enormous energy shielding ourselves from death, unlike in medieval times, when dancing skeletons were painted on the walls of churches and people wore skull brooches (known as 'memento mori') as a reminder that death could snatch them away at any moment.[7] We don't talk to our children about it, we shut the elderly away in care homes out of sight and out of mind, and the advertising industry tells us that we can be forever young. Perhaps it is time to start having more conversations about death.

It is also important to recognise what these studies don't show. They are not saying that we need to get better at imagining ourselves when we are much older, and that this would somehow be a stepping stone to caring about future generations. There is a growing body of research that presents people with computer-generated images of their elderly future selves, with wrinkles and grey hair, and reveals how doing so can prompt them to defer spending today and save more money into their pensions.[8] But none of it demonstrates that this form of imagining has any impact on their legacy giving. What's really needed is a prompt for thinking about mortality rather than retirement.

While it is clear that we should draw on the power of the death nudge, the lab experiments of behavioural psychologists can seem far removed from the realities of everyday life. For instance, they tend to frame leaving a legacy as an end-of-life financial decision, whereas it could equally involve planting a tree, switching to a plant-based diet or taking part in a street protest to protect the health care system.

To help think through such possibilities, it is worth giving yourself a death nudge with a penetrating question about the legacies we leave, which was first asked by the long-term thinker Stewart Brand: What might our descendants wish we had done better for them?[9]

Struggle with it, tussle with it, feel the piercing stare of the future. Whatever the answer, it is a call to action.

Paying It Forward: Passing on Gifts to the Next Generation

Giving people a death nudge might prompt immediate shifts in behaviour but still may not go far enough in creating the deep psychological shifts required to embed the values of the good ancestor in society. So how can we create a more profound connection with humanity's unborn and the planet they will inhabit? By delving into the ancient practice of giving gifts.

In most traditional societies, gift-giving originated as a ritual practice to reinforce community bonds and ensure good relations between tribal groups. Sometimes it was based on direct reciprocity: you gave a pipe and received an animal skin in return. But in many cultures, such as among the Massim peoples on the Trobriand Islands near New Guinea, gifts were not passed directly back and forth but rather travelled in a circle around the archipelago. In a ceremonial exchange known as the *kula*, first studied around a century ago by the anthropologist Bronisław Malinowski, red shell necklaces (worn by women) moved clockwise, while armshells (worn by men) were passed anticlockwise from island to island, community to community.[10]

Leaving a transcendent legacy for future people is a similar form of non-reciprocal gift exchange, but one that is passed through time rather than around space. Such exchanges already take place in everyday life, such as when parents pass used children's clothes on to other families: my children often wear jackets and shoes that have been handed down from older kids in our neighbourhood, and we will soon pass them on to the next cohort once they have outgrown them. More broadly, we are all recipients of gifts from previous generations: from the labourers of the past who built the roads and sewers we use every day, the medical researchers who found cures for smallpox and rabies, the campaigners who fought against slavery and for the voting rights we take for granted, and the composers who wrote music that can bring tears to our eyes. As the nineteenth-century anarchist geographer Peter Kropotkin wrote:

> For thousands of years millions of men have laboured to clear the forests, to drain the marshes and to open up highways by land and water . . . At the crossings of the highways great cities have sprung up, and within their borders all the treasures of industry, science and art have been accumulated. Whole generations, that lived and died in misery, oppressed and ill-treated by their masters, and worn out by toil, have handed on this immense inheritance to our century.[11]

Although we may often fail to acknowledge this inheritance, our lives are built on the gifts we have received from these ancestors we all share. Transcendent legacy is how we pay our dues. But instead of 'paying it back' we can 'pay it forward' by becoming givers of gifts to future generations.

Gift-giving is an ideal that resonates with the original meaning of the word *legacy*, which has its origins in medieval Europe. A legate – from the Latin *legatus*, meaning ambassador or envoy – was an emissary sent by the Pope to faraway lands, bearing an important message. So someone leaving a legacy can be thought of as being an intertemporal ambassador of the present sending a gift into the distant future.

There may be no higher calling than leaving a gift to the universal strangers of tomorrow, a gift that will offer us a place in the great procession of life that links us back to the first cellular organisms and forward to whatever we evolve into in the millennia ahead. We have already received extraordinary gifts from past generations of living beings, none greater than a planet on which we can live, breathe and flourish. At the very least, we can pass it on in a fit state for those who will follow us, so we are not looked back on as perpetrators of reckless bio-negligence or as agents of mass extinction. Is that really how we want to be remembered? 'We are the first generation to know that we face unprecedented global environmental risks, but at the same time we are the last generation with a significant chance to do something about it,' warns the earth system scientist Johan Rockström.[12] Time is running out for us to leave a legacy of which we can be proud.

The idea of leaving an intergenerational gift for posterity is a potent motivating force for many people, whether that gift is a thriving planet, an era of peace or takes some other form. Yet it can be difficult to feel a powerful and personal connection with the unborn inhabitants of the earth who we will never meet and can never look in the eye. Their lives can remain so distant, abstract and unknowable that it is almost impossible to step into their shoes and be moved to care about their prospects. Empathising with future generations may be one of the greatest of all moral challenges.

Is there any way of bridging this gap? There is, and it is rooted in ancient traditions of ancestor worship.

In Search of Whakapapa (With Help from My Daughter)

The veneration of ancestors is a thread that runs throughout the human story. The Christian Old Testament, the Hindu Mahabharata and the ancient Norse sagas of the Edda all contain long genealogical lists that trace bloodlines into the distant past. The Icelandic word *edda* itself means 'grandmother': these were stories told by generations of grandmothers to their kin. Among them were tales of Valhalla, the great hall roofed with shields, where those who died glorious deaths in battle would go to join their ancestors. The Vikings believed that they were being judged for their heroic deeds by their dead forebears and sought to be remembered well by those who were to come after them. Archaeologists have found signs of ancestor worship in China that go back over 4,000 years, including vessels used to serve the sacrificed flesh of enemies captured in war, as a ritual offering to the dead.[13] In contemporary China, past generations are fed in less gruesome fashion during the annual 'Festival of Hungry Ghosts', where empty seats are left for deceased family members who are given a sumptuous feast to satisfy their eternal appetites. Such rituals reinforce the Confucian ideal of filial piety – respect for one's elders – that remains powerful in Chinese culture.

Ancestor worship invites us to gaze from the present into the past, which at first appears very different from the notion of legacy, where we imagine our descendants looking back at us from the future to judge our actions in the present. Yet the veneration of ancestors typically creates a powerful chain of intergenerational linkage that travels forwards in time as well as backwards. This is evident in the time-bending Māori proverb, *Kia whakatōmuri te haere whakamua*: 'I walk backwards into the future with my eyes fixed on my past.' The Māori worldview is based on a liquid sense of time that dissolves yesterday, today and tomorrow into one another, and which requires a respect for the traditions and beliefs of previous generations while also being mindful of those who are yet to come. Everyone is in the room: the dead, the living and the unborn. 'We are all grandchildren and we are all ancestors,' says Māori lawyer and children's rights campaigner Julia Whaipooti. 'Personally I'm driven by our *mokopuna* ('future generations') to make the world a better place than when we found it.'[14]

The best-known expression of such thinking is the Māori concept of *whakapapa* ('genealogy'), which describes a continuous lifeline that connects an individual to the past, present and future.[15] In traditional Māori culture, a person's *whakapapa* or ancestral lineage can be represented in a *ta moko*, a facial or body tattoo. Nanaia Mahuta, the first female politician to wear a facial *ta moko* in the New Zealand parliament, describes it a marker of 'who I am, where I come from and the contribution I want to continue to make'.[16]

According to leadership expert and author James Kerr, the New Zealand rugby team try to live by a philosophy of *whakapapa*, which calls on them to both represent the players who came before them and create a legacy for those who will follow:

There's a fundamental Māori spiritual concept called 'whakapapa' – a long unbroken chain of humans standing arm in arm from the beginning of time to the end of eternity. And the sun shines for just a moment on this, our time. It's our obligation and responsibility to add to the legacy. Our first responsibility is to be a good ancestor.[17]

While *whakapapa* is best understood as part of a web of interlocking Māori concepts, such as *whānau* ('extended family') and *whenua* ('land' or 'placenta'), it is clearly a concept that has the potential to cross cultural boundaries, inspiring even non-Māori people to shine the light wider and picture their place in that long chain of the dead, the living and the unborn. Yet it may be difficult to absorb such thinking into our lives, since Western culture has been so devastatingly successful at severing a deep sense of intergenerational connection. Just as the children in Philip Pullman's *His Dark Materials* novels have been severed from their animal souls, or dæmons, we have been cut off from our ancestors and futurecestors. We are so busy living in the present, caught in the short now of work deadlines and instant messaging, that the idea of being just one link in a vast chain of humanity that stretches through cosmological time might feel hard to grasp. Our individualistic culture of self-help and 'looking after number one' makes it even more challenging. The result is to rupture our intergenerational ties and shrink our time horizons to the present tense. If we think of leaving a legacy at all, it is generally limited to just one or two generations from today, and within the boundaries of our family tree.

With imagination, however, we can find ways of connecting with the power of *whakapapa*. The most effective means I have ever encountered for doing so was through taking part in an immersive workshop on legacy thinking, part of a weekend convened by the Long Time Project. The workshop, which was called Human Layers, was created by cultural activists Ella Saltmarshe and Hannah Smith, and inspired by the deep ecologist Joanna Macy. Although it is best experienced in the company of others, it is possible to experience by yourself.

You begin by standing in an open space. The first instruction is to take a step backwards, with your eyes closed, and imagine someone you know and care about from an older generation, such as a parent or grandparent. You then step further back again and imagine them as a young adult, picturing their life, their thoughts and feelings, their hopes and struggles. After a minute, you take a third step backwards and imagine their fifth birthday – everyone who is there, the looks on their faces, the emotions in the air. When I did this, I was picturing my five-year-old father in his tiny village in Poland, just a year before the outbreak of the Second World War turned his life upside down. There was laughter, warm embraces from his grandmother, the first strawberries of spring from the forest.

For the next stage, you return to your original starting position and imagine a young person in your life who you care about and feel connected to, like a niece or godchild or one of your own children. Again with your eyes closed, you take a step forward and conjure up their face, their voice, the things they love doing. Then take another step forward and you've travelled 30 years into the future – what's happening in their life, what are their joys and troubles, what is the state of the world around them? Then take a final step and it's their ninetieth birthday party. You picture them surrounded by their own children and grandchildren, their closest friends, neighbours and work colleagues. They stand up, slightly doddery, with a stiff drink in their hand, about to make a birthday speech. Suddenly, over on the mantelpiece, they see a photograph of you, and decide instead to tell the gathered group about the legacy you left them: what they learned from you about how to live and the ways you inspired them.

At this point, the final instruction is to sit down and write out the speech they would give, a memorial to you, their departed ancestor.

Doing this exercise can be confronting, especially for those who have dark thoughts about our planetary future. It brings some people to tears. But it also offers an important way to visualise and personalise the future, when it can so easily remain a distant abstraction.

When I did it, imagining my then ten-year-old daughter turning into a ninety-year-old, it was a revelatory *whakapapa* moment.

Perhaps for the first time, I truly felt part of the interlinked chain of humanity. It made me consider not just the world I wanted to leave for my daughter, but what I wanted to leave for all future generations, who were symbolised by everyone who was at the birthday party with her. I realised that she was not an isolated individual but part of a whole interconnected web of life and relationships that constituted the future: all those people in the room, the air they were breathing, the living world outside the walls. To care about her life was to care about *all* life. A deep immersion in thinking about familial legacy, I discovered, can be a bridge to a more transcendent sense of legacy, prompting us to think beyond the confines of biological inheritance.

But it is not only a single child that can provide this transcendent link to the future; any set of relationships in which we are embedded has this potential. When we feel empathically bonded to a particular community, like the New Zealand rugby players do, we can develop a feeling of concern for, and solidarity with, its future members, and a desire to leave a legacy for their benefit. We can picture them; we almost know them. Whether it's a community based around sport, faith, culture, place or politics, we can feel motivated by a sense of shared history and a shared narrative towards acting in the interests of a shared destiny. This is how the power of empathy can work across the expanses of time, helping us escape from the straitjacket of the ego and the myopia of the now.

Growing a Legacy for Tomorrow

Of the six approaches to long-term thinking that appear in this book, the idea of a legacy mindset comes closest to Jonas Salk's original concern about being a good ancestor. It puts us into a relationship with future generations, so we feel their constant gaze upon us. We can be thankful that human beings possess a deep psychological drive to leave a legacy for posterity, and we know how to activate it: with the wisdom of *whakapapa*, the power of intergenerational gifts and timely death nudges to switch on our acorn brains.

We have an existential choice about how we want to be remembered and who our legacy will be for. We will never become good ancestors by simply pursuing an egocentric legacy that does little more than celebrate and immortalise our personal achievements, and nor can we only dedicate ourselves to a narrow sense of familial legacy, tempting though it may be. As a father of two children, I understand the desire to leave something behind for members of my own family, especially a financial inheritance that might offer them a semblance of security in this uncertain world. Yet if we hope for humankind – and that includes our own descendants – to survive and thrive into the twenty-first century and beyond, we must widen our vision to include a more transcendent approach to legacy.

There is an Apache saying, 'We do not inherit the land from our ancestors; we borrow it from our children.'[18] In the end it is not just our own children, but all children who will judge us from the future.

A legacy is not something that we *leave* but something we *grow* throughout our lives. It is not just a bequest written into a will, but a daily practice. We grow our legacy as parents and friends, as workers and citizens, as creators and activists and as members of communities. It is about being mindful of the consequences of our actions into the distant future, whether through the way we shop or the way we vote. It is about passing on a world that is fit for the flourishing of life. It is about planting acorns in the ground on behalf of those yet to come.

We can be inspired by all those who have chosen this path, such as the Kenyan medical professor Wangari Maathai, the first African woman to win the Nobel Peace Prize. In 1977 she founded the Green Belt Movement in Kenya, with the twin aims of promoting women's empowerment and restoring the country's natural wealth. By the time of her death in 2011, it had been responsible for training more than 25,000 women in forestry skills and planting over 40 million trees. And still her legacy continues to thrive, with the Green Belt Movement working with women in over 4,000 community groups around the country and campaigning for sustainable livelihoods across Africa. That is what it means to be a good ancestor.

Wangari Maathai, founder of the Green Belt Movement.

5

Intergenerational Justice

Reasons to Respect the Seventh Generation

'Why should I care about future generations? What have they ever done for me?' Although often attributed to Groucho Marx, this clever quip has in fact been circulating for more than 200 years.[1] But in our age of accelerating climate change, rapid species extinction and the spectre of AI and nanotechnology risk, the joke is starting to ring hollow: suddenly it is clear that the burning issue is what we are doing *to them*. There may no other moment in history when the actions of the present have had such monumental consequences for the future. We are now faced with one of the most urgent social questions of the twenty-first century: what obligations and responsibilities do we have to the generations who will succeed us?

The answer is obvious to Greta Thunberg, the teenage Swedish climate activist who has inspired an international movement of school students to strike until rich countries start reducing their carbon emissions in line with the 2015 Paris Climate Agreement. In December 2018 she stood before world leaders at the UN Climate Change Conference in Katowice in Poland, and admonished them for failing to tackle the global ecological crisis:

> The year 2078, I will celebrate my seventy-fifth birthday. If I have children, then maybe they will spend that day with me. Maybe they will ask about you. Maybe they will ask why you didn't do anything while there was still time to act. You say you love your children above all else, and yet you are stealing their future in front of their very eyes.[2]

Fired up by this blatant act of intergenerational theft, Greta is among the leaders of a growing movement of time rebels that has the potential to transform what modern democracy looks like. This movement is calling for intergenerational justice and equity – striking a fair balance between meeting the needs of current and future generations – and finding ways to represent the interests of the citizens of tomorrow in today's political institutions.

We can think of these generations to come as 'futureholders', a term coined by Juliet Davenport, founder of the renewable energy company Good Energy. Just as companies have shareholders, societies have futureholders: future citizens whose interests and welfare should be considered in the decisions that will affect their lives. Some you have already met – your children or other young people you know – while most are yet to be born. Securing their well-being requires creating a society based on intergenerational justice, which is one of the six approaches to long-term thinking that are at the core of this book. It offers a moral compass for becoming a good ancestor, expanding our ethical imaginations forward in time and helping to guide other forms of long thinking, such as cathedral thinking and holistic forecasting. In contrast to a legacy mindset, which can foster a sense of personal connection with futureholders, intergenerational justice encourages a sense of collective responsibility.

This chapter explores the four main grounds on which today's time rebels are making the case for intergenerational justice, and the inspiration they have found in the seventh-generation principle of indigenous cultures. Our starting point is one of the most formidable barriers they face: an extraordinarily influential economic practice that goes by the innocent name of 'discounting'.

The Dark Art of Discounting (or How We Turn Future Citizens into Slaves)

Discounting is a weapon of intergenerational oppression disguised as a rational economic methodology. Just as a person appears smaller and smaller the further from us they stand, discounting gives smaller and smaller weight to their interests the further in the future they stand. Policymakers use discounting to weigh up the costs and benefits of long-term investment decisions. If you really want to know how much a government cares for its future citizens, don't listen to eloquent ministerial speeches, just look at the discount rate. What you will discover is shocking.

The argument for discounting seems plausible at first. Human beings tend to value present rewards more than future ones, so we might prefer to be given $2,000 today rather than $5,000 in ten years' time. Discounting turns this time preference into a principle, whereby future benefits are given relatively less value compared to current ones. Take a government policy with the future benefit of saving human lives, such as investing in health care. Using a discount rate of 2 per cent, a single life today is given the same value as 2.7 lives in 50 years' time (this is calculated like compound interest: $1 \times 1.02^{50} = 2.7$). After 100 years, a life today has a value equal to 7.2 future lives. Raise the discount rate and the relative value of future lives falls rapidly: at a rate of 10 per cent, a life today is worth 117 lives in 50 years, and 13,781 lives after 100 years ($1 \times 1.1^{100} = 13,781$). So with that 10 per cent discount rate, a government would opt to save just a few lives today rather than invest the same amount of money to save nearly 14,000 lives a century from now.

What has this all got to do with intergenerational justice? Over the last hundred years, discounting has spread from finance and accounting to infiltrate policymaking in areas ranging from public health to climate change. Governments now often decide whether to invest in hospitals, transport infrastructure or a new flood barrier system by using a discount rate to calculate how the future benefits of such projects compare to their costs today. The discount rates they typically deploy – usually between 2 per cent and 4 per cent – might not sound very high, but they can be enough to tilt them against such investments even if they are likely to bring large benefits in the future, since distant benefits (beyond, say, 50 years) appear to be negligible.[3]

To see the problem of discounting in action, consider the UK government's controversial 2018 ruling against the approval of the country's first ever tidal lagoon energy project in Swansea Bay. Hopes for the project were high, especially given that the UK possesses around 50 per cent of Europe's available tidal and wave energy, with tidal power offering the potential to supply up to 20 per cent of the nation's energy needs. The government justified its decision by claiming that tidal power was less cost-effective than alternative options such as nuclear, but as critics swiftly pointed out, the cost-benefit analysis and discounting methodology employed did not include the long-term costs of nuclear decommissioning or waste disposal, while also failing to include the full benefits of the 120-year tidal project beyond the first 60 years. Including these longer-term costs and benefits would have likely tipped the balance in favour of the development.[4] As Good Energy CEO Juliet Davenport explained to me, one of the reasons why such large-scale renewable energy projects often struggle to get government backing is that their start-up costs are relatively high, while the long-term benefits get discounted away. The result is that future generations bear the ultimate cost of our statistical disregard.[5]

Discounting might have become standard government practice, but should it play such a dominant role in decision-making? One challenge to this was *The Economics of Climate Change*, the 2006 report written for the UK government by economist Nicholas Stern, which recommended that the future costs of global warming were so great that every year, 1 per cent of global GDP should be spent on mitigating them. Stern was widely praised for giving the interests of future generations significant weight by using an unusually low discount rate that averaged 1.4 per cent, compared to the more standard 3 per cent used by economists such as William Nordhaus or the 3.5 per cent typically used by UK government departments.[6] Yet was this really such a great victory for intergenerational justice?

In fact, the effect of a 1.4 per cent discount rate amounted to treating future generations as little more than slaves. How so? Under a notorious clause in the US Constitution of 1787, an African-American slave was assigned three-fifths of the value of a free white person for the purpose of calculating the congressional representation of Southern States. So how quickly do we give future generations a status equivalent to slaves under the rules of discounting, or in other words, after how many years is a future person given just three-fifths the value of a person today? Using Stern's 1.4 per cent discount rate, after just 36.5 years future people are treated no better than slaves: their interests are worth just 60 per cent of people's interests today. With Nordhaus's 3 per cent – the standard used by many governments – the results are even starker: future generations are 'enslaved' in a mere 17 years. So compared to 100 people in the present, 100 people in the future are valued at the equivalent of 60 people (three-fifths) after 17 years, 5 people after a century and just a single person after 150 years (see below). How could we treat our descendants with such callous disregard? Discounting is an iconic expression of the colonisation of the future, treating it as virtually empty of inhabitants.

Shouldn't we cease the practice of discounting and instead treat all people's interests equally, regardless of when they happen to be born? As the standard reply goes, discounting simply reflects our preference for parties today rather than pensions tomorrow. Yet an individual's preference for the present does not justify us collectively treating future generations in the same way. Who are we to diminish the value they will place on their own lives and welfare? A second

The enslavement of future generations

With a discount rate of 3%, what is the equivalent value given to 100 human beings at different points over the next 150 years?

Now: 100 people

After 17 years: 60 people (status of slaves)

After 50 years: 23 people

After 100 years: 5 people

After 150 years: 1 person

Graphic: Nigel Hawtin

response, often found in economics textbooks, is that discounting is justified because economic growth and technological advancements will equip future generations with better and cheaper means of tackling problems such as climate change, so we shouldn't overinvest in helping them out. Yet it is wishful thinking to assume that growth will continue decade after decade, especially once the impact of ecological breakdown begins to kick in. It is equally wishful to believe that with enough money and technology in their pockets, our descendants will be able to simply reverse cataclysmic events such as species extinctions, polar ice melt or the rampant spread of genetically engineered viruses.

While discounting may first appear to be a neutral and technocratic exercise, as the Nobel Prize-winning economist Amartya Sen points out, it inevitably involves a value judgement and should be 'a matter for public deliberation'.[7] The inventor of discounting, Frank Ramsey, went a step further and declared in 1928 that discounting the welfare of future generations was 'ethically indefensible and arises merely from the weakness of the imagination'.[8] This is not to say that discounting should have no place whatsoever in project appraisal, just that it may not be appropriate to use when assessing environmental projects with very long-term impacts like a tidal energy scheme, or in cases where there is the chance of irreversible and catastrophic risks that no promise of economic growth can make up for. But in order to justify putting discounting to one side, we also need to make the positive case for equality between the generations. Why exactly should we care so much about people from the future?

The Arrow, The Scales, The Blindfold and The Baton

If you were given $100 million and asked to allocate it for the welfare of humankind, how would you do it? Among the dilemmas you would face is not just how to share the funds between different countries or specific social groups to alleviate suffering in today's world, but how to distribute the funds *through time*. In other words, how much, if any, should be earmarked or invested for the benefit of future generations, and how many generations ahead? This question goes to the heart of debates about intergenerational justice and equity. There are, of course, no simple answers, and philosophers have been struggling with the issue for more than 50 years. But there is a growing consensus that the lives of future people – even those living decades or centuries from now – should matter in our moral deliberations and political decisions, and not simply be swept aside with a Groucho Marx witticism or an economist's discount rate.

This emerging consensus is partly visible in the avalanche of international accords that refer to future generations. Go back to the French Declaration of the Rights of Man (1789) or the Universal Declaration of Human Rights (1948), and you won't find any reference whatsoever to future generations.[9] This all began to change in 1987, when the UN's World Commission on Environment and Development published Our Common Future (known as the Brundtland Report), which famously defined sustainable development as 'development that meets the needs of the present without compromising the ability of future generations to meet their own needs'.[10] Since 1993 there have been more than 200 UN resolutions mentioning the welfare of 'future generations', as well as more than 40 national constitutions, in countries from Argentina to Estonia.[11]

Unsurprisingly, this outburst of official recognition has yet to be translated into significant political practice, but it undoubtedly signals that the issue of intergenerational justice has finally come of age. An extraordinary range of organisations is now advocating on the behalf of tomorrow's citizens. They include international campaigning groups like Greenpeace, whose mission is 'to ensure a peaceful and sustainable world for future generations', and think tanks such as the Foundation for the Rights of Future Generations. There are youth groups in Italy calling for a Court of Intergenerational Justice, while the organisation Our Children's Trust is fighting legal battles for the right of America's future generations to live on a healthy planet.[12] They are joined by direct action movements such as the Sunrise Movement in the US and Extinction Rebellion in the UK, and politically engaged midwives concerned with the fate of the babies they deliver.[13] There are experts on existential risk lobbying governments to mitigate the dangers that new technologies pose for humanity in the coming century.[14] Pope Francis has also come on board, speaking of the need for 'justice between generations'.[15] The struggle for the rights and interests of futureholders is fast becoming one of the most vibrant social movements of our time.

Just as campaigners against slavery in the eighteenth century drew on a powerful set of arguments to legitimise their cause and give it moral and intellectual firepower, so too do many of today's advocates for future generations. They realise that it is not good enough to simply state that the needs of future generations matter as much as the needs of those living in the present, as if it were an irrefutable fact, especially when there are so many pressing problems facing humanity today, from child poverty to civil war. We need to recognise the moral urgency of the issues in our own time – for instance, that there are 150 million children currently at risk of malnutrition-related mortality[16] – but we also need to grant future people fair treatment, so their interests are not ignored. Campaigners understand that it is vital to offer compelling grounds for bringing future generations into our circle of concern, in order to inspire action on their behalf.[17] So why should we care about them, or even sacrifice for them? The most popular arguments fall into four broad types, each expressing a different moral motive for intergenerational justice, which I've named The Arrow, The Scales, The Blindfold and The Baton (see below).

Four moral motives for intergenerational justice

The Arrow
Treat people of equal worth, independent of when they happen to be born

The Scales
Weigh up the well-being of those alive today against all those yet to be born

The Blindfold
Imagine the world you'd want if you didn't know into which generation you would be born

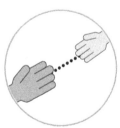

The Baton
Treat future generations how you would want past generations to have treated you

Graphic: Nigel Hawtin

The Arrow concerns the extent to which we are responsible for the future consequences of our actions. One of its best-known formulations appears in the writing of philosopher Derek Parfit:

> Remoteness in time has, in itself, no more significance than remoteness in space. Suppose that I shoot some arrow into a distant wood, where it wounds some person. If I should have known that there might be someone in this wood, I am guilty of gross negligence. Because this person is far away, I cannot identify the person whom I harm. But this is no excuse. Nor is it any excuse that this person is far away. We should make the same claims about effects on people who are temporally remote.[18]

To put it another way, if we have an obligation not to plant a bomb on a train that would harm a child now, we have the same obligation not to do so if it was timed to go off in ten minutes, or ten days or even ten years from now.[19] This argument is frequently used in debates about nuclear waste. We know there is a high probability that what is known as 'high-level' radioactive waste will be dangerous to people hundreds or even thousands of years from today, but just because they are distant in time doesn't mean we should be freely permitted to dump the risk on them. We should respect their welfare independent of when they happen to be born, a view that is completely at odds with the logic of discounting. Nuclear waste is like an arrow flying through the woods for centuries or millennia, posing a continual risk to human populations. There is a significant chance that at some point the arrow is going to land with devastating effects, just as is the case with our burning of fossil fuels or poisoning of the oceans. We have a responsibility to take action today to mitigate the future impact of the arrows we fire. In fact, the fewer we fire, the better.[20]

The Scales, a second rationale for intergenerational justice, asks us to imagine a set of scales where everyone who is alive today is on one side, and all the generations of people who are yet to be born are on the other. At least in terms of sheer numbers, the current population is easily outweighed by all those who will succeed us. By one calculation, around 100 billion people have lived and died in the past 50,000 years; if the average birth rate of the twenty-first century is maintained for the next 50,000 years, around 6.75 trillion human beings will be born. That is 877 times more people than the 7.7 billion who are alive today, and far outnumbers every human being that has ever lived (see below).[21] How could we possibly ignore their well-being and think that our own is of such greater value?

Some critics counter that in the coming millennia there may not even be humans like us to stand on the other side of the scales. *Homo sapiens* could morph into a cyborg race with artificially enhanced intelligence and manufactured organs that allow them to live centuries rather than decades, and they may have a completely different set of values and concept of well-being. How can we know what might even matter to them, or whether we would grant them the same moral standing as ourselves? But assuming that there will still be some *Homo sapiens* around, or beings who resemble us in significant ways that we recognise – feeling pain, fearing death, falling in love, wanting families and searching for purpose – it would be an act of colossal moral failure to disregard their welfare. Doing so would be to display an unashamedly colonial attitude to the future, treating it as a distant land empty of inhabitants that we are free to plunder with impunity.

The Blindfold refers to a thought experiment invented by the political philosopher John Rawls in his 1971 book *A Theory of Justice*. Imagine you stand behind a 'veil of ignorance', not knowing what position in society you will be born into – you have no idea what your wealth, sex, ethnic background, intelligence or values will be. In this 'original position', asked Rawls, how would you distribute the resources of society? Would you, for instance, allow some people to

The scale of unborn generations

Looking 50,000 years into the past and 50,000 into the future –
assuming that the twenty-first century's birth rate remains constant –
all human lives ever lived are far outweighed by all those
yet to come

The dead
100 billion

The living
7.7 billion

Unborn
generations
6.75 trillion

Based on UN estimate that
average births per year in the
twenty-first century will
stabilise at 135 million

Graphic: Nigel Hawtin

be very wealthy while the vast majority living in poverty? Rawls argued that we wouldn't since we would be risking our own destitution, and that we would instead opt for basic principles of equality and redistribution.[22] But now take the experiment further and imagine that you are not only ignorant of what social position you'll land in, but also of the generation into which you will be born. Perhaps it will be in 10 years, when life may be little different from today, but it could be in 200 years, when there is a massive global food and water crisis and the rich are mostly living off-planet. So now how would you distribute the resources? How much would you set aside or invest for future generations, just in case you happened to be born among them?

Rawls and many others have attempted to provide an answer to this conundrum. One response is that we should set aside only enough to ensure 'just institutions', so any future society is able to preserve basic rights.[23] A different approach is to guarantee that subsequent generations are able to meet their essential needs or make the kinds of choices that lead to a fulfilling life, which might require a minimum level of education or health care. Others argue that resource distribution misses the big environmental picture and that each generation should leave the planet in a condition of life-sustaining ecological health that is at least as good as when they were bequeathed it – a principle of 'regenerative justice' that echoes ideas of stewardship.[24] One might object that such a range of responses renders Rawls's thought experiment of little value. Yet whatever the answer, the key point is that when we are behind a veil of ignorance, we begin to consider the welfare of future generations as something that should matter to us today. The power of The Blindfold is that it expands the human imagination, inspiring us to extend our circle of care not just across space, but also through time.

A final popular argument, which I call The Baton, is based on the Golden Rule, 'Do unto others as you would have them do unto you.'

This empathic principle can be found in almost every major world religion, and we often teach it to children as one of their first moral lessons in life. A limitation of the Golden Rule is that we tend to think of it within the temporal confines of our own lives – treating other people around us as we would want to be treated too. But we can easily extend this idea to future generations, so that we also have a duty not to impose harm and dangerous risks on future people that we wouldn't be willing to accept ourselves. In other words, 'Do unto future generations as you would have past generations do unto you.'[25] Think of it as an intergenerational Golden Rule that can be passed on from one generation to another – that is to say, a 'golden baton'.

If we think back to our own forebears, there are many things that we might wish they had never passed on to us, from the inheritance of colonial-era racism and patriarchal attitudes that still have a hold in so many countries, to the environmental impacts of an industrial system based on fossil fuels. If we would wish that our 'bad ancestors' had not left us such legacies, what grounds do we have for passing on a similarly negative inheritance to the future, whether in the form of the ecological damage we cause, the potential risks of new technologies or the thoughtless dumping of nuclear waste? After all, we wouldn't want to be on the receiving end of such an inheritance ourselves. The Baton ensures that we are mindful about the consequences of our actions, and is among our best guides for becoming good ancestors. We can also think about it in relation to positive actions, so we make sure to pass on the public health institutions or great works of art and literature left to us by previous generations. In a story from the Jewish Talmud, a man is asked why he is planting a carob tree that will not produce fruit within his lifetime and replies, 'Just as my ancestors planted for me, I too am planting for my descendants.'[26]

These four arguments are founding principles that underpin the values of a long now civilisation. While it might be difficult to mentally envisage what tomorrow's world will look like and the precise challenges humanity will face, their crucial role is to bring the silent majority of future generations into the room when we are making choices, whether as individuals or as a society. They open our minds to respecting the interests of futureholders and ensuring their fair treatment in a world where they are largely ignored by existing political institutions. These arguments cannot in themselves provide an exact formula for how we might allocate resources between current and future generations, but they do tell us that the needs of future people should be duly considered alongside the injustices and suffering faced by people today. Their concerns deserve a fair hearing.

How might we transform these philosophical arguments into practical action? Perhaps the most powerful and effective way of doing so is to adopt an indigenous cultural practice that embodies their intent in a single unifying vision: seventh-generation decision-making.

Seventh-Generation Thinking and the
Value of Deep Stewardship

If you asked a typical career politician to make a major policy decision based on looking 200 years into the future, they would probably laugh you out of their office. But for many indigenous peoples, this is a deeply respected cultural tradition. According to Oren Lyons, a Native American chief of the Turtle Clan of the Onondaga Nation, part of the Iroquois Confederacy:

> We are looking ahead, as is one of the first mandates given us as chiefs, to make sure every decision that we make relates to the welfare and well-being of the seventh generation to come, and that is the basis by which we make decisions in council. We consider: will this be to the benefit of the seventh generation?[27]

This seventh-generation thinking, says John Borrows, a Canadian law professor and member of the Chippewas of Nawash First Nation band in Ontario, 'is a significant principle of Indigenous Law' that ensures a healthy environment for their descendants, especially by restricting the exploitation of natural resources: 'Living within our limits demonstrates affection for our children. It also shows our respect and love for the earth.'[28]

Such customary practices are not limited to the Americas and can also be found among indigenous peoples worldwide, although not always expressed in relation to a specific number of generations. When I met Tanzanian Maasai leader Samwel Nangiria, he told me that in their struggles to preserve their traditional way of life the Maasai are planning a century ahead, unlike some of the NGOs who want to help them, whose projects only last two or three years. 'We need to think about the present, the past and the lives of future people,' he said. 'This is not just about land – it's about all life. We have a Life Plan that looks forward 100 years. We are fighting for our people, our wildlife, the next generation.'[29]

Underlying this indigenous worldview is a philosophy of deep stewardship, in which the earth is not something that is 'owned' by the current generation and available for them to dispose of as they wish but rather a living entity, a Mother Earth that must be preserved intact and thriving for their descendants and all of life itself. It's an idea that is familiar in the teachings of many religions, such as Christianity, which see the earth as a gift from God that is temporarily 'on loan' to each generation.[30] But the indigenous perspective runs deeper, for it does not treat human beings as superior creatures with a special duty to stand guard over Creation, but rather as an integral part of a planetary living whole. Acting as a steward for the seventh generation is a profound expression of biosphere consciousness.

Among the leading advocates of seventh-generation thinking is ecologist and geneticist David Suzuki. In his view, our politicians ought to be asking, 'Look, if we pass this bill, what's that going to do seven generations down the line?'[31] Suzuki recognises that seeing humans as interdependent with the living world lies at the heart of the seventh-generation principle. The environment is not something 'out there'; as he puts it, 'we *are* the environment'. We are connected to the landscape, just as we are to future generations, through the air we breathe, the water we drink and the soil in which we grow our food.

The oxygen we breathe in, for instance, circulates in our bloodstream and around half remains in our lungs, so there is no clear line separating where the air ends and we begin. When we exhale, our breath mixes with the air and is taken in by other people, birds, mammals and reptiles. 'If I am air and you are air, then I am you,' writes Suzuki. But the atoms in the air also persist through time. According to one study, there are 3×10^{19} (three followed by nineteen zeros) argon atoms in a breath of air. These quintillions of atoms are continually being blown around the planet, so wherever you are, you will breathe in around 15 argon atoms that you breathed in a year earlier. And that's not all. Each breath we take contains argon atoms that were probably once inhaled by Cleopatra and Gautama Buddha, and will be breathed in by our descendants seven generations from today. 'Air,' says Suzuki, plays an essential role 'linking all life in a single matrix, and joining past, present and future in a single flowing entity.'[32]

Seventh-generation thinking is powerfully compelling, but it also carries some myths. The Iroquois Great Law of Peace, a 500-year-old 'constitution' of the six Iroquois nations, is often cited as the origin of the principle, yet it does not actually make any specific mention of considering the seventh generation.[33] Nevertheless, the principle is undoubtedly alive and well in indigenous decision-making practices today, such as among the Oglala Lakota Nation in South Dakota.[34] Secondly, it suggests an ideal of indigenous people always living in harmony with nature and caring about their future generations, but it is well known that some native peoples have sold logging and mining rights to the highest bidder rather than acting as ecological stewards. Of course, even indigenous communities are subject to the lures of short-termism, but this is the exception rather than the rule.

Is it realistic to take a practice like seventh-generation thinking out of the context of indigenous cultures and give it meaning and traction in the high-velocity, consumer-driven modern world? Could it really be taken seriously by the shoppers of Shanghai, the oil executives of Dubai or the politicians of Miami?

Yes, much more than one might imagine. Over the last two decades, 'seventh-generation thinking' has become a popular shorthand for a long-term approach to sustainability and intergenerational justice that is spreading its influence far beyond traditional indigenous communities. The global youth organisation Earth Guardians aims to 'protect our planet and its people for the next seven generations'.[35] In Japan, Future Design, a political movement that works to incorporate the interests of future generations into policymaking, is inspired by the Iroquois seventh-generation principle.[36] Deep ecologist Joanna Macy has devised a 'Seventh Generation' workshop, where participants engage in a paired dialogue, with one person speaking from the present and the other representing someone from seven generations in the future.[37] Chief Oren Lyons himself helped found the Swedish urban farming company Plantagon in 2008, which began issuing unique 'seventh-generation shares' that could only be cashed in after they had passed through seven generations of a family or seven people who had each held them for at least 33 years.[38] There is even a sustainable cleaning product company called Seventh Generation, which has the principle stencilled on the window of the main conference room at its Vermont headquarters.

No government has yet made the seventh-generation principle a cornerstone of public policy, yet adopting it may sooner or later become a matter of necessity rather than choice. In a 2008 speech, Elinor Ostrom, winner of the Nobel Prize in Economics, raised the question of how we could create societies that sustainably manage the natural resources we have inherited so we can pass them on to our descendants:

> I am deeply indebted to the indigenous peoples in the US, who had an image of seven generations being the appropriate time to think about the future. I think we should all reinstate in our mind the seven-generation rule. When we make really major decisions, we should ask not only what will it do for me today, but what will it do for my children, my children's children, and their children's children into the future.[39]

Empowering the Silent Majority

No matter how compelling the case to respect the interests of future generations, there remain formidable forces lined up to deny them fair treatment and neglect their needs, from politicians looking to boost their popularity in the next poll, to fossil fuel and biotech companies wanting to make a quick buck. Yet the greatest challenge remains invisible: the billions of unborn citizens of tomorrow are not here to make their case for themselves. They cannot chain themselves to a corporate headquarters or stage a sit-down protest on a busy city bridge. They cannot take a government to court, write a newspaper column in their defence or refuse to be discounted by economists. They are a majority condemned to suffer in silence.

Hope lies in a growing global movement for intergenerational justice dedicated to their cause, which is backed up by the moral force of The Arrow, The Scales, The Blindfold and The Baton, and inspired by the practice of the seventh-generation principle. It includes the hundreds of thousands of schoolchildren – among them my own – who have joined Greta Thunberg in multi-nation strikes, the direct-action protesters compelling countries and cities worldwide to declare climate emergencies and the advocates for citizens' assemblies that give a voice to the interests of future generations. This is just the beginning of what may turn out to be one of the most powerful progressive social movements of our time.

Until now, representative democracy has systematically ignored the rights of future generations, who have been relegated to the position of a powerless and neglected silent majority. Overturning this temporal discrimination would create the most seismic change in the history of democracy since the enfranchisement of women in the early twentieth century. With this ambition in mind, my partner and I now give our electoral votes to our 11-year-old twins: we scrutinise the party manifestos, watch political debates and discuss the issues together, and then they instruct us how to vote.

Will the intergenerational justice movement succeed? Its strategies and struggles, which will be explored in Part Three of this book, offer hope. So does the evidence from human history. Until the middle of the twentieth century, Europeans showed little interest in the plight of people living in developing countries. There were few advocacy organisations devoted to them, they gained little media attention and politicians barely gave them a thought. That has all changed. By the mid-twenty-first century, it is possible that our attitude to the futureholders will have undergone a similar transformation. They will have become part of our moral and political mindscape.

6

Cathedral Thinking

The Art of Planning into the Distant Future

'When we build, let us think that we build forever.
Let it not be for the present delight, nor for present use alone;
let it be such a work as our descendants will thank us for.'

– John Ruskin[1]

There is a story about New College, Oxford, that often comes up in conversations about long-term thinking. Apparently, it was discovered in the 1860s that the long oak beams holding up the roof of the ancient dining hall were rotten and needed replacing. Nobody knew where they might find such huge timbers. It then came to light – thanks to the college woodsman – that when the hall was built in the fourteenth century, the college's founder William of Wykeham had planted a grove of oaks that were reserved expressly for replacing the beams. And so, thanks to Wykeham's incredible foresight, 500 years later the college had the oaks it needed for the job and the fellows and students have been dining happily under the replacement beams ever since.

It's a wonderful story. The only problem is that it isn't true. 'It seems some myths will never die,' I was told by New College archivist, Jennifer Thorp, when I asked her about its authenticity.[2] It turns out that the oaks for the beams came from a woodland that was not purchased by the college until decades after the original hall had been built, and that they had never been especially earmarked for restoring the roof. William of Wykeham had not been so far-sighted after all.

My point is not to highlight yet another example of fake news. Rather, the popularity of this story shows just how much we want to believe in the human capacity for long-term planning. A tale about planting trees for the benefit of people half a millennium in the future feels like the perfect antidote to our age of pathological short-termism. If only our politicians would stop obsessing about the latest opinion poll and become a little more like William of Wykeham, we might take measures to invest seriously in public health care, put a brake on global warming or prepare for the risks of biological warfare. We might even stop dumping nuclear waste on future generations too. That, in any case, is the hope.

This chapter demonstrates that the historical record is on the side of hope. We don't need to invent stories about our ability to plan for the long term, because human beings have been surprisingly good at it over the past 5,000 years. It may be one of the greatest skills of our species and the clearest practical expression of our acorn brains in action. According to Jared Diamond, 'successful long-term planning' is vital if a society is going to survive and flourish rather than collapse.[3] That's why the art of planning into the distant future – sometimes known as 'cathedral thinking' – is among the six essential strategies for forging a culture of long-termism. So what does successful long-term planning look like, and what does history teach us about the conditions under which it can emerge? Insights can be found in three unexpected areas: sacred architecture, a Japanese moonscape and a dramatic sewerage crisis.

Five Thousand Years of Long-Term Planning

Planning, defined simply, is about mapping out a practical course of action to achieve a specific goal. My focus is not on making immediate plans, such as what to have for dinner this evening or even where to be living in five years' time, but on our potential to plan projects with time horizons lasting decades or longer, even beyond our own lifetimes.

If you have any doubts about our ability to do so, walk through the doors of Ulm Minster, a Lutheran church in southwest Germany, where you will find a foundation stone dated 1377. In that year, the city's inhabitants decided to build a new church under the watchful eye of architect Heinrich Parler the Elder, which they planned to finance themselves through individual contributions. But none of them would ever see the finished building, for it wasn't completed until more than 500 years later, in 1890.

Ulm Minster surely ranks as one of the most impressive crowdfunding projects in history. It is also a classic instance of long-term planning, a project that its founders knew would never be finished within their own lifespans. And yet they embarked on it anyway, driven perhaps by a mixture of spiritual conviction and dogged determination. Its closest contemporary rival is the Sagrada Familia, Antoni Gaudí's fantastical basilica in Barcelona. Begun in 1882, it may be the longest continuous building project in the world today, with completion finally expected in 2026. Gaudí, who worked on the site for the last 43 years of his life, was never an architect to rush things, and would happily have a wall knocked down if he didn't think it looked right. 'My client is not in a hurry,' he used to say, referring to his divine overseer.[4] Yet the fact that religious buildings are among the best-known examples of long-term planning may be due less to having a client as patient as God and more to do with the longevity of religious institutions themselves. Most Catholics expect that their ancient order, which is already 2,000 years old, will be around for centuries to come, so it makes perfect sense to build for the benefit of its future flock.

The concept of cathedral thinking acts as a shorthand for the kind of long-term vision evident in sacred architecture but largely absent from politics or business. According to Greta Thunberg, 'it will take cathedral thinking' to tackle the climate crisis.[5] Another populariser

The Sagrada Familia in 1905. Gaudí worked on the building from 1883 until his death in 1926, regularly sleeping in the basement of the construction site. It was only a quarter finished when he was killed by a tram on his daily walk to confession, aged 73.

of the concept is astrophysicist Martin Rees, who has pointed out that the far-sighted outlook that inspired the builders of the eleventh-century Ely Cathedral could not be more different from the prevailing myopia of our current moment: 'In today's runaway world, we can't aspire to leave a monument lasting a thousand years, but it would surely be shameful if we persisted in policies that denied future generations a fair inheritance.'[6]

Yet is it only cathedrals that we should look to for inspiration? The table below catalogues a range of long-term projects that human societies have undertaken over the past five millennia, with time horizons stretching from decades to several centuries.

Long-Term Planning in Human History

RELIGIOUS BUILDINGS

Step Pyramid, Saqqara, Egypt	The oldest pyramid in the world, built c.2600 BCE in 18 years, where King Djoser could be eternally reborn in the afterlife. The engineer Imhotep was revered as a god.
Ulm Minster, Germany	Lutheran church constructed 1377–1890. Funded by local residents, it was the mother of all crowdfunding projects lasting over 500 years.
Sagrada Família, Spain	Gaudí's basilica in Barcelona. Begun in 1882, completion is expected in 2026. It is currently the longest continuous building project in the world. Gaudí spent 43 years on it.
Ise Jingū, Japan	A Shinto shrine that has been torn down and rebuilt to exactly the same design every 20 years since 690 CE. A building forever new and forever ancient.

INFRASTRUCTURE

Qanats of Gonabad, Iran	Water tunnel system built 700–500 BCE, over 33km long and still in use. Supplies water for around 40,000 people in arid areas.
Segovia aqueduct, Spain	One of the best-preserved examples of Roman civil engineering. Built in the first century CE from granite with no mortar. Used until the nineteenth century.
Great Wall of China	Dates back to the third century BCE. From the fourteenth century, the Ming dynasty spent 200 years building 8,850km of wall and 25,000 watchtowers to keep out Mongols.

Polder water management system, Netherlands	Land protected from flooding by dikes, covering a quarter of the country. The oldest existing polder dates from 1533. Managed by democratic water boards.
Canal du Midi, France	The first great European canal, 240km long, linking the Mediterranean with the Bay of Biscay. Built 1665–81. The designer Pierre-Paul Riquet became a national hero.
Panama Canal	Construction 1881–94 under the French but then abandoned, with 22,000 worker deaths. Completed 1904–14 by the US, which controlled the canal zone until 1979.
Trans-Siberian Railway, Russia	Built 1891–1916. The longest railway in the world, from Moscow to Vladivostok on the Sea of Japan; 62,000 labourers constructed the 9,289km line.
Channel Tunnel, UK–France	50km tunnel first proposed in 1802, supported by Churchill in 1920s and finally built 1988–94, with a lining designed to last 120 years.
South–North Water Transfer Project, China	Conceived under Mao in 1952. Construction 2002–50. Three canals, 1,553 miles long, transporting the equivalent of 50 per cent of the annual flow of the Nile.

URBAN DESIGN

Miletus, Greece	In 479 BCE Hippodamus of Miletus, the inventor of formal urban planning, creates the first grid plan for his home city of 10,000 people. It becomes the model for later Roman cities.
Haussmann's renovation of Paris, France	Vast public works programme, 1853–70: boulevards, sewers, aqueducts and parks. Haussmann's projects continued to be built until 1927.

London's sewers, UK	Built following the 'Great Stink' of 1858 and deadly cholera outbreaks. Chief Engineer Bazalgette took 18 years, with 22,000 workers and 318 million bricks. The system is still in use.
Brasilia, Brazil	Brazil's capital city, planned and developed by Lúcio Costa, Oscar Niemeyer and Robert Burle Marx in 1956–60. The ultimate modernist planned city.
Freiburg eco city, Germany	Renowned for sustainable urban development since the 1970s. In the Vauben district, cars must be parked in garages on the outskirts. One-third of city journeys are made by bike.
British Library, UK	Built 1982–99 and designed to last 250 years. The largest public building constructed in the UK in the twentieth century.
North Vancouver 100-Year Sustainability Vision, Canada	Started in 2007. Extends city plan from 30 to 100 years, to achieve 80 per cent reduction in greenhouse gas emissions by 2050 and make the city carbon neutral by 2107.

PUBLIC POLICY

Tokugawa reforestation, Japan	One of the world's first long-term plantation forestry schemes, between the 1760s and 1867, saving Japan from environmental and economic catastrophe.
US Constitution	Created 1787 and amended 27 times. The oldest written and codified constitution still in force.
Yellowstone National Park, USA	Established in 1872. The world's first national park and a key development in US environmental conservation history. Famous for the reintroduction of wolves in the 1990s.

Soviet Five-Year Plans	Five-year development plans between 1928 and 1991, part of a decades-long economic strategy. Replicated in other countries, including China, India and Indonesia.
New Deal, USA	President Roosevelt's 1933–9 public works and social policy recovery programme to rescue the United States from the Great Depression.
National Health Service, UK	Established in 1948 as part of a post-WW2 welfare state, to provide medical care for all residents, free at the point of use. Employs around 1.5 million people.
European Union	Political and economic union of 27 nations and nearly 500 million people. Founded to prevent repeat of nationalist conflict following WW2. Has its roots in the European Coal and Steel Community founded 1952.
Global eradication of smallpox	Programme begun by World Health Organization in 1958, when around 2 million people died from it each year. Completed in 1980.
One Child Policy, China	Population control programme, 1979–2015. Criticised for encouraging the sex-selective abortion of female foetuses.
Sovereign Wealth Fund, Norway	Established in 1990, using surplus revenues from the oil and gas industries, mostly for distribution to future generations. Valued at $1 trillion ($200,000 per citizen).
Onagawa nuclear plant, Japan	Built in the early 1980s and survived 2011 tsunami (unlike Fukushima) due to its construction on high ground and the provision of extra-high flood defences.

Onkalo nuclear waste repository, Finland	An underground nuclear waste facility. Construction began 2004, with completion due in 2023. Designed to accept waste for 100 years and store it for 100,000 years.

SOCIAL MOVEMENTS

Suffragettes, UK	A movement started around 1867 to obtain voting rights for women in Britain. Achieved its aim for women over 30 in 1918, and for those over 21 in 1928.
Marxist revolutionary organisations	Movements with their origins in *The Communist Manifesto* (1848), pursuing decades-long revolutionary class struggles worldwide. Lost impetus after 1989.
Neoliberalism	Seeded in the 1940s by the Mont Pelerin Society (members included Friedrich Hayek and Milton Friedman), implemented by Thatcher and Reagan in the 1980s.
Green Belt Movement, Kenya	An organisation founded in 1977 by Nobel laureate Wangari Maathai, for women's empowerment and conservation. Over 51 million trees planted to date.

SCIENTIFIC ENDEAVOURS

Vavilov Seed Collection, Russia	Founded in 1921. During WW2, a dozen botanists starved to death in a secret vault while guarding its 370,000 seeds from German soldiers, never eating a single one.
ITER nuclear fusion reactor, France	Nuclear fusion power generation project involving 35 countries. Started in 1988, with full operation expected in 2035 (if the technology works).

Svalbard Global Seed Vault, Norway	Seed bank opened in 2008 in the remote Arctic, with over 1 million seeds from 6,000 species. Designed to last at least 1,000 years in an indestructible rock bunker.

CULTURAL PROJECTS

Mormon missionaries	Over 1 million Mormons have been missionaries since 1830. There are currently 70,000 a year attempting to spread their gospel in 150 countries.
10,000 Year Clock	Clock designed to run for 10,000 years, currently being built in the Texas desert, a project of the Long Now Foundation. First prototype was built in 1999.
Future Library, Norway	From 2014 every year for 100 years, a famous author deposits a unique written work. They will all be published in 2114, on paper from 1,000 specially planted trees.

This table offers several instructive lessons about the human capacity for long-term planning and how it works in practice. Most obviously, this is something that *Homo sapiens* are remarkably good at. Our short-term brains might encourage us to grab the marshmallow in front of us, but our long-term acorn brains have enabled us to plan and execute breathtaking and monumental projects, such as the Roman aqueducts, Haussmann's public works programme in Paris, the Panama Canal and the Channel Tunnel. Beavers might be good at making dams, but no animals can match humans for their skills as visionary builders and engineers.

Looking at the table more closely, we can see that planning clearly comes in two distinct varieties. There are those projects that take a long time to complete, such as the building of a cathedral or a canal system, and thus require complex, multi-stage planning spread over many years. Typically those behind the project would prefer it to be finished sooner rather than later, but may be limited by financial or other constraints: there is little doubt that the burghers of Ulm would rather have had their minster erected in five decades than five centuries. In the second category are projects that are intended to have a long-lasting lifespan once they are complete, such as a library or seed vault.[7] Occasionally there may be an overlap between the two categories, as in the Great Wall of China, a long-term construction feat designed to last through successive generations of the Ming dynasty. There are also some examples – such as the Qanat water tunnels of Iran – which may not necessarily have been planned to endure centuries, but have managed to last so long due to successful intergenerational maintenance.

A third lesson is that long-range planning extends far beyond cathedrals and other large-scale construction projects, to areas such as public policy, science and culture. In the policy realm there are examples such as Britain's National Health Service, founded in 1948 to provide free medical care for generations to come, and which is still operating more than 70 years later, with a workforce of 1.5 million people (although under growing constraints due to factors such as increasing longevity). Then there are political entities such as the European Union, the origins of which go back to the European Coal and Steel Community established in 1952, which has gradually evolved into a set of long-term governance institutions that have managed to weather periodic economic and political crises. In 1990 Norway created a Sovereign Wealth Fund, which has accumulated over $1 trillion from government oil and gas production revenues for distribution to future generations, who will ironically need the funds to mitigate the environmental impact of fossil fuels (in 2019 the fund began divesting its holdings in overseas fossil fuel exploration companies, but more for financial than environmental reasons). Other examples include scientific projects such as the ITER nuclear fusion research facility in France and artistic endeavours like the 10,000 Year Clock. Perhaps nothing can rival the Onkalo nuclear waste repository in Finland, with its ambition to keep radioactive waste safe for 100,000 years – though will there be anyone around then to check?[8]

Fourth, long-term planning is not just a top-down practice in which architects, engineers and other planners impose their blueprint visions: it is also embodied in the grassroots struggles of social and political movements. For example, leaders of the suffragette movement, which founded its first formal organisation in Manchester in 1867, were prepared for a long political battle that was unlikely to last just a few months or even years. It turned out to take more than half a century to achieve their aims.[9] The table could include many other political struggles, from the movements against slavery that arose in Europe in the eighteenth century, to the US civil rights movement and the campaigns for indigenous rights today.

A final insight is that cathedral thinking isn't always good for us. In fact, it has been responsible for unmitigated planning disasters, as well as plans with utterly malign intent. This is not just a reference to Hitler's megalomaniac plan to conquer Europe and establish a thousand-year Reich, or the inefficiencies and mismanagement of Soviet five-year economic plans that led to colossal waste of resources and shops lacking basic foodstuffs but full of skis and pencil sharpeners.[10] Around the world, the building of hundreds of dams, canals and roads over the last century has resulted in untold ecological damage in the name of 'development' and 'progress'. Enough concrete has now been poured to encase the entire planet completely in a spherical concrete coffin two millimetres thick, even extending over all the world's oceans (and that's not all: the cement industry produces around 5 per cent of global carbon dioxide emissions).[11] Then there are planned cities like Brasilia, which might be celebrated for Oscar Niemeyer's brilliant modernist architecture but is now widely considered one of the most lifeless, dysfunctional examples of urban planning of the twentieth century. For this we can quite fairly blame Le Courbusier, whose authoritarian vision was the inspiration for Brasilia, a city designed to a single, rational, top-down blueprint. His famous dictum says it all: 'The Plan: Dictator'.[12]

Long-term planning has its dangers, especially when imposed from above in a linear, dictatorial fashion that is insensitive to human needs and fragile ecosystems. Yet tackling the ecological, technological and social crises of our age cannot be done on an ad hoc, improvised basis devoid of any planning. So how can we learn to plan wisely for the challenges of the future? A good place to start looking for answers is ancient Japan, which offers one of history's most remarkable examples of the power of planning to avert civilisational collapse.

Do We Need Benign Dictators? A Story from Ancient Japan

'Japan today should be an impoverished, slum-ridden, peasant society subsisting on an eroded moonscape, rather than a wealthy, dynamic, highly industrialised society living on a luxuriant green archipelago.'[13] It seems hard to believe this picture of a devastated wasteland drawn by the environmental historian Conrad Totman, yet for centuries Japan seemed bent on accomplishing its own destruction. Some 80 per cent of the country might now be covered by forested mountains, but between the 1550s and the 1750s its woodlands were so severely decimated that it was on the verge of ecological and social collapse. Pre-industrial Japan was a wooden-structured civilisation as dependent on timber as we are on oil today. The country's elite razed whole forests to build thousands of wooden castles, palaces and shrines. The growth of cities like Edo (modern-day Tokyo) led to a surge of demand for construction timber that resulted in acute short-ages, while peasants raided the forests for firewood. At the same time, the expansion of agriculture required chopping down vast swathes of ancient old-growth woodlands, and deforestation created erosion and flooding of Japan's fragile lowlands. The consequence was a series of major famines from the 1600s.[14]

There was no way that natural tree regrowth could keep pace with this unrelenting ecological warfare. Eventually the ruling Tokugawa shoguns, who ran a hereditary military dictatorship with the help of 250 subordinate barons, realised they had to act. Their initial response was to limit forest depletion through laws that banned the logging of scarce species or the use of precious woods for new buildings. But such regulations, often poorly enforced, were far from enough. Then between the 1760s and the late 1860s they embarked on a new approach: one of the world's first systematic programmes of mass plantation for-estry. Officials paid villagers to plant up to 100,000 seedlings a year, while new laws encouraged commercial tree planting, making trees a profitable, albeit slow-growing, crop (usually taking a minimum of 50 years between planting and harvesting). Advances in silvicul-tural techniques helped saplings survive and maximised timber yields. It was a long-term plan implemented over decades, which required the ruling authorities to envision at least 50 to 100 years into the future, as it would take that long for substantive reforest-ation to occur.[15]

The results were slow but spectacular. For centuries the country had been sucked into the classic 'progress trap', pursuing a path to civilisational decline by undermining the ecological resource base on which the society was founded. But thanks to reforestation, by the late nineteenth century Japan had reverted to a green archipelago, avoiding the fate of collapse.

On one level this is a story of hope for today, offering a model for how we might harness the power of long-term planning to tackle our own ecological crises. On another level it raises a challenging political question: is effective long-term planning most likely to thrive under an authoritarian regime?

Japan's reforestation programme was largely possible because the Tokugawa shoguns were feudal dictators who could impose new laws with limited opposition, and who had the power to draft in forced peasant labour when necessary to undertake the arduous task of planting. And we shouldn't fall for the comforting argument that their actions were inspired by a Japanese love of nature or a Buddhist respect for life; if true, why would they have decimated their forests in the first place? The shoguns were probably willing to pursue such a long-term project because they wanted to ensure their descendants had a prosperous society over which they could reign. Japan's long-term planning was a result of being controlled by an authoritarian family dynasty that was bent on preserving its own power through the generations.[16]

Few of us would freely choose to live under such a dictatorship today, especially if it had sword-wielding samurai to enforce the laws. But in recent years I have heard a growing number of people suggest that some kind of 'benign dictatorship' is just what we need to deal with the crises we face, since democratic politics is so hopelessly short-sighted. They include scientist James Lovelock, who has argued that 'it may be necessary to put democracy on hold for a while' to deal with the global ecological emergency. Similarly, in an article on the critical threats posed by climate change and bioweapons, astrophysicist Martin Rees has written that 'Only an enlightened despot could push through the measures needed to navigate the twenty-first century safely'.[17] It is a surprising statement, given that Rees patently has some faith in the democratic process, evident in his being a founder of the All-Party Parliamentary Group on Future Generations (in his capacity as a member of the UK's House of Lords). When I asked him in a public forum whether he was offering dictatorship as a serious policy prescription to deal with short-termism and suggested that he might have been joking in the article, he replied, 'Actually, I was semi-serious.'[18] He then gave the example of China as an authoritarian regime that was incredibly successful at long-term planning, as it was now demonstrating through huge investment in solar technology and other policies. I could see plenty of heads in the room nodding in agreement.

Mine was not among them. History has few, if any, examples of dictators who remain benign and enlightened for very long – witness, for example, China's record on human rights. Moreover, as the Intergenerational Solidarity Index discussed in Chapter 9 demonstrates, there is little evidence that authoritarian regimes have a better record on long-term thinking and planning than democratic ones. Sweden, for instance, manages to generate almost 60 per cent of its energy through renewable sources without having a despot in charge, compared to 26 per cent in China.[19]

In fact, looking through the historical record, there are powerful examples of democratic regimes making long-term planning a policy priority. But under what circumstances are they willing to do so? To answer this question, we must descend deep into the sewers of Victorian London.

The Great Stink (or How a Crisis Can Kickstart Radical Planning)

Picture London in the 1850s. In fact, don't picture it – smell it. Since medieval times, the city's human waste had been deposited in cesspools – stinking holes in the ground full of rotting sludge, often in the basements of houses – or flushed directly into the River Thames. While thousands of cesspools had been removed since the 1830s, the Thames itself remained a giant cesspool that also happened to be the city's main source of drinking water: Londoners were drinking their own raw sewage. The result was mass outbreaks of cholera, with over 14,000 people dying in 1848 and a further 10,000 in 1854.[20] And yet city authorities did almost nothing to resolve this ongoing public health disaster. They were hampered not just by a lack of funds and the prevalent belief that cholera was spread through the air rather than through water, but also by the pressure of private water companies who insisted that the drinking water they pumped from the river was wonderfully pure.

The crisis came to a head in the stiflingly hot summer of 1858. That year had already seen three cholera outbreaks, and now the lack of rainfall had exposed sewage deposits six feet deep on the sloping banks of the Thames. The putrid fumes spread throughout the city. But it wasn't just the labouring poor who had to bear it: the smell also wafted straight from the river into the recently rebuilt Houses of Parliament and the new ventilation system conspired to pump the rank odour throughout the building. The smell was so vile that debates in the Commons and Lords had to be abandoned, and parliamentarians fled from the committee rooms with cloths over their faces.

What became known as the 'Great Stink' was finally enough to prompt the government to act. Prime Minister Benjamin Disraeli rushed through a bill in a record 16 days that provided the Metropolitan Board of Works with the long-term financing it needed to construct a modern sewer system for London, and extensive new powers necessary to make it happen. Finally, thanks to a crisis from which MPs themselves were unable to escape, Britain embarked on one of the most radical public health reforms of the nineteenth century. As *The Times* reported, 'That hot fortnight did for the sanitary administration of the Metropolis what the Bengal mutinies did for the administration of India.'[21]

The sewers, however, were still to be built. Enter one of the heroes of the Victorian age, the Chief Engineer of London's Metropolitan Board of Works, Joseph Bazalgette. Over a period of 18 years, Bazalgette

DIPHTHERIA. SCROFULA. CHOLERA.

FATHER THAMES INTRODUCING HIS OFFSPRING TO THE FAIR CITY OF LONDON.

(A Design for a Fresco in the New Houses of Parliament.)

Punch magazine published this cartoon at the height of the Great Stink in July 1858, describing it as 'a design for a fresco for the new Houses of Parliament'. Father Thames, a personification of the river, introduces his offspring (Diphtheria, Scrofula and Cholera) to 'the fair city of London'.

masterminded a network of sewers 82 miles in length, using 880,000 cubic yards of concrete and 318 million bricks, which transported sewage to pumping stations downriver, where it could be safely washed out to sea by the ebb tide. Remarkably, almost the whole system is still in use today, and tourists who stroll down the broad Victoria and Albert Embankments along the Thames are actually walking on promenades built by Bazalgette's 22,000 workers to house the sewers just a few metres below.

How have the sewers survived intact for so long? The answer lies in the chief engineer's capacity for long-term planning. Bazalgette foresaw the growth of the city's population and constructed the sewers to carry more than twice the volume than was required at the time. He also insisted on using the newly invented Portland cement, which was 50 per cent more expensive than regular cement but far longer-lasting, actually getting stronger following contact with water. Moreover, he made sure expensive but durable Staffordshire Blue bricks were used rather than fragile factory-made pipes. Although we cannot know for certain – unfortunately, he left no personal diaries – Bazalgette seemed to be planning for his sewerage system to last at least a hundred years. He was undoubtedly one of the great time rebels of Victorian Britain.

Bazalgette's legacy is extraordinary. According to historian John Doxat, 'though perhaps less remembered than his contemporary Isambard Kingdom Brunel, this superb and far-sighted engineer probably did more good, and saved more lives, than any single Victorian public official'.[22] We should respect both these figures for their long-term vision, having been responsible – with the help of their labourers' sweat – for building bridges, sewers, railways and other infrastructure that is still used by millions of people every day. What drove them to plan for posterity? Perhaps it was a kind of 'empire psychology', a cultural confidence that their Victorian age would stretch out into the distant future as a triumphant and eternal civilisation. Yet it may also have been the long-term mentality common among the profession of civil engineers itself.

Today's engineers enjoy little renown compared to their Victorian counterparts. For instance, how many people know the name of the chief engineer of the Channel Tunnel or of pioneering solar power engineers? Engineering is certainly far from an innocent profession: engineers have been responsible for designing nuclear warheads and oil pipelines, as well as more benign creations like sewerage systems. Yet there is something to admire in their tendency to think long rather than short – in their desire to build to last. The code of conduct of the UK's Institution of Civil Engineers states that 'all members should have full regard for the public interest particularly in relation to matters of health and safety, and in relation to the well-being of future generations.'[23] Wouldn't it be good if our politicians and business leaders had to make a similar pledge, and were held to account for it?

One of the key lessons to draw from Bazalgette's sewers is that successful long-term planning needs to be based on building adaptability, flexibility and resilience into the original design. In his book *How Buildings Learn*, Stewart Brand points out that the most long-lasting buildings are those that can 'learn' by adapting to new contexts over time: they can accommodate different users or be easily extended, retrofitted or upgraded. He draws an analogy with biology: 'the more adapted an organism to present conditions, the less adaptable it can be to unknown future conditions.'[24] This is exactly where the London sewers were exemplary. By making the tunnels double the size needed at the time, Bazalgette designed long-term adaptability into the system, just as his use of the finest building materials gave the sewers enough resilience to survive over a century of constant wear and tear. Of course, we can learn about resilience not just from cases like the Victorian sewers, but from natural phenomena such as a delicate spider web that manages to survive a storm or the way sweating and shivering help regulate human body temperature.[25] All of them, however, raise the question of how we can design an evolutionary learning capability into our political, economic and social systems so they are not crippled by rigidity in the face of changing circumstances or external shocks. Part Three of this book offers real-world examples of such systems in action, from decentralised political institutions that are sensitive to changing local needs, to the nimble economic design of 'cosmo-local production'.

An equally vital lesson from London's sewerage system is that it often takes an acute crisis to activate long-term planning. Without MPs directly suffering the effects of the Great Stink, it could have been decades before London's sewerage problem was tackled seriously, with possibly hundreds of thousands of people losing their lives. In fact, throughout history, long-term planning has frequently emerged from moments of crisis, especially when it has affected those in political and economic power. This would come as no surprise to Karl Marx or Milton Friedman, who are among the many thinkers who have argued that fundamental system change is typically a product of crisis, which can recast the rules of the game, challenge old orthodoxies and open up new possibilities. Well-known examples include the New Deal in the United States, a response to the crisis of the Great Depression, and the British government's introduction of food and petrol rationing in the Second World War, which was made possible by the very real threat of German invasion.[26] Or consider the unprecedented range of long-term institutions that arose out of the ashes of that war: the European Union, the United Nations, the Marshall Plan, the Bretton Woods financial system, and in Britain the welfare state, mass public housing and the nationalisation of industry.

One of the reasons we fail to take substantive action on an issue such as climate change – for instance, through massive long-term investment in renewable energy or punitive carbon taxes – is that most people (especially in the West) don't experience it as a severe crisis like the Great Stink or the Second World War. The impacts are too gradual: like a frog that gets slowly boiled alive in water that rises only gradually in temperature, the planetary heat is getting turned up slowly and we're failing to jump out of the pot. Even the growing number of climate-related disasters – from drought in Kenya to wildfires in Australia – haven't been damaging enough to provoke the serious response required. Might it take a quick succession of genuinely cataclysmic events that affect powerful political and economic actors for humanity to wake up – perhaps a single year in which New York City and Shanghai are devastated by hurricanes that kill tens of thousands of people, food riots sweep European capitals following mass crop failures and Britain's MPs have to escape a flooded West-minster Palace in life rafts, after the Thames Barrier overflows and leaves London under water?

This could come as disheartening news to ecological campaigners who believe that positive and optimistic messages of a better future are far more effective than visions of apocalypse in rousing people to action. While that may be true for motivating action among the general public, it is less obviously the case for the privileged and powerful, who are more likely to respond to crisis and even fear. The chances are that they will only take radical action if they feel they have something to lose.

This may be the ultimate historical lesson of the Great Stink: that radical long-term planning can be kickstarted by a crisis. It is the essence not of cathedral thinking but what I think of as 'sewer thinking'. Sometimes nothing but a crisis can shake dominant actors and institutions out of their slumber. It's a lesson absolutely understood by activists such as Greta Thunberg. 'Our house is on fire,' she told the World Economic Forum in Davos in Switzerland in 2019, 'I don't want your hope, I want you to panic . . . and act.'[27] Generating a genuine sense of crisis and emergency may be the most effective antidote to our deadly sleepwalk into civilisational breakdown.

Recognising the importance of crises does not mean, however, that we should sit back and wait for a catastrophe to happen. It is vital to prepare ourselves for any forthcoming ecological or other rupture by creating a ready roadmap for long-term system change. As Milton Friedman put it, while a crisis provides the opportunity for change, 'when that crisis occurs, the actions that are taken depend on the ideas that are lying around.'[28] The tragedy of the 2008 financial crisis was that there was no obvious alternative economic vision on offer. It was an opportunity to completely recast the global financial system, and yet governments ended up bailing out the banks and propping up the obsolete economic structures that created the crisis in the first place. It is a mistake that should not be repeated: alternative models need to be at the ready. That is why it is so crucial to begin seeding the values and practices of long-term thinking in the here and now.

Keeping the Pumps Running

With no plan, humanity will have no span. We urgently need long-term planning to confront the ecological and technological challenges of our time, as well as social policy issues, such as the lack of investment in mental health care. On the one hand, we can be assured of our capacity to do it: ever since the ancient Egyptians, we have been making plans and executing projects with time horizons stretching decades and even centuries into the future. On the other hand, we have seen that planning is a many-headed hydra: it can be malign and misdirected, it can generate tremendous environmental damage, it can thrive under dictatorship and, without a devastating crisis to set it off, it might never happen at all.

Much of human planning to date has been driven by the Holocene imperative of economic progress. All the concrete, plastics and toxins we produce might be giving us roads, buildings and other long-lasting infrastructure of modern civilisation but they are simultaneously choking the planet. This is hardly the kind of planning we need to negotiate the trials of the Anthropocene. We might be satisfying John Ruskin's credo to build as if we are building forever, but it cannot claim to be 'such a work as our descendants will thank us for'.

Long-term planning is also something we should be doing together, as a society. We might look to the Netherlands, whose citizens have been communally managing the polders – low-lying reclaimed land protected by dikes – for over 800 years. A quarter of the country is on this vulnerable land below sea level, which must be continually drained and pumped to avoid flooding (that's what all the windmills were originally for). Many older people remember the floods of 1953, when over 2,000 people were killed, and schoolchildren learn about St Lucia's flood of 1287, in which at least 50,000 people died. Such events, etched into the Dutch historical imagination, make the risk of inundation a lived reality; crisis could be just around the corner. In response to this constant threat, they have developed a sophisticated system of *waterschappen* or water boards, local democratic bodies that have existed for centuries to manage and maintain the polder flood defences. If the dikes fail, then everyone drowns together. Hence the Dutch saying, 'You have to be able to get along with your enemy, because he may be the person operating the neighbouring pump in your polder.'[29]

We are all, in one way or another, operating the pumps for each other. We live in an interdependent world, our actions having consequences not just for our neighbours or people in distant lands, but for the generations to come. Like the Dutch, we must learn to manage our planetary home together if we hope for it to have a long and thriving future, and to avoid being swept away in the deluge. Only then will we deserve the thanks of our descendants.

7

Holistic Forecasting

Long-Term Pathways for Civilisation

The world's first professional forecasters may have been Ancient Egyptian priests in the upper reaches of the River Nile over 3,000 years ago. Each spring, they gathered near the point where the river's three main tributaries met, to predict the size of the annual flood that would supply water to farmers a thousand miles downstream. If the water was clear, then the White Nile emerging from Lake Victoria would dominate the flow, producing a mild flood and low crop yield. If the water was dark, the Blue Nile would dictate the flow and be likely to supply the perfect amount for an abundant harvest. If the green-brown waters of the Atbara River streaming down from the Ethiopian highlands were prevailing, the flood would probably be early and catastrophically high, devastating the crops. Based on the priests' predictions, officials in the agricultural heartlands further down the Nile Valley were able to plan months in advance – storing grain, setting taxes or spending funds with a sense of what the future might hold.[1]

Nobody knows how accurate the priests were in foretelling the floods. What we do know, however, is that all human societies have developed priesthoods to predict the future – soothsayers, oracles, astrologers, shamans and prophets – who have searched for its secrets in the movement of the stars or the toss of bones, in the interpretation of dreams or the pattern of past events. Today such priests have titles that possess the aura of science and rationalism. They are forecasters, futurists, trend spotters or foresight experts.[2] While they typically disavow any ability to predict specific events like Nostradamus or the

Oracle of Delphi and prefer to talk about scenarios and probabilities, their role is the same: to tame the uncertainties of the future and provide a vision of what landscapes may lie ahead.

These modern seers generally only look a few months or years ahead, especially if they are engaged in the business world. Corporate forecasting also frequently displays little, if any, concern for future generations: when an oil company makes projections about its production figures, its gaze is set more firmly on its share price than on the price humanity will eventually pay for its actions. Yet forecasting is undeniably valuable. It is difficult to imagine practising the art of long-term thinking without making any predictions about the future at all. Failing to do so would simply feed a reactive short-term culture where we only dealt with events as they hit us in the present. We need to prepare and plan for what is likely to be on the horizon, whether it's the prospect of summer forest fires, the political tinderbox of growing far-right populism or the slow burnout of a whole civilisation.

This chapter presents what I call 'holistic forecasting' as the fifth of six key tools for long-term thinking. It offers a much longer time frame than traditional forecasting, stretching into decades and centuries. It is also wider in scope, focusing on the big-picture prospects for people and planet on a global scale, rather than on the narrow institutional and corporate interests that prevail in mainstream forecasting. It is not about predicting particular events in the near term but sketching out a broad range of pathways that our planetary civilisation may follow over the long term.

The Rise of Networked Uncertainty

Uncertainty about the future has always been a barrier to long-term forecasting. Moreover, the further forward we project in time, the greater the range of possibilities and pathways, which multiplies the levels of uncertainty. As futures thinkers like to put it, the 'cone of uncertainty' keeps widening.[3]

Since the turn of the millennium, however, we have shifted from a cone-shaped future to a new era of networked uncertainty: 'networked' because the events and risks we face are increasingly interdependent and globalised, raising the prospect of rapid contagion and butterfly effects and rendering even the near-term future almost unreadable. A perfect storm of factors have combined to create this interlinked, non-linear structure of radical uncertainty: the accelerating pace of technological innovation, the increased speed of information flow, geopolitical instabilities that have developed since the end of the Cold War, growing job insecurity, financial market volatility and interconnectedness, and wildcard threats from AI, bioweapons, cybercrime and genetically engineered diseases.

The evidence of networked uncertainty is all around us. How many economists foresaw the 2008 crash and its global knock-on effects, like the Occupy movement? How many political pundits predicted Brexit and Trump? And the uncertainty is unlikely to be reduced any time soon. Climate scientists warn of tipping points that will lead to the sudden collapse of ice shelves or entire species. We have also witnessed a proliferation of 'black swan' events – things that are not only difficult to predict and highly consequential, but which the experts can only retrospectively claim they saw coming all along – from 9/11 to the rise of Google.[4]

We appear to have entered the age of an unknowable future. As Yuval Noah Harari suggests, in 1020 it was relatively easy to predict what the world of 1050 would look like, but in 2020 it is almost impossible to know what kind of world we will inhabit in 2050, let alone beyond that date.[5]

Professional forecasters still like to give the impression that they can shine a light into the darkness of the future, yet there is startling evidence that their ability to make accurate predictions is extremely limited. In a famous 20-year study by political scientist Philip Tet-lock, 284 foresight 'experts' – from think-tank brains to World Bank analysts – were asked to make a series of relatively long-term geopo-litical and economic forecasts, such as whether the European Union would lose one of its members over the coming ten years or what the size of the US deficit would be in a decade. After mapping their 82,361 predictions against real-world outcomes, his conclusion was that the experts were not just extremely inaccurate in their judge-ments, but actually performed worse on average than even the simplest rule of thumb, such as 'always predict no change' or 'assume the current rate of change continues uninterrupted'. In fact, Tetlock found an inverse relationship between their accuracy of prediction and their level of public renown and professional qualifications.[6]

One could fairly conclude that long-term forecasting is a lost cause. Why not just accept uncertainty, put all our plans on the back-burner, and simply deal with the future when it happens?

Because there are patterns in history, if only we know where to look for them.

The Wisdom of the S-Curve

Human beings are pattern-seeking creatures. From Archimedes' principle and the theory of evolution to the second law of thermody-namics, we have endeavoured to discover universal laws in the natural world. We have equally sought to find the underlying patterns in the social world: Aristotle, Polybius, Ibn Khaldun and Karl Marx all believed they had identified cyclical patterns in history that deter-mined the rise and fall of states and empires, classes and economic systems. Today the search for patterns goes on, with Google and Face-book hoping to use Big Data to discover laws of human behaviour that will make us click on more advertisements and share more videos.

But are there really any patterns out there? Everything we know about networked uncertainty should make us sceptical. Yet I want to take a stand against the sceptics and highlight one crucial pattern that has occurred repeatedly in human societies in the past and will almost certainly continue to appear in the future. In fact, it is so integral to the philosophy of long-term thinking that it should be seared into the brain of anyone aspiring to be a good ancestor.

The pattern is the fabled S-curve, sometimes known as the sigmoid curve (see below). It will not tell you who will win the next presidential election, or when the stock market will crash, or whether we will colonise Mars. Rather, it offers a simpler yet more profound message: *nothing grows forever*. The classic version begins with an upward curve of accelerating growth or 'take-off', then reaches an inflection point where the rate of growth of the phenomenon in question starts to slow down, eventually levelling off into a period of 'maturity'; it then typically hits a second inflection point where it gradually descends into 'decline'. A more extreme version of the curve follows a steep upward trend, reaching a sharp peak that leads to a precipitous 'collapse'.

S-curves can be found throughout the living world, from the growth of an ant colony and the spread of cancer cells to the growth of a forest or your children's feet. Such patterns are equally prevalent in human systems. Empires and economies, dictatorships and democracies, social movements and fashion fads – all of them in the end succumb to the logic of the S-curve. They grow, they peak, they decline.

Over the past half-century, recognition of the sigmoid curve has become one of the most important and widespread insights of the social and applied sciences. For organisational behaviour expert Charles Handy, the S-curve is the essential form of how businesses, social organisations and political systems develop over time, 'it is the line of all things human'.[7] Tech analyst Paul Saffo advises to 'look for the S-curve,' noting that the uptake of new technologies – from

The S-curve: nothing grows forever

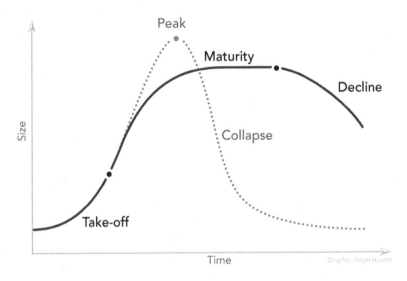

personal robots to driverless cars – is destined to follow its shape.[8] Scholars have used the sigmoid curve to describe the rise and fall of ancient civilisations like the Roman Empire, but also to predict modern-day shifts, such as the decline of the United States as a global superpower.[9] In the field of systems thinking, the authors of the Club of Rome's 1972 report *The Limits to Growth* put the S-curve at the heart of their analysis.[10] More recently, economist Kate Raworth has shown that mainstream economics assumes that GDP growth follows an 'exponential curve left hanging in mid-air', when the reality is that it is far more likely to level off into the shape of the S-curve.[11] Energy expert Ugo Bardi has found inspiration in the Roman philosopher Seneca's observation that 'growth is slow, but ruin is rapid', to coin the concept of 'the Seneca cliff': large structures, such as financial systems or animal populations, tend to follow a skewed S-curve in their development, reaching a peak and then suddenly collapsing.[12]

Among the greatest exponents of the sigmoid curve was Jonas Salk, who described it as the most important 'thinking tool' of our age of change.[13] In the early 1980s, Salk began to see that the long-term trend in human population would follow the curve's contours. Global population had remained below one billion people for most of the last 8,000 years, but following the population explosion that occurred from around 1800 – sending the curve rapidly upwards – it was starting to decelerate and would likely level off at ten to eleven billion towards the end of the twenty-first century (a forecast remarkably similar to current UN projections). Splitting this S-curve into two sections around its first inflection point, Salk believed that a radical transformation would be needed from the way society worked in Epoch A, the early growth part of the curve, to how it functioned in Epoch B, the growing-up part (see below).[14]

Jonas Salk's S-curve

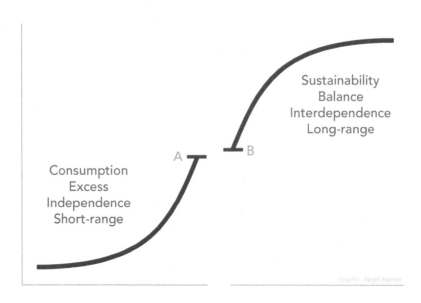

Jonas Salk believed that the values that dominated in Epoch A, especially during the past two centuries, would need to be replaced by the values of Epoch B as we moved into the twenty-first century.

In Epoch A there were few limits on growth, resource use and available energy. It was a period characterised by high levels of material consumption, a largely individualistic culture and a dominance of short-range thinking. But in Salk's view, with a global population approaching ten times its earlier historic level, society was moving into Epoch B, where we will only be able to survive by adopting a new set of values and institutions based on sustainable resource use, an awareness of limits, higher levels of social cooperation and much longer-range thinking. He was convinced that to be good ancestors we must recognise that we are heading towards the top of the sigmoid curve and thus need to adopt a mindset fit for Epoch B, rather than clutch on to the outdated attitudes and practices of Epoch A. If we failed to make this transition, human civilisation would be heading for a calamitous breakdown.[15]

As a thinking tool, one of the powers of the S-curve is that it challenges the deepest assumption of our prevailing Enlightenment culture: that growth and progress will continue indefinitely. Such an assumption pervades psychologist Steven Pinker's global bestseller *Enlightenment Now*, which presents 75 graphs to demonstrate humanity's apparently enormous progress over the last 200 years: increased longevity, improved public health, declines in crime and violence, reductions in poverty, better access to education and even improved environmental protection. While there is some truth in his argument about the shape of progress in the past (though many dispute his environmental claims), when it comes to the future, he is on particularly shaky empirical ground.[16] Pinker is unashamedly optimistic and believes that 'the cold, hard facts' point to a simple truth: 'that what has already happened will continue to happen'. In other words, the path of progress is set to continue ever upwards. He is dismissive of the 'romantic Green movement' and others who are concerned with the perils of climate change, biodiversity loss, wealth inequality or technological risks such as bioweapons, instead putting his faith in the wonders of geoengineering and economic growth to solve all our problems. He even quotes the nineteenth-century historian Thomas Macaulay to reinforce his quasi-religious faith in endless progress: 'On what principle is it that, when we see nothing but improvement behind us, we are to expect nothing but deterioration before us?'[17] Pinker's arguments represent linear thinking at its most extreme, a wilful blindness to the compelling evidence of the S-curve that defies the Enlightenment rationalism he claims to champion. He is like a child who believes they can keep blowing up the balloon, bigger and bigger, without any prospect that it could ever burst.

'It is difficult to make predictions, especially about the future,' says an old Danish proverb.[18] While forecasting particular events may be an elusive science, the sigmoid curve puts us on firmer ground by identifying a pattern of growth and decay that is found repeatedly in human affairs (although certainly not everywhere, nor is the curve always smooth). Wait long enough, and what might at first sight appear to be a continuously upswinging J-curve will eventually turn into an S-curve, whether we are looking at the long-term path of economic growth, technological innovation, population change, urban expansion or some other phenomenon. The S-curve cannot itself tell us when we will reach an inflection point of slow down or decline, but it warns us that they are likely to happen. And that can only make us wiser in our planning for the future: it readies us to prepare, to adapt, to build resilience, to reinvent.

At the same time, the sigmoid curve can prompt us to consider alternative pathways of development. Are there ways of ensuring that we mature gradually rather than peak and crash? Can we slow the pace of decline once it sets in? And might it even be possible to leap off an unsustainable pathway onto a different curve altogether? In this sense, the sigmoid curve offers an invitation and a motivation to reconsider how we organise our economies, our societies and our daily lives, and the values and beliefs that underpin them. There might be a range of curves for our global civilisation to follow. But if we hope to fully grasp what these might be, we will need to summon help from another thinking tool that good ancestors should have at their disposal: scenario planning.

A Brief History of Scenario Planning

In 1948, a young physicist named Herman Kahn found himself a job at the RAND Corporation, a new research institute established with funding from the US Air Force. RAND effectively operated as a think tank for government defence policy, devising military strategy for the increasingly hot Cold War.[19] It soon also became a hothouse for innovative long-term forecasting techniques based on insights from new fields such as game theory, cybernetics and computing, and Kahn was among its brightest stars.

During the 1950s, Kahn began developing what has come to be known as 'scenario planning'. He realised that rather than trying to predict specific future events, it was more effective to sketch out a set of plausible scenarios that might emerge. He put this thinking to work in his controversial 1960 book *On Thermonuclear War*, which explored the possible scenarios that could result in the event of a nuclear war with the Soviet Union. In some, tens of millions of Americans died, generations of children were born with birth defects and portions of the planet became uninhabitable for millennia. In others, only a few major cities were destroyed, radiation sickness was limited and the US economy was able to recover within a few decades or even faster.

Although it was a striking exercise in long-term thinking that highlighted the devasting possible consequences of an atomic war,

Kahn's book was certainly not presented as an argument against pressing the nuclear button. Kahn believed that nuclear war was not only possible; it was winnable. In a notorious table (see below) labelled 'Tragic But Distinguishable Postwar States', he listed the number of US citizens that might be killed under various scenarios and the length of time required for America's economic recovery. Kahn's chilling conclusion was that a loss of up to 20 million lives was 'acceptable' in a nuclear conflict if the US were to emerge victorious. Despite being a great tragedy, the majority of survivors would be able to lead 'normal and happy lives' and would not suffer so much that they would 'envy the dead'.[20] For Kahn, 20 million deaths, or 10 per cent of the then US population, might be a price worth paying

Tragic but distinguishable postwar states

Dead	Economic Recuperation
2,000,000	1 year
5,000,000	2 years
10,000,000	5 years
20,000,000	10 years
40,000,000	20 years
80,000,000	50 years
160,000,000	100 years

Will the survivors envy the dead?

Possible scenarios for the US in the event of a US-Soviet nuclear conflict, from Herman Kahn's book *On Thermonuclear War*.

for defeating the Russians. The growing anti-nuclear movement quickly labelled his book 'a moral tract on mass murder'. It is no wonder that Stanley Kubrick used Kahn as one of his models for the mad scientist played by Peter Sellers in his 1964 nuclear satire *Dr Strangelove*. Kahn is said to have asked the director for royalties because so many lines from his book appeared in the movie.[21]

Following Kahn, scenario planning only took off after it was used with spectacular success by Pierre Wack, head of planning at the oil company Royal Dutch Shell. In the early 1970s, Wack refined Kahn's approach into a coherent methodology. The aim, he said, was not to make the 'right forecast' – an impossible task in an increasingly uncertain world – but 'to accept uncertainty, try to understand it and make it part of our reasoning'.[22] There was not one single future out there, waiting to happen, but rather many possible futures were in the offing. Wack began by identifying three or four of these different futures, at least one of which was business as usual and another being a low-probability but high-impact alternative. He then developed detailed storylines of how each might play out. The purpose was to ensure that the organisation was prepared for these multiple scenarios, for instance by devising ways to be resilient to a range of outcomes. Doing so was a means of resisting the 'fallacy of extrapolation', where the future is assumed to be a linear continuation of past trends.

Wack shot to fame among corporate strategists after he used scenario planning to foresee the possibility of the oil price shock in 1973. He had realised that the Arab states in the OPEC cartel might try to restrict supply in order to significantly push up the global price of oil, which had been relatively stable for decades. Royal Dutch Shell eventually took Wack's advice and prepared for the possible price hike, for instance by cutting back their operations costs. As a result, they were able to weather the storm of the oil crisis and become one of the world's largest and most profitable companies by the end of the decade.[23]

Scenario planning soon took the business world by storm. By 1977 around 20 per cent of Fortune 1000 companies in the US were using it, a figure that jumped to nearly 50 per cent by 1981.[24] Gradually it began to spread outside the corporate realm and was increasingly deployed by demographers, government planners, environmental campaigners and development NGOs. Yet it was still primarily used as a business tool to enable companies to gain competitive advantage through identifying market trends, commercial opportunities and mitigating against financial risk.[25]

That all began to change around the turn of the millennium, due to the rise of climate science, which took the old human obsession with predicting tomorrow's weather to a totally new level. In the wake of the Rio Earth Summit in 1992 and the Kyoto Protocol in 1997, there were soon thousands of researchers making climate forecasts 50 or 100 years in the future, and frequently drawing on the tools of scenario planning in their analyses. The likely impact of different planetary warming scenarios began seeping into public consciousness. Which parts of Florida or Bangladesh would be under water if we hit two, three or even six degrees of warming by 2100? How much would different levels of ocean acidification affect global food supply by 2050? How might potential tipping-point events interact with one another, from the melting of the Greenland ice sheet to the thawing of Siberian permafrost and the mass dieback of the Amazon rainforest? The reports of the Intergovernmental Panel on Climate Change served to redefine the public meaning of 'long term', taking it far beyond the five- or ten-year horizons of corporate thinking. Scenarios and projections to 2030–40 were now considered 'near term', with those for 2080–2100 designated 'long term'. Some extended further still, making predictions about sea-level rises and atmospheric carbon dioxide to the year 2500.[26]

In effect, a generation of climate scientists and environmental risk researchers rescued scenario planning and other forecasting methods from the clutches of the marketplace, while simultaneously catapulting the public imagination forward in time.

By expanding the time frame in which society thought about the future of the planet, they also opened the mental space for contemplating the long-term pathways of humanity itself. The fate of human civilisation became a subject of films, novels and scholarly tomes. Would we be able to ride out the firestorms and ice storms of the ecological crisis, as well as the myriad technological threats that were now emerging? Or were we destined for social collapse or even extinction? Armed with the twin tools of the S-curve and scenario planning, these are the questions to which we will now turn.

Three Pathways of Human Civilisation

An understanding of the likely future trajectories of human society is central to the art of long-term thinking. The assumptions we make about the possibilities of civilisational progress or breakdown will influence the plans we make, the movements we create, the careers we follow and even choices such as whether or not to have children. Having a picture of the potential long-range pathways in our minds is essential mental scaffolding for negotiating our collective and personal journeys into the future. Yet it is difficult to know where to start when thinking about these pathways, which exist on the vast scale of a complex global civilisation comprised of billions of people.

A helpful place to begin is with what we know about the fate of past civilisations. The underlying historical truth is that they tend to follow the logic of the S-curve: civilisations are born, they flower and then they die. According to Cambridge University risk researcher Luke Kemp, 'collapse may be a normal phenomenon for civilisations, regardless of their size and technological stage.' His view is based on a unique study of 87 ancient civilisations stretching over a period of more than 3,000 years. Kemp defined a civilisation as a society with agriculture, multiple cities, a continuous political structure and military domination of a geographic region, and specified collapse as a phase where there is a rapid and enduring loss of population, identity and socio-economic complexity. After looking at examples ranging from Phoenicia and the Shang dynasty in China to the Roman Empire and the Olmecs, he concluded that the average lifespan of an ancient civilisation was just 336 years (see below).[27]

Why exactly do civilisations collapse? A fascinating body of scholarly literature has grown up around this question. Take a classic case, such as the Sumerian civilisation that rose up in what is now Southern Iraq around 3000 BCE, which boasted sophisticated irrigation systems and impressive cities like Ur and Uruk. By 2000 BCE it had largely disappeared. Why? A leading explanation is that their predominant agricultural technique of diverting enormous quantities of water onto arid land led to mass salt deposits in the soil. Archaeological records reveal that after an early period of abundance, crop yields of wheat and later barley began to fall drastically due to this salination, yet the dynastic rulers took little heed. Especially during the Akkadian Empire period, they continued extending the canals, intensifying agricultural production and embarking on lavish building projects, indulging in luxury and glory. But doing so required them to hugely overextend their resource use beyond the carrying capacity of the local ecology. Eventually, like so many other early civilisations, such as the Mayans of Copán, it collapsed by destroying the natural environment on which its progress had been based.[28]

While environmental degradation has been a widespread cause of civilisational breakdown, the Sumerian story hints at another explanation: elite domination and inequality. When ruling elites are able to insulate themselves from the problems they create, those problems multiply and eventually catch up with them, whether in the form of economic collapse or destabilising social unrest. Some scholars, such

Ancient civilisations

The average lifespan of a civilisation is 336 years ⊢———⊣

3000BCE   2000   1000   0   1000CE

Norte Chico

Akkadian

Ancient Egypt, New Kingdom

Phoenicia

Carthage

Classical Greek

Roman Empire

Byzantine

Western Turk

3000BCE   2000   1000   0   1000CE

Graphic: Nigel Hawtin

as Joseph Tainter, argue that civilisations ultimately collapse under the weight of their own complexity. For instance, there came a point at which administering and controlling the vast Roman Empire became so expensive, so bureaucratic and required so much military muscle, that it could no longer sustain itself. Others point out that civilisations can die when there are major climatic changes, such as sustained drought, or due to external shocks, as occurred when the Spanish conquest of Central and South America brought deadly violence and equally deadly epidemics to the Aztec Empire. Debate rages over controversial cases such as Easter Island: was its demise due to the environmental catastrophe of deforestation, as Jared Diamond contends, or some other reason such as an infestation of rats or the impact of Europeans when they arrived in the eighteenth century?[29]

It may be some time before we have a full-blown theory of civilisational collapse. Meanwhile, we are left with the burning question of whether we are heading for it ourselves. Evidence for the impending breakdown of today's highly interdependent globalised civilisation, which can be traced back to the rise of European capitalism in the sixteenth century, grows by the day.[30] Melting ice caps, devastating wildfires, disappearing species, water shortages. The timing may be uncertain but all the ecological warning signs are there that we are crossing critical boundaries of earth system stability that will send us over dangerous tipping points: we are on course for a new epoch, which scientists Will Steffen and Johan Rockström describe as 'Hothouse Earth'.[31] At the same time, existential risk experts warn that threats from runaway technologies like AI and synthetic biology loom ever larger, with the possibility of causing a megadeath-scale loss of life this century.[32] Despite all the evidence, we remain in a state of denial. We know the Roman Empire fell into oblivion but can scarcely imagine let alone admit that we might face a similar fate.

Yet the likelihood that all civilisations eventually die does not mean that our current pathway is unalterable. Human history is not

Three pathways for civilisation

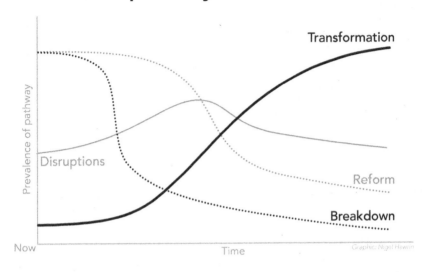

a linear story but an unpredictable drama full of actors, ideas and events that can shape its narrative and bend its arc. It is useful to consider three possible pathways for the future of civilisation that are on the horizon, which I call Breakdown, Reform and Transformation (see above). While each follows the familiar contours of the S-curve, together they depict a range of likely scenarios that we may face. These three paths are not an exhaustive array of possible futures, but represent the dominant trajectories identified by experts in the field of global risk studies.[33]

One route we may follow is towards Breakdown. This is the path of 'business as usual', where we continue striving for the goal of material progress but soon reach a point of societal collapse in the near term, as we fail to respond to rampant ecological and techno-logical crises, and cross dangerous tipping points that send civilisation over a cliff edge. Breakdown could take a number of different forms. It could be a new dark age of social chaos, mass starvation and institutional collapse (a possibility that is discussed in the next chapter), or it might take us towards a state that global scenarios analyst Paul Raskin describes as 'Fortress World', where the rich retreat into protected enclaves, leaving the impoverished majority to suffer outside the gates (think *The Hunger Games*).

The most likely trajectory is Reform, where we respond to global crises but in an inadequate and piecemeal way that merely extends the curve outwards, to a greater or lesser extent. We manage to maintain our current civilisational pathway, with all its existing problems and inequalities, for some decades or possibly longer, but eventually hit an inflection point that sends us down the curve, though perhaps not as steeply as in the Breakdown scenario. It might look as if we are in an era of relative stability, yet in the long run we are merely prolonging the life of the old system and postponing our demise.

This is the pathway currently being pursued by most national governments, especially countries in the Organisation for Economic Co-operation and Development (OECD). Their response to the climate crisis, for instance, is to put their faith in reformist ideas such as 'green growth', 'reinventing capitalism' or a belief that technological solutions are just around the corner. They busily set woefully inadequate targets for reducing carbon emissions, and engage in international negotiations that result in weak compromise solutions lacking mechanisms for enforcement. While some implement more extensive reforms than others, they share an unwillingness to make far-reaching changes to the economic or political system that would allow them to adjust to the new reality. The Reform path is one where keeping below 2°C of planetary heating is seen as a worthy achievement, even though studies show that living in a world that is 2°C hotter rather than 1.5°C hotter would result in an extra 150 million human deaths from air pollution alone. As David Wallace-Wells notes, 'numbers that large can be hard to grasp, but 150 million is the equivalent of twenty-five Holocausts.'[34]

The third pathway, Transformation, represents a radical shift in the values and institutions that underpin society. As the diagram illustrates, the seeds of this possible future are already visible in the present. The question is whether we can jump onto this curve and contribute to its upward trajectory, so a new system replaces the old. It requires actively drawing history towards the outcomes we desire, unlike much scenario planning, which often involves adjusting to emerging futures rather than aiming to create them. This proactive approach is sometimes known as 'backcasting': identify the future you want and then work out the likely steps required to get there.

There may be competing visions of this Transformation pathway. Some envisage it as a technological path, with major high-tech breakthroughs redirecting the course of civilisation, such as those that allow humankind to conquer space and colonise other worlds, thereby ensuring the longevity of our species. Paul Raskin pins his hopes on a transformative path he calls 'New Paradigm', imagining a scenario where a global citizens movement emerges and helps create a new system of planetary-level governance to tackle the ecological crisis. In his narrative, written from the vantage point of 'Mandela City, 2084', a tumultuous period of 'general emergency' between 2023 and 2028 is eventually followed by the foundation of a 'Commonwealth of Earthland' in 2048.[35] This book aspires to a Transformation path that I have described as a long now civilisation. Its ambition is to safeguard and promote conditions to allow the flourishing of life on earth for the generations to come, based on a deeply embedded ethos of long-term thinking. It is a world where the old institutions of representative democracy and growth-dependent economics lose their dominant position and are replaced by the new political, economic and cultural forms explored in Part Three of the book.

The civilisational trajectory we follow will be influenced by disruptive innovations or events (indicated by the line on the diagram), which offer an opportunity to switch from one curve onto another.

These could take the form of a new technology like blockchain, a natural disaster like an earthquake or the rise of new political movements. The recent climate strikes by students around the world are a prime example of such a disruption. It is possible that these time rebels fighting for intergenerational justice will be co-opted by the existing dominant system, with politicians inviting young protesters onto public platforms but only paying lip service to their demands. In that case, it would merely stretch out the Reform pathway, prolonging the moment before decline sets in. Yet the strikes could equally be harnessed by advocates of Transformation, helping to fire up new radical movements for change, as we have witnessed with climate strikers and Extinction Rebellion activists combining forces in many countries.

All three pathways are likely to co-exist in a messy amalgam as we traverse the coming decades: there will be cities and organisations that are engaged in Transformation alongside nations pursuing Reform and communities facing the impact of Breakdown. We confront a choice about the civilisational pathway we want to follow, whether acting in our personal lives, communities, workplaces or as citizens. The longer we wait to jump onto the path of Transformation, the greater the amount of suffering humanity will have to endure as our societies slide inexorably down the S-curve. A good ancestor recognises a dying system when they see one, and rather than trying to pass on their own dysfunctional civilisation to the next generation, they take part in the historic act of seeding a new civilisation that can grow in its place and maintain the conditions conducive to life into the long future.

Dreams of Psychohistory

In Isaac Asimov's 1951 sci-fi classic *Foundation*, a brilliant statistician named Hari Seldon invents a new science known as 'psychohistory'. Through the analysis of huge datasets, Seldon discovers a method for predicting the broad future of galactic civilisation, from the approach of wars to the rise or demise of empires. Using the insights of psychohistory, Seldon realises that the Galactic Empire, which currently rules over millions of worlds, is in a process of decline, bringing with it a descent into a period of barbarism that is likely to last 30,000 years before a new empire can emerge from the ruins. Although it is too late to stop this dark age from happening, with wise planning its length can be reduced to just a thousand years, so Seldon establishes two new colonies, known as foundations, at opposite ends of the galaxy, from which the seeds of a new galactic civilisation can grow.

Psychohistory is a myth. But this does not mean that the future of humanity is a black box of uncertainty. Holistic forecasting reveals the pattern of recurring S-curves that rise and fall over time, echoing the cycles of life and death in the natural world. To claim that we know nothing of the future can too easily become an excuse for apathy, almost an ideology of inaction. Our knowledge of its likely contours is plain to see in thousands of scientific studies of our planetary and living systems. The impact of the ecological emergency is already here in the form of droughts, extreme weather events and growing food and water insecurity for millions of people, especially among poor and marginalised communities in both the wealthy North and the Global South, who are being hit hardest and fastest. The future is all too present.

I have often thought of Asimov's story in the darker moments of writing this book, when it has seemed that we may be too late to prevent the breakdown of our own myopic civilisation. It offers hope that it might be possible to leap onto the path of transformation, enabling a less short-sighted and self-destructive civilisation to arise in its place – one that reflects the long-range mindset of Jonas Salk's Epoch B. We must find ways to create our own foundations not on the far edges of the galaxy but right here in the tumult of our existing societies.

8

Transcendent Goal

A Lodestar to Guide Humanity

One of the greatest discoveries in philosophical thought over the past 2,000 years is that human beings thrive on striving for meaningful future goals that give their lives purpose and direction. Aristotle was convinced that each of us should have 'some object for the good life to aim at ... since not to have one's life organised in view of some end is a mark of much folly.' The German philosopher Friedrich Nietzsche advised, 'He who has a why to live for can bear with almost any how.' Viktor Frankl, Auschwitz survivor and founder of existential psychotherapy, believed that we find meaning by dedicating ourselves to what he called a 'concrete assignment', a future project or ideal that transcends the self.[1]

The Ancient Greeks referred to this ultimate goal or purpose as a *telos*. It functions as a compass for our thoughts and actions, helping us make choices among the sea of possibilities. As individuals, our telos could be anything from discovering a cure for cancer or following the principles of a religion, to caring for an ailing parent or becoming a concert pianist. The astronomer Carl Sagan argued that whole societies should also adopt a telos to guide them – what he called 'a long-term goal and a sacred project'.[2]

Identifying such a transcendent goal for humankind, and striving to achieve it, ranks as the most fundamental of all six strategies for long-term thinking, offering a lodestar to guide our actions into the distant future. This is especially important given that long-term thinking can be hijacked and directed towards self-seeking ambitions, such as creating a political dynasty, amassing endless wealth

Transcendent goals for humankind

Perpetual progress
Pursue material improvement and endless economic growth

Utopian dream
Create an ideal society based on political, economic or religious beliefs

Techno liberation
Colonise other worlds and use technology to transcend the limits of the human body

Survival mode
Adapt to civilisational breakdown and develop the skills for basic human survival

One-planet thriving
Meet the needs of all current and future people within the means of a flourishing planet

or maintaining power and privilege.[3] There may be nothing more essential than answering the question, 'Long-term thinking: to what end?'

This chapter highlights five possible transcendent goals for humanity that are at the forefront of public debates about our collective future (see above). They are fascinating in their diversity: each of them is based on a very different vision of the world to which we might ultimately aspire, ranging from the highly technological to the deeply ecological. They are all powerfully motivating and have committed advocates who believe that their transcendent goal is the best one for ensuring the long-term well-being of humankind. While all five possess compelling qualities, it is worth exploring each one to see whether it offers not just a far-sighted and inspiring goal, but whether it also makes us good ancestors. Which of them have what it takes to safeguard the best interests of future generations?

Perpetual Progress: Keeping the Curve Rising Ever Upwards

The pursuit of material progress has been the dominant long-term goal of Western societies for more than two centuries, and has gradually spread its influence across the globe. An inheritance from the Enlightenment, its objective has been to secure continuous economic development and modernisation that improves the quality of our daily lives. As a telos for humankind, it is best represented by a curve of economic growth rising ever upwards into the future. There is no doubt that material progress has been delivering the goods for large portions of the human population. Since the eighteenth century, it has given us longer lifespans, public health, reductions in poverty, mass education, faster transport and consumer comforts from air conditioning to mobile phones. As Steven Pinker puts it, 'The Enlightenment has worked,' and progress has been one of its leading ideals.[4]

Yet this story of progress is undercut by an inherent short-termism that exists in tension with its long-term ambitions.

The origins of human progress go back 50,000 years, to the invention of new hunting technologies and techniques during the Upper Palaeolithic Period. With sharper weapons and smarter strategies, our Stone Age ancestors could now kill not just a single bison or mammoth, but trap and kill scores of them in an enclosed valley or drive them off a cliff edge to their deaths. Clever if you wanted to feast today, but not if you wanted to eat for the next hundred seasons. While modern-day hunter-gatherers, such as the San peoples of the Kalahari and the Inuit, have mastered how to live in tune with their ecologies, this was not always the case with prehistoric peoples, whose early waves of migration across the continents frequently led to the mass extinction of other species as they literally hunted them out of existence. Archaeologists have found industrial-scale slaughter sites, including a thousand mammoths at one, and a hundred thousand horses at another.[5] Magnificent megafauna such as woolly rhinos and straight-tusked elephants fast disappeared from Europe (remains of elephants, hippopotamuses and lions have been found deep beneath Trafalgar Square), giant wombats and kangaroos vanished from Australia, and giant bison and beavers were among the casualties in North America. While climatic changes may have led to the disappearance of some species, there is now a widespread consensus that humans played a major role by carrying out an ecological blitzkrieg. As historian Ronald Wright notes, 'a bad smell of extinction follows *Homo sapiens* around the world.' Palaeontologist Tim Flannery puts it even more starkly, describing our rapacious species as 'the future eaters'.[6]

The development of industrial capitalism in the eighteenth century ramped up the pursuit of progress.[7] The Industrial Revolution and urbanisation wiped out the vestiges of feudalism by creating a proletariat to sweat in the factories and toil down the mines. Over time, the benefits of this new system were palpable: despite deepening wealth inequality, millions of people were lifted out of poverty. Yet its costs were enormous, for it was powered by the burning of fossil fuels that had been stored within the earth for millions of years, locking the pursuit of material progress into an energy system that has depleted resources, destabilised the climate and caused untold damage to the life-support systems of the living world. 'The powers unleashed by the Industrial Revolution,' concludes economic historian Tony Wrigley, 'have proved to possess the capacity to bestow blessings without earlier parallel but also to cause harm on a scale previously unknown'.[8]

In the second half of the twentieth century, industrial capitalism was joined by consumer capitalism, which focused less on the exploitation of labour and more on the manufacture of desire – getting people to buy things they didn't really need, from second cars to napkin rings. This fostered a short-term culture of instant consumer gratification that tapped into our marshmallow brains and is evident in everything from the rise of the fast-food industry to today's expectation of same-day delivery of online shopping. It also displayed a reckless attitude towards long-term consequences: so long as firms achieved their immediate financial goals, it didn't matter if this polluted the air, deforested the landscape, poisoned rivers, created nicotine and sugar addictions or plunged households into long-term debt.

This consumer-driven version of progress has been fuelled by the drive for endless GDP growth. As economist Tim Jackson has argued, 'The pursuit of economic growth has been the single most prevalent policy goal across the world for the past 70 years.'[9] Governments across the political spectrum have become obsessed with keeping the growth curve rising ever upwards, quarter after quarter, as if it were the only measure of progress that matters and no matter the social and ecological costs.

The great acceleration

Human impacts on the living world have accelerated rapidly since the 1950s, which is often considered as the start date for the Anthropocene era

Human population: Global total (billions)
GDP: Gross domestic product (2005 $US)
FDI: Global foreign direct investment ($US)
Energy: Primary energy use (exajoule EJ)
Water use: Agricultural, industrial and domestic consumption (thousand km³)
Paper: Paper production (million tonnes)
Transport: New motor vehicles per year (millions)
CO₂: Carbon dioxide (parts per million)
Ozone: Statospheric ozone (percentage loss)
Temperature: Global surface temperature anomaly (°C)
Forest: Loss of tropical forests compared to 1700 (%)
Species: Decrease in mean species abundance (%)

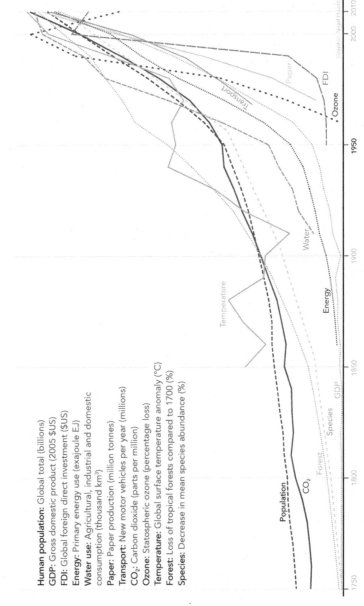

The widespread faith in progress as a goal for humanity is perfectly understandable. Compared to the grinding poverty of the Middle Ages, the material benefits it has produced over the past 200 years are an extraordinary achievement. But it has now become too difficult to ignore the collateral damage. Earth system scientists have a name for it: the Great Acceleration. Especially since the 1950s, rising GDP, car ownership and other indicators of material progress have been accompanied by rapidly increasing levels of carbon dioxide, species extinction and other forms of ecological degradation (see above).[10] All those steeply rising curves have become an iconic image of the dangers inherent in the pursuit of progress.

It is hard to imagine our descendants thanking us for this inheritance; in fact, they are more likely to condemn us for it. If we aim to be good ancestors and create a world fit for the generations to come, it is time to leave perpetual progress as a goal of the past that is no longer suited to the future. So where, then, should we direct our long-term aspirations?

Utopian Dream: Visions of an Ideal Society

'A map of the world that does not include Utopia is not worth even glancing at,' wrote Oscar Wilde.[11] Utopias, by their very nature, are suffused with long-termism: they offer a vision of an ideal society to which we might aspire, with no illusion that it can be achieved overnight. Karl Marx knew that a workers' paradise would not be a quick win in the face of an entrenched capitalist system, and the revolutionary movements he inspired pursued decades-long class struggles in their quest to forge a better society. Similarly, utopian religious movements, such as Mormonism, have taken the long view in their efforts to create a vision of heaven on earth, building up their communities of believers gradually and often in the face of persecution and prejudice.

What is sometimes called 'social utopianism' – focused on reconfiguring society around ideals such as equality, freedom and social justice – has particularly strong long-term credentials. Throughout history it has been remarkably successful at motivating and sustaining movements for change, even when the odds have been heavily stacked against them. There would have been no anti-slavery organisations, no trade unions, no suffragettes, no anti-colonial movements and no welfare states without utopian visions that challenged the assumptions and beliefs of their times and painted a picture of a better world as a long-term goal to strive for. As Jeremy Rifkin argues, 'Images of the future are the single most powerful socialising agents that exist in Western culture.'[12] That is why Martin Luther King Jr proclaimed, 'I have a dream'. Social utopias have helped to reframe the human story, offering fresh pathways along which our imaginations can travel and creating beacons of hope for radically transforming the future.

A powerful feature of these utopian visions is that they tend to focus on shared goals and principles to live by, giving them the potential to tackle the global crises of our age that require a collective, coordinated response. Yet aspiring good ancestors should be wary of social utopias that were formulated before we entered the Anthropocene epoch of ecological breakdown in the late twentieth century. The potential melting of the Greenland ice sheet simply wasn't on the radar of early utopian thinkers such as Karl Marx, Charles Fourier, William Morris and Thomas More. Their long-term thinking typically lacked awareness of the fragility of earth's life-supporting systems. However, there are some exceptions, such as the nineteenth-century anarchist Peter Kropotkin, whose writing displays a keen ecological awareness.

Contemporary utopian thought has changed with the times and become much more attuned to the long-term challenges that are facing humanity. Since the 1970s there has been an explosion of 'ecotopian' fiction from writers such as Ursula Le Guin and Ernest Callenbach, often inspired by earlier authors such as Aldous Huxley. Moreover, there are now plenty of progressive rabbis, cardinals and imams who have incorporated environmental thinking into their religious visions of the future, with the planet being considered a gift from God that must be protected and preserved for future generations.[13]

An exemplar of this new mode of utopianism, which combines established social themes with modern ecological ones, is Jonathon Porritt's book *The World We Made*. Written from the perspective of a school teacher in the future, it aims 'to tell the story of how we got the world back from the brink of collapse to where we are now in 2050'. This new world is full of worker cooperatives, a 25-hour working week, vertical urban farms and electric planes. Porritt's originality is to describe the protracted struggles required to create it, including the rise of a global social movement called Enough! that kickstarted the shift to a more sustainable society.[14] By presenting a utopian vision that includes both the ends and the means, it offers a clear and credible long-term pathway that good ancestors might follow.

Long-term thinking will always require utopian ideals to set inspiring goals for humankind, and to energise and empower movements for change. Today's movements focused on the crises of our age, such as Extinction Rebellion, are part of a long history of social struggles that have found motivation and determination in dreams of a better world. As the Uruguayan writer Eduardo Galeano remarked, 'Utopia lies at the horizon. When I draw nearer by two steps, it retreats two steps. If I proceed ten steps forward, it swiftly slips ten steps ahead. No matter how far I go, I can never reach it. What, then, is the purpose of utopia? It is to cause us to advance.'[15]

As we set out to reach utopia, might the long-term interests of future generations be best secured not by aspiring to reinvent this world, but by escaping to a different one?

Techno-Liberation: Is Our Destiny in the Stars?

When it comes to technology, our brilliance as a species is unparalleled. From the first stone axe to the latest advances in genome sequencing, we have managed to radically alter the pathway of humankind. Despite well-founded public scepticism about the virtues of technology, including concerns about tech giants stealing our personal data or the problems of digital addiction, many long-term thinkers still believe that our ultimate goal should be a technological future. This long-term objective comes in three main forms, Techno-escape, Techno-split and Techno-fix, each of which offers a compelling telos to guide humanity.

Techno-escape provides one of the most alluring transcendent goals for our species: our destiny is in the stars, and we must set our sights on escaping the confines of earth and colonise other worlds. The argument behind it typically goes something like this: in the long run every planetary society will face the threat of annihilation – due to asteroid impact, or resource depletion, or perhaps blowing themselves up – so any civilisation that wants to survive in the long term needs to spread itself out across multiple planets, not out of some romantic zeal, but for the practical reason of staying alive. As Carl Sagan put it with characteristic eloquence:

> The moon was where the tree of immortality grew in ancient Chinese myth. The tree of longevity if not of immortality, it seems, indeed grows on other worlds. If we were up there among the planets, if there were self-sufficient human communities on many worlds, our species would be insulated from catastrophe . . . If our long-term survival is at stake, we have a basic responsibility to our species to venture to other worlds.[16]

This vision is shared by tech entrepreneur and SpaceX founder Elon Musk, who believes that colonising Mars is the next great step for humanity (presumably in rockets owned by his company). 'I want to die on Mars, just not on impact,' says Musk.[17]

One issue facing the techno-escapers concerns the length of time it will all take. Mars is a lifeless and radiation-prone desert enveloped by carbon dioxide, which is subject to temperatures of minus 100°C and over 30 million miles from earth. We may have to wait until 2040 before a single person sets foot on it. And most experts believe that even if we could get enough people there safely, making it habitable for a substantive human population by artificially creating a new atmosphere (known as 'terraforming') would probably take hundreds or maybe thousands of years, and could in the end be impossible.[18] Yet the advocates of space colonisation contend that this is precisely the kind of long-term thinking we need: if we truly aspire to be good ancestors, we should embark as soon as possible on the cosmic task of settling Mars and other planets. It might take a long time, they say, but it's the best way to guarantee the survival of our species.

A more serious challenge is that the goal of techno-escape may create serious collateral damage: the more we set our hopes on escaping to other worlds, the less likely we are to make the effort required to preserve our existing planetary home. In fact, while tackling a problem like climate change might seem daunting, it is far easier than the task of colonising Mars. As Martin Rees points out, 'No place in our solar system offers an environment even as clement as the Antarctic or the top of Everest.'[19] Our first priority should be to learn to live within the biophysical means of the only planet we know that sustains life. Once we have mastered this challenge, then we can do as much terraforming of Mars as we like. As any mountaineer will tell you, make sure your base camp is in good condition with ample supplies before you attempt a risky summit. We've still got a long way to go before our base camp is in order. Until then, we should consider voyaging to Mars as an elite minority sport for Elon Musk and other super-rich space adventurers rather than as an ultimate goal for the human race.

The growing transhumanist movement offers an alternative long-term telos, known as techno-split. This is the idea that the future of our species lies in using technology to upgrade ourselves to the point where we are able to make an evolutionary jump to a new kind of human, in effect splitting off from our biological forebears.[20]

While it may take several centuries to make the leap onto a new evolutionary plane, the advocates of techno-split point out that the seeds of this transformation are already appearing. Some are excited by the prospect of medical advances, such as body part transplants and genetic manipulations to stop our cells ageing, that would enable us to achieve what they call 'longevity escape velocity'. This is where for every passing year, progress in medical research increases the average human lifespan by more than one year, which should theoretically allow us to outrun death and achieve immortality (unless we get run over by a bus). Other transhumanists await the day when we can upgrade our brains with implants that enhance our memory and other cognitive functions to a level of 'superintelligence'. A third strand is betting on the possibility of 'whole brain emulation', where we create artificial versions of our brains that can be uploaded into the cloud. Once we are fully online, claim its enthusiasts, it will then be easy to send our digital selves to colonise the far corners of the galaxy and travel for aeons through the cosmos.[21]

Techno-split is heady stuff, but is it science or science fiction? There is no doubt that artificially enhanced humans are on the horizon – many people already have pacemakers that are connected to the internet, and the colour-blind artist Neil Harbisson has an audio antenna implanted into his head. Yet the idea that we can create electronic replicas of ourselves is based on the false analogy that humans are essentially computers whose minds are software that can be separated off from their flesh and blood hardware.[22] Decades of neurological research has shown that the mind and body are intimately intertwined: we learn through our whole sensory apparatus, a

Are we on the verge of techno-split? Colour-blind artist Neil Harbisson, who is known as the 'world's first cyborg', has an antenna implanted permanently in his skull that allows him to feel and hear colours as audible vibrations inside his head. Wi-fi enabled, he can also receive satellite data.

sculptor can project her mind into her fingertips, we feel our emotions coursing through our whole physical being, mental stress can cause diabetes, the beat of our hearts and the sweat on our palms are part of who we are.[23] We are not just bits and bytes of information that can be copied and pasted into a big server in the sky. And we still have no idea about how consciousness really works, and whether it could ever materialise from a clever arrangement of zeros and ones embedded in a microchip. Would it really be 'me' up there in the cloud?

There is also growing concern about the rise of an engineered cyborg race of superhumans. Especially in the early stages, it will only be the wealthy who will be able to afford artificial enhancements (it currently costs around $80,000 to have your brain cryonically frozen and kept in a warehouse in Arizona – and nobody knows how, when, or if unfreezing will ever be possible). The danger is that a new kind of inequality will eventually emerge, a genuine techno-split that leaves those who haven't been upgraded as a subservient underclass. As Yuval Noah Harari argues, if we really want to understand how this might play out, we should think about how Europeans treated their colonial subjects in the nineteenth century, or how we treat animals today.[24] Are we really prepared to condemn future generations to a world based on a technological version of the Nazi ideology of the Untermensch? Far from gaining us accolades as good ancestors, this would represent a tragic failure to consider the long-term risks posed by our actions.

The final form of techno-liberation is far less spectacular than either techno-escape or techno-split. Call it techno-fix, which can be defined as the belief that humans will always devise new technologies to solve the problems they face. When cities became too crowded, we invented skyscrapers. When we needed more food, along came the Green Revolution. And so, the argument goes, we will find ways to wriggle out of the ecological crisis we have created for ourselves. Top of the list are technologies like carbon capture and storage (CCS) and geoengineering a clean and healthy atmosphere. Techno-fix may not sound like a grand long-term goal for humankind, but it smuggles one in through the back door: namely, that the goal of our species should be to continue doing whatever we are already doing. In other words, we can maintain the highly materialistic consumer society we currently have into the distant future because technological solutions will emerge to solve the environmental problems it generates.

Is such optimism justified? Consider geoengineering, which might take the form of spraying light-reflecting sulphate aerosols into the stratosphere, in the hope of creating a global cooling effect that counterbalances the heating effect of burning fossil fuels. This solution could never be tested at the planetary scale, and so might have devastating and irreversible side effects that we cannot predict, such as disturbing the seasonal monsoon rains that billions of people rely on for food production. Moreover, geoengineering would be politically complex, requiring unprecedented global coordination to keep the thermostat at an agreed level and the technology functioning not just for a few years, but indefinitely through wars, famines and whatever else the future throws at us.[25] Geoengineering might work, but is a gamble of colossal proportions that we would be thrusting upon generation after generation.

This gamble conflicts with a basic tenet of environmental policy-making known as the precautionary principle: 'When an activity raises threats of harm to human health or the environment, precautionary measures should be taken even if some cause-and-effect relationships are not fully established scientifically.'[26] This is really a sophisticated way of restating the ancient medical principle 'first, do no harm'. We might as an individual take the risk of a new cancer treatment that could kill us faster than the disease itself, but do we have the right to impose a similarly risky treatment on billions of people, both today and in the future, in order to restore our planetary health?[27]

Technology offers visionary goals for our species that can send our imaginations forward by centuries and even millennia. Yet as the economic historian Carlota Perez points out, 'technology provides the options, but society chooses the future'. Our priority must be to make wise choices about which of them will best serve the well-being of future generations and not pose threats to their lives and livelihoods.

Survival Mode: Gearing Up for Civilisational Breakdown

The ideals of perpetual progress, utopian societies and technological liberation are little more than fantasies according to advocates of a fourth overarching goal for humankind, best described as 'survival mode'. They argue that we have spent far too long in denial about the fate of the earth and must face the reality that the collapse of civilisation as we know it is inevitable and that our ultimate existential task is to prepare ourselves for the worst by developing the skills for basic survival.

The underlying premise of this idea is that the planetary ecological emergency is far more severe than we are willing to admit: bodies such as the Intergovernmental Panel on Climate Change systematically underestimate the extent of the crisis, due to their need to reach consensus; all indicators suggest that we face the prospect of severe global food and water shortages within the next few decades; and we are on the verge of ecosystem collapse (in fact, it's already happening, from coral bleaching to 'insectageddon'). We have made no serious progress on reducing greenhouse gas emissions since the early 1990s, and there is no reason to think that this pattern will change. As such, we will never keep below the international target of 1.5°C warming, and are in fact heading towards calamitous levels of at least 3–4°C. Our civilisation, claims sustainability academic Jem Bendell, faces 'inevitable near-term collapse due to climate change', probably within the next ten to twenty years. It is 'too late to avert a global environmental catastrophe in the lifetimes of people today . . . we are set for disruptive and uncontrollable levels of climate change, bringing starvation, destruction, migration, disease and war.' Climate philosopher Roy Scranton puts it even more succinctly: 'We're fucked. The only questions are how soon and how badly.'[28]

Some adherents of 'survival mode' envisage a future resembling the violent and pitiless post-apocalyptic world of Cormac McCarthy's novel *The Road*, a Hobbesian state of nature, where life is solitary, poor, nasty, brutish and short. For them, the best strategy is to grab a gun, head for the high ground and pull up the drawbridge. A less individualistic response, described by Bendell as 'Deep Adaptation', is that we should immediately start working together to prepare for the far-reaching impacts of the coming collapse. His suggested actions include withdrawing populations from coastlines that will be flooded, shutting nuclear facilities that could face meltdown due to technological breakdown and social chaos, increasing community-level food production, and psychologically preparing ourselves for the 'climate tragedy', including the very real possibility that 'you will fear being violently killed before starving to death.'[29]

While the ecological crisis is likely to hit harder and faster than most people think, does it therefore follow that the collapse of civilisation is 'inevitable'? Human societies are unpredictable, complex, nonlinear systems: there is nothing inevitable about them. Who could have foreseen the rise of Christianity, the spread of Buddhism from India, Europe's economic recovery after losing a third of its population due to the Black Death, the birth of Renaissance humanism, the social impact of the spinning jenny, the doubling of human longevity since the nineteenth century, the end of Apartheid and state socialism in Eastern Europe or the growth of the internet? It is absolutely possible that due to climate change, we face the prospect of hundreds of millions of people starving to death, the disintegration of international trade, multiple failed states, outbreaks of civil war and systematic breakdowns of trust and other social norms. But it is also possible that this civilisational collapse won't happen, or at least not on the scale that the adherents of 'survival mode' assert.[30] We have never faced a planetary-level ecological crisis before, so we simply don't know what impact it will have on the vast web of human organisations that have developed over the past 10,000 years.

What we do know is that humans can be extremely effective at responding to a crisis. Even the Americans and Russians managed an alliance against Germany in the Second World War, just as extraordinary social cooperation emerged in communities hit by disasters such as Hurricane Katrina and 9/11. 'The image of the selfish, panicky or regressively savage human being in times of disaster has little truth in it,' writes Rebecca Solnit in her book *A Paradise Built in Hell*. 'The prevalent human nature in disaster is resilient, resourceful, generous, empathic and brave'.[31] It is too early to say that it is game over. We need to be agnostic about the prospect of civilisational collapse: realistically prepared that it might happen, but open to the possibility that it might not. If that possibility exists, it is morally inexcusable to turn our backs on future generations by not acting on it. They would never forgive us if we chose to give up when there was still a chance of averting disaster and jumping onto a transformative civilisational pathway.

The idea that collapse is inevitable is not only empirically unproven but also promotes a fatalistic inertia and apathy. 'By turning people's attention toward preparing for doom, rather than focusing on structural political and economic change,' argues cultural thinker Jeremy Lent, 'Deep Adaptation threatens to become a self-fulfilling prophecy, increasing the risk of collapse by diluting efforts toward societal transformation.'[32] If we are told we will fail at something and keep repeating this to ourselves, we typically make such an outcome more likely. Framing collapse as 'inevitable' creates feedback loops of passive despair rather than of radical hope that inspires action. 'If we assume we are doomed, then we will definitely be doomed,' writes philosopher Rupert Read, one of the leading figures in Extinction Rebellion. 'We need to feel a confidence: that a change of course remains eminently *possible*.'[33]

Survival mode replaces the denial of the climate crisis with another form of denial: the denial that change can happen, that taking action could make a substantive difference to the fate of human civilisation. This is not a moment for false optimism. It is a moment for recognising that through collective effort, determined will and inspiring vision, humankind can think long, act long and reconfigure the contours of history.

One-Planet Thriving: Living Within the Boundaries of the Natural World

Over the past half-century, a fifth long-term goal for humanity has emerged out of fields such as sustainability science, systems design and ecological thought. It can be summed up by the concept of 'one-planet thriving', the idea of meeting the needs of all current and future people within the ecological means of a flourishing planet. In practice, this requires living within the life-supporting systems of the natural world, so we don't use more resources than the earth can naturally regenerate (for instance, only harvest timber as fast as it can grow back), or create more wastes than it can naturally absorb (so don't burn fossil fuels more rapidly than they can be absorbed by the oceans and other carbon sinks). In other words, it is about thriving in balance for the centuries and millennia to come.

This is an undeniably ambitious telos, but also one that is readily measurable: we currently use natural resources at a rate that is nearly double what earth is able to regenerate and absorb each year. Once we hit 29 July – so after just seven months – we begin to overshoot the planet's biocapacity, largely due to deforestation, biodiversity loss, soil erosion and carbon dioxide build-up in the atmosphere.[34] Ultimately, we need to shift what has come to be known as 'Earth Overshoot Day' from the middle of the year back to 31 December, so we are truly thriving within the means of this one planet and not running down the ecosystems on which future generations must, like us, depend for survival.

One of the most profound expressions of this ideal appears in the work of biologist and biomimicry designer Janine Benyus. In her view, we should draw our lessons for long-term survival from the 3.8 billion years of research and development that nature has to offer:

The answers we seek, the secrets to a sustainable world, are literally all around us. If we choose to truly mimic life's genius, the future I see would be beauty and abundance and certainly fewer regrets. In the natural world the definition of success is the continuity of Life. You keep yourself alive and you keep your offspring alive. That's success. But it's not the offspring in this generation. Success is keeping your offspring alive for ten thousand generations and more. That presents a conundrum because you're not going to be there to take care of your offspring ten thousand generations from now. So what organisms have learned to do is to take care of the place that's going to take care of their offspring. Life has learned to create conditions conducive to life. That's really the magic heart of it. And that's also the design brief for us right now. We have to learn how to do that.[35]

This passage offers a unique insight into long-term thinking: that it can be pursued by *stepping outside the realm of time itself*, and that it is about caring for *place* as much as rethinking *time*. The best way for any species – including our own – to ensure its longevity is to fully adapt to and preserve the ecosystem in which it is embedded. That means caring for the rivers, the soil, the trees, the pollinators, the very air that we breathe. It means respecting the intricate relationships that sustain the web of life and have enabled us to evolve. If we overshoot nature's biocapacity, we are failing in the task of taking care of the place that will take care of our offspring.[36]

Put simply: if we want to survive and thrive for thousands of generations, don't foul the nest.

Yet this is precisely what human beings have been doing since they made their first tool, since they became set on accumulation, since they lost the capacity to say 'enough' and became a species addicted to ascending the perilous curves of the Great Acceleration in the pursuit of material progress.

The goal of one-planet thriving has been reinforced by a growing recognition that human beings are not separate from nature but an interdependent part of the living planetary whole. Such holistic thinking is evident among indigenous cultures in their worship of Mother Earth and practices such as the seventh-generation principle. But it has also been finding its way into the Western mind. In 2011, Ron Garan spent six months living on the International Space Station. Amid his gruelling schedule of scientific experiments and technical repairs, he was sometimes able to gaze at the 'fragile oasis' of the earth below:

> One of the really interesting things about a long-duration space flight is that you get to watch the earth transform over the weeks and the months that you're up there. You get to watch the ice break up, the seasons change. And from that perspective over time, you really get the sense that we have this living, breathing organism hanging in the blackness of space just riding through the universe.[37]

Others who have observed earth from space have had similar epiphanies, which have come to be known as the 'overview effect'. They suddenly see it as a single living system, a rare and fragile organic whole that deserves reverence and preservation, with humans as just one small part of its interconnected web of life. Many people experienced the overview effect in 1968 when they first saw 'Earthrise', a partial image of the planet taken from the Apollo 8 spacecraft, and then in 1972, when astronauts on Apollo 17 beamed back the whole-planet photo known as 'The Blue Marble', which soon became an iconic symbol of the environmental movement. This holistic perspective was also evident in James Lovelock and Lynn Margulis's Gaia hypothesis, which first emerged in the 1970s and suggests that our planet functions like a self-regulating, living organism. Gradually over recent decades, we have been developing a sense of what Brian Eno calls 'the Big Here' – a sister concept he invented to accompany 'the Long Now'.[38] The Big Here expands the spatial realm of where our responsibilities for the future lie, to encompass a here that is bigger than our own home, or neighbourhood, or country. A here that is the size of the earth itself.

The transcendent goal of one-planet thriving calls on us to recognise our symbiotic relationship with the planetary whole and to respect its natural boundaries and capacities. It sets our sights on place rather than time as the key to ensuring the longevity of our species. One-planet thriving stands apart from the other forms of telos described earlier, through its elemental concern with safeguarding the possibility of life itself, generation after generation, drawing on nearly four billion years of evolutionary learning and wisdom. It is about protecting 'base camp earth' and ensuring a viable future for our descendants on the one and only planet that has evolved to sustain them. And that is why it is the long-term goal that can best guide us along the pathway of the good ancestor.

Let the living world act as the compass for humanity, as so beautifully expressed in the Mohawk blessing, 'Thank you, Earth. You know the way.'[39]

———

We stand at a turning point in our journey. By now, our acorn brains should be well and truly switched on and fired up: we have gained the cognitive skill set we need for long-term thinking. Our minds have travelled across the expanses of deep time. They have traversed the boundaries of death in search of a legacy. They have become grounded in the principles of intergenerational justice. They have been inspired by cathedral thinking and discovered the

S-curves of holistic foresight. And they have gained a telos of one-planet thriving to guide them, which is not a detailed blueprint of a specific form of government or economy but a lodestar to ensure that our long thinking remains directed towards the interests of future generations. We are poised and prepared to take the next step of turning ideas into action. The moment has come to meet the time rebels who are putting the six ways to think long-term into practice in an ambitious attempt to launch humanity onto a new civilisational pathway.

PART THREE

BRING ON THE TIME REBELLION

Ideas have the power to change the world, but only when people put them into practice. The following chapters reveal how a committed network of activists, organisers, academics, policymakers and students are seeding the six ways to think long in three realms: politics, economics and culture. These time rebels face formidable barriers and their victory is far from assured, yet they are determined to decolonise the future and reshape the contours of history.

9

Deep Democracy

Is There an Antidote for Political Myopia?

Just imagine if tomorrow's generations could have their voices heard in today's political debates. If there was a way to represent their interests and ensure their futures were not trampled on by the short-termism that rules in the cut and thrust of modern political life. If it was possible to expand the boundaries of the 'demos' (from the Ancient Greek for 'the people'), so it included not only young people who are currently excluded from voting, but the multitude of potential citizens waiting to be born.

You may not have read about it in the media, but a quiet revolution has been taking place with precisely this intention, led by a pioneering generation of time rebels who have embarked on a radical project to create a new political model that I call 'deep democracy'. Their ambition is to extend the time horizons of democratic government and rescue it from the myopic politicians who fail to take the long view as they get swept up in the whirlwind of elections, opinion polls and 24/7 news.

Just as the idea of deep time expands our temporal imagination across the cosmos, deep democracy expands our political imagination beyond the short-sightedness at the heart of government. To do so, it draws on the long-term ideals discussed in Part Two, such as intergenerational justice, cathedral thinking, the seventh-generation principle and the transcendent goal of one-planet thriving.

The vanguard rebel movement to reinvent democracy still has no official name and remains fragmented, but it is rapidly gaining momentum across the globe. To fully gauge its prospects, we need to answer several questions. What are the underlying drivers of political myopia? Is democracy the best system for dealing with long-range challenges, or might authoritarian systems be a more effective option? And how are the time rebels putting deep democracy into practice, in the face of powerful opposition?

Few people see this democratic revolution coming. But like the protests that brought down the Berlin Wall in 1989, there is a chance – admittedly slim but undoubtedly possible – that the progressive forces of history will align and break the barriers that are holding back a new era of long-term politics.

Political Presentism: How Future Generations Are Excluded from the Democratic Deal

'The origin of civil government,' wrote David Hume in 1739, is that 'men are not able radically to cure, either in themselves or others, that narrowness of soul, which makes them prefer the present to the remote'.[1] The Scottish philosopher was convinced that the institutions of government, such as elected representatives and parliamentary debates, were needed to temper our impulsive and selfish desires and foster society's long-term interests and welfare.

If only.

Today, Hume's view appears to be wishful thinking, since it is so startlingly clear that politicians and the political system itself have become a cause of rampant short-termism rather than a cure for it. While representative democracies in the Western world have evolved long-lasting institutions such as civil services, police forces and judiciaries, they equally exhibit what can be called 'political presentism': a bias towards prioritising short-term political interests and decisions, and in favour of current over future generations.[2] When the Czech prime minister Andrej Babiš was asked in June 2019 why he had blocked an agreement to commit EU member states to reducing their carbon emissions to net zero by 2050, he replied, 'Why should we decide 31 years ahead of time what will happen in 2050?'[3] The ruling political class typically refuse to see the future as their responsibility.

The affliction of political presentism has roots in five factors that pervade the nature of democracy itself. First is the temporal trap of electoral cycles, an inherent design limitation of democratic government that produces short political time horizons.[4] Time itself has been cycled into the ballot box, with politicians and their parties focusing with blinkered attention on whatever it will take to entice voters at the next election. Back in the 1970s, the economist William Nordhaus identified this problem as the 'political business cycle', noticing that governments would repeatedly expand their spending in the run up to elections and then introduce austerity measures once they had gained office to rein in their now overheating economies. His concern was that this could generate 'purely myopic policy, where future generations are ignored'.[5] The result is that long-term issues from which politicians can make little immediate political capital, such as dealing with ecological breakdown or pension reform, are often kept permanently on the back-burner.

A second factor is the power of special interest groups, and especially corporations, to secure near-term political favours for themselves, while passing the longer-term costs onto the rest of society.[6] This is hardly a new problem: in 1913 an exasperated Woodrow Wilson declared that 'the government of the United States is the foster child of special interests . . . the big bankers, the big manufacturers, the big masters of commerce.'[7] More recently, Al Gore announced that 'American democracy has been hacked – and the hack is campaign finance.'[8] When fossil fuel companies successfully lobby governments for the right to drill and frack on public land or manage to block carbon-cutting legislation, they are holding the future to ransom in the name of shareholder returns. Similarly, in the wake of the 2008 financial crisis, US and UK banks that were responsible for the crash used their political influence to secure massive taxpayer-funded bail-outs that amounted to a short-term fix rather than long-term reform. According to Jared Diamond, one of the key causes of the collapse of civilisations is when 'the interests of the decision-making elite in power clash with the interests of the rest of society. Especially if the elite can insulate themselves from the consequences of their actions'.[9] We would be wise to take note.

The deepest cause of political presentism is that representative democracy systematically ignores the interests of future people. The citizens of tomorrow are granted no rights, nor – in the vast majority of countries – are there public bodies to represent their interests or potential views on decisions taken today that will undoubtedly affect their lives.[10] This is a blind spot so enormous that we barely notice it: in the decade I spent researching democratic governance as a political scientist, it simply never occurred to me that future generations are disenfranchised in the same way that slaves and women were in the past. But that is the reality, and that is why hundreds of thousands of school students around the world have been striking to get rich nations to reduce their carbon emissions: they have had enough of democratic systems that render them voiceless and powerless. It is also why so many young people in the UK – especially those below the voting age – felt betrayed by the result of the Brexit referendum: since over-65s were more than twice as likely as under-25s to vote to leave the European Union, older voters had a major impact on a decision with long-term consequences that they would scarcely have to live with themselves.[11]

Digital drivers, such as social media and 24/7 news cycles, have magnified the problem of political presentism. While the growth of television as a medium of mass communication from the 1950s helped launch a new age of sound bites and political spin, we now find ourselves living in 'Twitterocracies', where our political representatives spend much of their time giving instant opinions on social media and cable news channels, and engaging in constant reputational warfare to ensure they are trending.[12] A single tweet from Donald Trump can quickly cascade into a full-blown political drama that occupies politicians and the media for days. The result is to foreshorten political time by distracting public attention from longer-term and less tweetworthy 'slow news', whether an intensifying drought in sub-Saharan Africa or a new intergovernmental report on the growing resistance of common diseases to antibiotics.[13]

A final political challenge lies not with democratic government directly but with the larger body in which it exists: the nation state. When nation states first emerged in the eighteenth and nineteenth centuries and replaced the old order of empires and principalities, they were not an especially dangerous source of short-termism. Italy and France, for instance, had long-term visions to create a strong sense of national identity, along with public institutions including civil services and education systems.[14] But times have changed. Many of today's most acute long-term concerns, such as the climate crisis, are global in nature and require global solutions. There may be no greater problem of collective action than trying to get scores of countries, which often have vastly different cultures, histories, economies and priorities, to overcome their differences and find common ground. On rare occasions cooperation takes place, as with the Montreal Protocol to protect the ozone layer in 1987, but more typically, individual nation states focus on their particular interests rather than on shared long-term risks. A country like the US or Australia might refuse to ratify a global agreement on carbon reductions because it threatens its mining industry or a slowdown of its economy. Another (think India, Pakistan or Israel) might opt out of a nuclear non-proliferation treaty if it wants to develop its own nuclear weapons. Even relatively homogenous regions, such as the European Union, have trouble reaching agreements on issues like the number of refugees each member state should take or how many fish they are allowed to catch.

Just like my 11-year-old twins, nation states are constantly bickering, always wanting the largest slice of cake, and doing their best to avoid their share of the housework. Unlike my twins, nation states show no sign of growing out of it.

The Intergenerational Solidarity Index: Measuring the Long-Term Policy Performance of Democracies and Autocracies

The problem of short-termism in democratic politics has become so acute that a growing chorus of voices has begun speaking in favour of 'benign dictatorship' or 'enlightened despotism' as the solution to our problems, especially to take the tough measures required to deal with the climate emergency. Such sentiments, mentioned in Chapter 6, have become increasingly common not only among well-known figures like scientist James Lovelock, but also among the general public; terms such as 'eco-authoritarianism' are beginning to appear with growing frequency in online forums and on social media feeds, while audience members in my talks on long-term thinking often suggest autocratic government as an antidote to political myopia.[15] The standard argument is that we need to become more like China, which appears to have a proven track record on long-term policymaking, especially regarding investment in green technologies. Or like Singapore, which may put some limits on civil and political liberties but manages to take a far-sighted approach to everything from education reform to urban planning.

It all starts to sound very enticing: let's just bypass those squabbling democratic politicians, who are mostly interested in advancing their own careers, and put our faith instead in authoritarian regimes that are willing and able to take concerted long-term action on the multiple crises facing humanity.

The problem with such thinking is that it cherry-picks the best policies of countries like China or Singapore, while ignoring the records of other one-party states and authoritarian-leaning regimes around the world such as Saudi Arabia, Russia and Cambodia. Examining the evidence is crucial: could it really be true that autocracies perform better than democracies when it comes to long-term public policy that benefits future generations?

Over the past decade, academics and policy experts have begun to devise quantitative indices that measure and compare the long-term policy orientation of national governments. Such indices, which focus on assessing policy outcomes rather than policy promises on paper, have been produced by organisations including the World Economic Forum and the Intergenerational Foundation, as well as individual scholars.[16] The following analysis is based on what I consider to be the most conceptually coherent, methodologically rigorous and geographically comprehensive of these indicators: the Intergenerational Solidarity Index (ISI), created by the interdisciplinary scientist Jamie McQuilkin, and first published in the peer-reviewed journal *Intergenerational Justice Review.*[17]

What does the ISI look like, and what does it tell us about the virtues of democracies versus authoritarian regimes? The ISI provides scores for 122 countries each year between 2015 and 2019, and is a composite index that combines ten indicators of long-term policy practice in environmental, social and economic realms (details of its construction are set out in the Appendix).[18] The environmental dimension rewards countries that have low depletion of their forests, a small carbon footprint and a significant share of renewables in their energy system. They are also penalised for high levels of fossil fuel production. On the social dimension, countries receive higher scores for small class sizes in primary schools, low child mortality for a given level of GDP, and a population growth rate just below replacement rate. The three economic indicators reward low wealth inequality, high net savings and a healthy current account balance.

To create the final index score, which ranges from 1 (low intergenerational solidarity) to 100 (high intergenerational solidarity), the indicators are given equal weighting and are aggregated arithmetically within dimensions (environmental, social and economic) and then geometrically between them. This method ensures that no single indicator or dimension dominates the index.

As a first step, it's worth taking a snapshot view of the scores of individual countries. Which nations in the world can justifiably claim to be acting with regard to future generations? The table below presents the 24 highest-ranked countries for the 2019 index. It is striking that the highest-scoring nations, such as Iceland, Nepal, Costa Rica and Uruguay, come from a wide range of geographical regions and income levels. While wealthy OECD countries occupy many of the top spots, some of them are far down the rankings: Germany is ranked only 28th, with the UK 45th and the US 62nd. It is equally striking that China doesn't make it into the top tier, being ranked only 25th largely due to its poor scores on measures such as carbon footprint and renewable energy (the country is still burning plenty of fossil fuels per person, despite its growing renewables sector). Singapore is even further down the league table at 41st, partly as a result of its weak performance on renewable energy generation.

Having spent several years as a political scientist specialising in the measurement of government performance, I am well aware that the results of any index should be taken with a pinch of salt.[19] Data is often patchy, and each component of an index is only ever a proxy for the underlying concept it attempts to reflect. Difficulties inevitably arise with any attempt to quantify the complexities of the real world, which is why an index like the ISI functions best to show broad patterns rather than to be revealing about specific cases.[20]

What about the big question of whether authoritarian governments think longer than democracies? This analysis, which I conducted jointly with McQuilkin, required selecting among the large number

The Intergenerational Solidarity League Table

Rank	ISI Score	Country	Rank	ISI Score	Country
1	86	Iceland	13	72	Slovenia
2	81	Sweden	14	72	Spain
3	78	Nepal	15	72	Sri Lanka
4	77	Switzerland	16	72	Finland
5	76	Denmark	17	72	Croatia
6	76	Hungary	18	71	Netherlands
7	76	France	19	71	Bulgaria
8	75	Costa Rica	20	71	Belarus
9	75	Belgium	21	70	Vietnam
10	75	Uruguay	22	70	New Zealand
11	74	Ireland	23	70	Italy
12	73	Austria	24	70	Luxembourg

Note: Scores on the Intergenerational Solidarity Index (ISI) range between 0 (low) and 100 (high). All data is from the 2019 index.

of democracy indices created in recent years. We chose one of the gold standards among political scientists: the V-Dem Liberal Democracy Index, produced at the University of Gothenburg in Sweden. Governments are given scores by expert assessors, who rank them on a scale of 0 to 1 based on the presence of free and fair elections, freedom of expression and information, equality before the law, civil liberties, and checks and balances between the executive, legislature and judiciary. Countries that don't make the grade are classified as autocracies. This index gauges what is commonly known as 'liberal democracy' or 'representative democracy', rather than alternative forms such as 'participatory democracy'.[21]

By plotting each country's democracy score against its intergenerational solidarity score, we created a unique global picture of political systems and their long-term policy performance at the national level (see below). Each index was also divided at its midpoint, enabling the classification of the countries into the four categories of 'Long-Term Democracies', 'Short-Term Democracies', 'Long-Term Autocracies' and 'Short-Term Autocracies'.[22]

Several clear patterns are visible in the data:

Out of the 25 countries with the highest scores on the ISI, 21 of them – 84 per cent – are democracies. Out of the 25 countries with the lowest scores on the ISI, 21 of them are autocracies.

Out of all 60 democracies, 75 per cent are Long-Term Democracies, while out of all 62 autocracies, only 37 per cent are Long-Term Autocracies. The average intergenerational solidarity score for democracies is 60, while the average for autocracies is just 42. So autocracies tend towards short-termism, while democracies tend towards long-termism.

The most populous quadrants are Long-Term Democracies and Short-Term Autocracies. If authoritarian regimes were significantly better at delivering long-term policy performance, we would have expected Long-Term Autocracies and Short-Term Democracies to be the most populous, which is clearly not the case.

This analysis reveals the fundamental weakness of the claims in favour of autocracies: there is no systematic empirical evidence that authoritarian regimes perform better than democratic governments when it comes to long-term policies that serve the interests of future generations. In fact, the data suggest the opposite: the average ISI score for democracies is far higher than for autocracies. In other

Which best serve future generations – democracies or autocracies?

Scores for countries on the Intergenerational Solidarity Index plotted against their scores on the V-dem Liberal Democracy Index, including dotted trend line

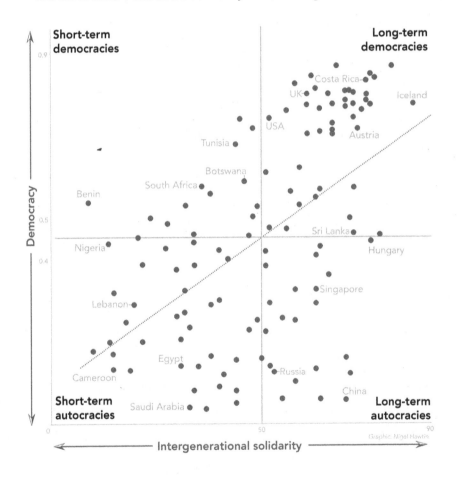

Short-term democracies

Long-term democracies

Costa Rica
UK
Iceland
USA
Austria
Tunisia
Botswana
South Africa
Benin
Sri Lanka
Nigeria
Hungary
Singapore
Lebanon
Egypt
Russia
Cameroon
China
Short-term autocracies
Saudi Arabia
Long-term autocracies

0.9
0.5
0.4
0

Democracy

0
50
90

Intergenerational solidarity

Graphic: Nigel Hawtin

words, you are much more likely to find high levels of intergenerational solidarity in a democracy than an authoritarian regime, whether it is a classic military dictatorship or a one-party state. Moreover, the trend line through the data, which runs from bottom left to top right, suggests that more democracy is accompanied by more long-termism. And let's not forget the obvious point that authoritarian regimes are also unlikely to be high-performing in terms of other things we might value, such as political freedom and human rights.

Yet none of this implies that democracies can sit back and relax. Every democratic government in the world could be striving to get a higher score on the ISI, even top performers such as Sweden, France and Austria. There is an urgent need to redesign democracy so it can respond far more effectively to the long-term challenges of our era. That's easy enough to say, but how exactly should it be done?

The Design Principles of Deep Democracy

Over the last two decades, political activists, policymakers and engaged academics have proposed more than 70 different ways to embed long-term thinking within democratic institutions.[23] Many of them have launched campaigns, organisations and legal actions to turn their ideas into reality. Join the dots, and it starts to look like a movement for a new kind of politics: deep democracy. Their most powerful and innovative proposals fall into four main areas: guardians of the future, citizens' assemblies, intergenerational rights and self-governing city-states (see below). These should not be thought of as a blueprint to be imposed on existing political systems, but rather as a set of design principles with the potential to inject democratic structures with a far deeper sense of time. The unifying feature of all these principles is that there are committed time rebels already

Design principles of deep democracy

Guardians of the future
Political institutions that represent and safeguard the interests of disenfranchised youth and future generations

Citizen assemblies
Civil society participation in deliberative assemblies, based on sortition, to shape policy on long-range issues

Intergenerational rights
Legal mechanisms to guarantee the rights and well-being of future generations and ensure intergenerational equity

Self-governing city-states
Radical devolution of power to cities from the national level to limit the influence of short-termist political and economic elites

Graphic: Nigel Hawtin

putting them into practice. The real question is whether they can be spread wide enough and scaled up fast enough to overcome the corrosive effects of political presentism.

But is there really any need to redesign democracy, when electorates could simply vote in politicians who support long-term policies? The problem with this view is that there would be nothing to stop an incoming government from simply reversing the long-term initiatives that a previous far-sighted administration may have pursued. Moreover, it underestimates the extent to which short-termism is structured into the DNA of representative democracy, for instance through a myopic focus on the electoral cycle. It is too risky to cross our fingers and hope that our existing democracies might spontaneously abandon their short-term ways and become champions of intergenerational justice. The value of the four design principles, as we are about to see, is that they help design myopia out of the political system.

GUARDIANS OF THE FUTURE

Among the most popular options is the creation of 'guardians of the future'. These are public officials or institutions with the specific remit to represent future citizens – not just children, but also unborn generations – who are left out of traditional democratic processes.

Many of these bodies have found inspiration in Finland's parliamentary 'Committee for the Future', which was established in 1993. Comprising 17 elected members of parliament, the committee reviews government policy for its impact on future generations – especially around technology, employment and environmental issues – and engages in long-term scenario planning. In 2001, the Israeli parliament took the bold initiative of appointing a Commissioner for Future Generations with the power to scrutinise and delay legislation on long-term concerns, such as air pollution and genetic biology. Ironically, the position was short-lived, being abolished by the Knesset in 2006 on the grounds that the commissioner was becoming too powerful.[24] But this setback hasn't stopped other countries picking up the intergenerational baton. Between 2008 and 2011, Hungary had an Ombudsman for Future Generations with considerable influence over environmental policy, and Malta created a similar post in 2012.[25] Tunisia's 2014 constitution instituted a Commission for Sustainable Development and the Rights of Future Generations, while in 2015 Sweden established a Council on the Future, whose leader Kristina Persson became known as the world's first 'minister of the future'. The United Arab Emirates has followed suit, with its own Ministry of Cabinet Affairs and the Future.

Among this expanding ensemble of guardians, the best-known today is the Future Generations Commissioner for Wales, a role which was established under the Well-Being for Future Generations Act in 2015. Its current holder, Sophie Howe, is a leading time rebel in the growing global movement for intergenerational justice. In her role as commissioner she is charged with reviewing policy in areas ranging from housing and education to environment and transport, and ensuring it accords with the internationally recognised definition of sustainable development: to meet the needs of the present, without compromising the ability of future generations to meet their own needs. As Howe puts it, 'Intergenerational justice is about prioritising the long-term needs over the short-term gains.' She is a political realist and the first to admit that her influence is limited. 'I can't force anybody to do anything and I can't force government to stop doing something,' she told me in a discussion about the political challenges of her role, 'but I have review powers to name and shame, so they do have to sit up and take notice. Would I like more powers? Yes, I would – who wouldn't!'[26]

Despite the constraints, she has managed to catapult future generations issues into the mainstream of public debate. Her opposition to the £1.6 billion extension of the M4 motorway, on the grounds that it was a 'twentieth-century solution' that failed to promote a low-carbon society, was considered instrumental in scrapping the scheme.[27] She has also been a vocal advocate of preventative health care, arguing that the National Health Service is really a 'national illness service' when it should be a 'national well-being service'. While it can be tough to convince today's voters to allocate their taxes to benefit tomorrow's citizens, Howe has pragmatically focused on issues like health care and the environment where the benefits accrue to both current and future generations.

Her greatest impact, however, may turn out to be in inspiring others to follow her lead. In 2019, the British anti-poverty activist and founder of the *Big Issue* magazine John Bird launched a campaign in the House of Lords to establish a Future Generations Commissioner for the whole United Kingdom, based on the Welsh model. Driven by a conviction that climate change will hit the poor the hardest, Lord Bird made a powerful and personal case for future generations to his fellow peers:

> We have a real problem: we are not the only ones hyperventilating about the future. The public is hyperventilating more. My 12-year-old daughter, who has organised strikes about the environment, is hyperventilating. My 14-year-old son, my 43-year-old son, my 53-year-old daughter and my 42-year-old daughter – everyone around me – are hyperventilating and getting excited about the possibility of changing the future, and that means we have to bring the future nearer. The best methodology is to adopt a Future Generations Act.[28]

While watching the ensuing debate from the viewing gallery, I was surprised by how many eminent public figures spoke in support of the initiative, among them sociologist Anthony Giddens, economist Richard Layard and astrophysicist Martin Rees. It was strikingly clear that the issue of intergenerational justice has finally come of political age: there were mentions of cathedral thinking and even the long-term lessons of Joseph Bazalgette's Victorian sewers.

Yet the challenges are huge: even if the UK gets its own commissioner, in order to have any serious impact they will need substantive powers, such as being able to take government bodies to court if they fail to meet their public duty to pursue long-term policies in areas such as child poverty alleviation or carbon reduction. Convincing MPs in the House of Commons to grant these powers will require enormous public pressure – and perhaps a crisis like the Great Stink of 1858. Some campaigners have taken a different approach, focusing instead on establishing international guardians, such as the appointment of a UN High Commissioner for Future Generations or a high-level council of Global Guardians for Future Generations. Yet it may be even more difficult to grant them enforceable powers than at the national level.[29]

The biggest challenge, however, is that the very idea of having guardians of the future can be criticised for lacking democratic legitimacy. Why shouldn't angry teenage climate strikers have a say themselves rather than having to rely on proxy adult representatives? Moreover, who is going to hold the guardian to account and ensure that they really voice the multiple perspectives of future citizens from different social backgrounds?[30] That is why the guardian model might best be seen as a first step towards a more radical and participatory form of democratic renewal: citizens' assemblies.

CITIZENS' ASSEMBLIES

In an interview about the Canadian government's continued support for the fossil fuel industry despite its promises to decarbonise the economy, the ecologist David Suzuki expressed his frustration with a political system where 'principles and ideals don't mean a goddam thing'. When asked what he would do to fix the problem of political short-termism, he replied:

> We need a system where politicians are drawn from a hat, the same way we set up our juries. People should be charged to serve for six years – they have no political party, their only job is to govern to the best of their ability. There's no chance in hell of that ever happening, but when you think about it that's the only system that would work.[31]

Suzuki's dream is not so far from political reality. In 2016, the Irish parliament established a Citizens' Assembly made up of 100 randomly selected members of the public, who spent several months deliberating on issues including abortion, climate change and the ageing population. Their recommendation to legalise abortion was taken on board by parliament, with the resulting referendum making constitutional history when voters overturned the ban. Cities in Spain and Belgium now have permanent citizens' assemblies that feed into municipal government, while nearly 1 in 60 Canadians have been invited to take part in them in towns throughout the country.[32] In 2019, the British parliament agreed to establish Climate Assembly UK, a citizen body that will discuss how the UK should respond to the climate emergency and implement the government's target of achieving net-zero carbon emissions by 2050.

The rise of citizens' assemblies signals an extraordinary development in the history of modern democracy: a revival of the ancient Athenian model of participatory democracy. But unlike Athenian bodies such as the Council of Five Hundred, which was only open to male citizens, today's assemblies are designed to be far more demographically inclusive.[33]

Experts in deliberative democracy argue that citizens' assemblies can be extremely effective at transcending short-termism for three main reasons. Firstly, by selecting members from a wide variety of backgrounds, they ensure that the assembly doesn't simply reflect the future concerns of privileged groups in society. Secondly, the practice of randomly selecting ordinary citizens (known as 'sortition') effectively limits domination by powerful political and economic actors who are often driven by short-term, self-serving interests. Thirdly, citizens' assemblies are an exercise in 'slow thinking', allowing participants the time and space to learn about and reflect on long-term issues facing society. Such factors, points out political scientist Graham Smith, help explain why citizens' assemblies 'outperform more traditional democratic institutions in orientating participants to consider long-term implications'.[34]

But can today's citizens really step into the shoes of future generations and represent their interests effectively? The Future Design movement in Japan is attempting to answer this very question. Led by economist Tatsuyoshi Saijo of the Research Institute for Humanity and Nature in Kyoto and inspired by the Native American seventh-generation principle, the movement has been pioneering a unique form of citizens' assembly in municipalities across the country. One group of participants takes the position of current residents, and the other group imagines themselves to be 'future residents' from the year 2060, even wearing special ceremonial robes to aid their imaginative leap forward in time. Multiple studies have shown that the future residents devise far more radical and progressive city plans compared to the current ones, particularly on environmental policy and health care. Although the participants are usually adults, Future Design practitioners in cities such as Tokyo are now starting to experiment with including high school students. In April 2019, the movement scored a major victory when the town of Hamada adopted their approach as the basis for its long-term city planning. Ultimately the movement aims to establish a Ministry of the Future as part of central government and a Department of the Future within all local government

City residents from the year 2060, wearing their ceremonial robes.

authorities, which would use their assembly model for policymaking. 'We must design social structures that activate the futurability we have within us,' says Saijo. 'If we don't do this, our continued existence itself is at stake.'[35]

Here's a future I would like to see across the democratic world: every few years, citizens aged 12 and over would be randomly selected to take part in a 'good ancestor' citizens' assembly, broadly based on Japan's Future Design movement and Ireland's Citizens' Assembly.[36] These 'intergenerational juries' would debate the long-term issues of the day – perhaps whether the government's target for reaching net-zero carbon emissions should be brought forward by a decade, or whether new regulations are needed on AI technologies. The assemblies, which would take place across the country, would draw on expert witnesses and give an equal voice to all participants, including young people. They would have powers rivalling elected legislatures or town councils, with the authority to delay or veto policies that impacted negatively on the basic rights of future people, and the ability to initiate legislation in key long-term policy areas such as energy, water, housing and child poverty. The assemblies would supplement the role of other institutions such as future generations commissioners, but would be far more inclusive and democratic. In some countries they might even replace legislative upper houses, becoming a people's chamber of good ancestors.[37]

Democracy has taken many forms and been reinvented many times over the past 2,500 years. Representative democracy, which emerged in the eighteenth century, is now so dominated by short-termism that it may be past its sell-by date, with little capacity to tackle the long-term challenges we face. This could be the moment to take advantage of the political momentum behind citizens' assemblies and inject a new stream of participatory democracy into the system.

INTERGENERATIONAL RIGHTS

A third design principle of an effective deep democracy is to embed the rights of future generations in the legal system, especially in constitutional law. Law matters not just because it is a way to ring-fence the interests of futureholders and protect them from the short-termism of incumbent politicians, but because it acts as a reference point against which future generations commissioners and citizens' assemblies can judge governments and hold them to account.

Is it feasible to grant rights to people who are not even alive or able to claim them? While there are already laws to protect the rights of an unborn foetus or person in a coma who isn't able to speak for themselves, it might still sound unrealistic to grant legal protection to people who may not be born for decades and who only exist in our imaginations. And yet legal activists around the world are starting to make it happen.

In 1993, environmental lawyer Antonio Oposa, acting on behalf of 43 children (including his own), won a landmark case in the Supreme Court of the Philippines to cancel government-issued timber licences to chop down old-growth forests because they violated the rights of current and succeeding generations to a healthy environment that preserves the 'rhythm and harmony of nature'. In the more recent Urgenda case in the Netherlands, the courts drew on the European Convention on Human Rights with a ruling in 2019 that the government has a legal duty of care to protect its citizens from the future impact of climate change by meeting its own stated targets to reduce greenhouse gas emissions.[38] The idea of intergenerational rights is now being put to the test in the United States, where a group of 21 youths aged between 12 and 23 are attempting to secure 'the legal right to a safe climate and healthy atmosphere for all present and future generations' by suing the federal government for supporting the fossil fuel industry. The case, brought by the organisation Our Children's Trust, is backed by such heavyweight figures as climate scientist James Hansen and economist Joseph Stiglitz, as well as Earth Guardians, the youth-led campaigning group inspired by the seventh-generation principle.[39]

Among the plaintiffs is the indigenous hip-hop artist Xiuhtezcatl Martinez, who began his environmental activism at the age of six and first addressed the UN General Assembly aged 15. His sense of stewardship and legacy run deep. 'My dad taught me that protecting the earth is a responsibility, the same way our ancestors had the responsibility to do so,' he says. 'As young people we ask, what do we want to build, what do we want to leave behind?'[40] Although the 21 time rebels may not succeed in their David versus Goliath battle against the Trump administration, which is making desperate efforts to block the court case, the huge public support and media attention they have gained means that they are already creating an inspiring legacy for intergenerational justice campaigners worldwide.[41]

A challenge facing all such rights-based campaigns is the lack of enforcement mechanisms. Across the world, governments continue to violate the human rights of indigenous people, ethnic minorities, women, trade unionists, journalists, children and many others, despite the existence of national laws and international documents such as the Universal Declaration of Human Rights. Why would we expect governments to protect the rights of future people if they so manifestly fail to protect the rights of those who are alive today? In fact, shouldn't we focus first on securing the rights of current generations before we even start with future ones? These struggles are not, however, mutually exclusive. Today's children are in themselves part of our future generations: by working to realise their rights, for example by investing in their health care and education, we are enacting the values of intergenerational justice. That is precisely why the Intergenerational Solidarity Index includes measures such as child mortality rates and primary school class sizes. In other words, fighting for children's rights is a stepping stone to securing the rights of future citizens more broadly. Similarly, the Urgenda case was won based on the rights of living Dutch citizens to a safe climate in the future, rather than on the rights of unborn generations, but the benefits will accrue to many generations to come. Although we still may be some way from securing full recognition of rights for future people in most countries, we should grasp every opportunity to take legal systems in that direction.

An alternative legal approach has been to focus not on establishing rights for future generations but for the earth itself. If giving rights to a non-human entity like a planet sounds fanciful, don't forget that corporations have enjoyed legal personhood since 1886, when the US Supreme Court deemed that they should be granted 'due process of law', a right originally established to protect freed slaves.[42] In 2010, Bolivia began leading the way in a new struggle for planetary rights with its Law of the Rights of Mother Earth, which gives nature equal rights to humans. New Zealand followed suit in 2017 by granting the

Whanganui River, which is sacred to Māori people, the same legal status as a person, ensuring that it will be better protected from mining and other forms of ecological violation.[43]

The next logical step in this process would be to establish 'ecocide' – the extensive destruction of the natural living world – as a crime under international law. Its leading advocate, British environmental lawyer Polly Higgins (who died in 2019), described ecocide as 'the missing international crime of our time'. She made a compelling case that it should be considered a legal equivalent of genocide or ethnic cleansing, with the individuals primarily responsible, such as CEOs or government ministers, being liable for prosecution by the International Criminal Court (ICC) in The Hague. Making it law, she argued, would be eminently feasible, simply requiring two-thirds of ICC member states to sign up to it. There is broad agreement among legal scholars that actions such as a logging company damaging the Amazon rainforest ecosystem, or an oil corporation knowingly destabilising the climate, would meet the definition of ecocide. As Higgins pointed out, the switch in legal mindset to treating the earth as a living being rather than as inert private property, 'shifts dramatically how we look into the long term because once we see ourselves as trustees, as guardians, we start taking responsibility for future generations.'[44]

Critics of ecocide argue that the ICC is hardly an institution to inspire confidence. Since being established in 2002, it has indicted fewer than 50 people on charges such as war crimes and genocide, and has convicted only a handful of them. It should be remembered, however, that legal institutions, like laws themselves, are not immune to change; the ICC may become more effective over time. The growing movement to criminalise ecocide resembles the early movement to abolish slavery in the 1780s for its ambition and potential impact, not to mention the strength of opposition from business. Polly Higgins may come to be remembered like the great anti-slavery campaigners of the eighteenth century. She may also be remembered as a good ancestor.

SELF-GOVERNING CITY-STATES

In Ancient Greek myth, Perseus was able to slay Medusa by avoiding her gaze, using the canny trick of looking at her reflection in his shield. Today we may be able to slay the Medusa of short-term thinking by adopting a similarly oblique strategy: a radical devolution of power away from nation states. This final way of redesigning democracy is not aimed directly at expanding the voice or rights of future generations, but would serve their interests by dispersing decision-making power from central government, where it is typically captured by corporate interests and other power brokers bent on short-term gains. Analysis based on the Intergenerational Solidarity Index supports this: the more decentralised a government is in its decision-making, the better it performs in terms of long-term public policy (so a highly federalised country such as Switzerland scores particularly well).[45] Making this shift would promote what the Nobel Prize-winning economist Elinor Ostrom called 'polycentric governance', where political authority is spread among multiple nested layers of governance from the local to the global levels.[46]

It isn't easy to take power away from national governments. So how could we turn this vision into reality? There is one approach worth pursuing above all others: to revive the Ancient Greek ideal of the 'polis' or self-governing city-state. The most obvious reason for doing this is that it is already happening. Across the globe, the growing disaffection with national-level democratic politics is being accompanied by the increasing prominence and autonomy of cities on a scale not seen since the age of Renaissance city-states such as Florence or Venice.

The human future is urban. An ever-expanding proportion of the world's population is living not just in cities but in 'megacities' of over ten million inhabitants, from Greater São Paulo, with a population of 21 million, to the Tokyo–Nagoya–Osaka megalopolis (known as the

'Taiheiyō Belt'), which is home to over 80 million people. China is currently reorganising itself around two-dozen clusters of megacities, each with a population of up to 100 million. The United Nations predicts that by 2030 there will be 43 megacity clusters containing two-thirds of the world's population and concentrating the vast majority of global wealth.[47]

Cities are not only absorbing more people but are becoming more politically powerful too. In June 2017, just a week after Donald Trump announced the US withdrawal from the Paris Climate Agreement, 279 US mayors – representing one in five Americans – defiantly pledged to uphold the agreement in their own cities such as Boston and Miami. In England, there were no directly elected mayors at the start of the millennium but now there are 23, including in major cities like London and Manchester, and their electoral contests are attracting an increasing number of high-profile candidates. This new generation of autonomous cities have been organising into interdependent networks, such as the C40 cities committed to taking action on climate change, the Global Parliament of Mayors and Rockefeller's 100 Resilient Cities. These networks are crucial for overcoming the stalemate between nation states on collective challenges such as creating binding international agreements on greenhouse gas reductions. International relations expert Parag Khanna argues that we are seeing the emergence of 'diplomacity', where cities bypass national governments and make independent agreements on trade and other issues with each other, much like the nearly 200 cities of the Hanseatic League did in northern Europe in the fifteenth and sixteenth centuries. 'We are moving into an era where cities will matter more than states,' Khanna concludes.[48] Devolution is becoming political destiny. Just imagine Europe as a confederation of twenty-first-century city-states (see below).[49]

This renaissance of city power is partly due to a growing recognition that they are far more effective than nation states at tackling

Europe reimagined as city-states

Size of metropolitan areas with over 1 million people
(based on Eurostat 2018)

1 million   5 million   10 million

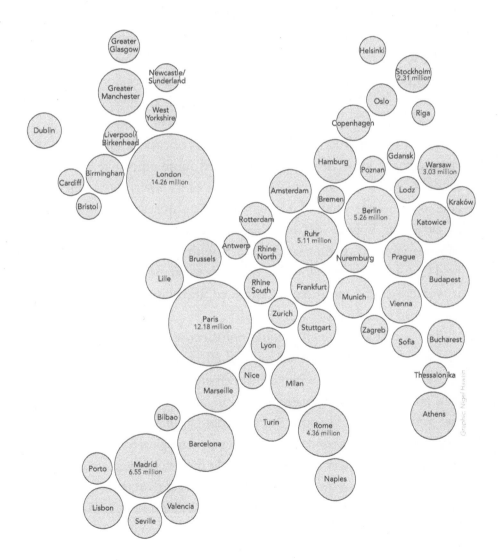

Greater Glasgow

Newcastle/Sunderland

Greater Manchester

West Yorkshire

Dublin

Liverpool/Birkenhead

Birmingham

Cardiff

Bristol

London
14.26 million

Helsinki

Stockholm
2.31 million

Oslo

Riga

Copenhagen

Hamburg

Gdansk

Poznan

Warsaw
3.03 million

Amsterdam

Bremen

Lodz

Berlin
5.26 million

Kraków

Katowice

Rotterdam

Ruhr
5.11 million

Antwerp

Rhine North

Nuremburg

Prague

Brussels

Lille

Rhine South

Frankfurt

Budapest

Munich

Vienna

Zurich

Stuttgart

Zagreb

Paris
12.18 million

Lyon

Sofia

Bucharest

Nice

Milan

Thessalonika

Marseille

Bilbao

Turin

Rome
4.36 million

Athens

Barcelona

Porto

Madrid
6.55 million

Naples

Lisbon

Valencia

Seville

Graphic Nigel Hawtin

long-term problems such as ecological overshoot, migration pressures and wealth inequality. They have a flexibility and an adaptability that makes them resilient in the face of change, unlike so many centralised national governments, which often suffer from institutional rigidity and being distant from the lived experiences of their citizens. That is not to say that cities are a pristine political form: every city has its corrupt officials and businesses bent on short-term gain. But if you are looking for innovative long-term vision, the place to find it is at the city-level. We need more cities like Freiburg in Germany, where private cars have been banished to car parks on the edge of housing developments, 40 per cent of families don't own a car and over one-third of all journeys are made by bike. We need more cities like Paris, where mayor Anne Hidalgo has infuriated motorists by constructing hundreds of miles of cycle lanes and converting roads into public parks. We need more cities like Inje in South Korea, which generates 93 per cent of its power from renewable sources, nearly half of it from wind. We also need the creativity of cities like Bogotá in Colombia, where former mayor Antanas Mockus replaced corrupt traffic officers with 400 mime artists who held up football-style yellow and red cards to offending drivers. And it worked: traffic violations plummeted and within a decade the number of road fatalities had halved.[50]

The potential of the city should not surprise us. Cities have been sites of pragmatic problem solving and effective long-term planning ever since the first great urban centres emerged in ancient Mesopotamia, providing their populations with drainage systems, public baths and grid-based street layouts. But the cities of today still have a lot of work to do. Most high-income cities have an ecological footprint – the area of land and water required to supply their needs and assimilate their wastes – that is several hundred times larger than their political areas. What we really need, argues ecologist William Rees, is to create self-sustaining 'bioregional city-states' that are integrated into their local ecosystems rather than parasitic upon them.[51] Such initiatives should be supplemented with the power of digital democracy, giving local people a say in decision-making through electronic voting and other forms of online public engagement. Innovative examples include Decide Madrid, a technology platform that has registered over 200,000 citizens who take part in participatory budgeting processes allocating over 100 million euros of city funds annually.[52] Every city should be striving to empower its citizens so their phones become a pocket-sized tool for grassroots democratic renewal.

Nation states are a recent historical invention and have only been the dominant form of political organisation for the past two centuries. Cities, in contrast, are the greatest and most enduring social technology ever invented by humankind. That is why cities such as Istanbul have lasted thousands of years, while empires and nations have risen and fallen around them. The nation state will be with us for some time yet, drawing us into its vortex of short-termism. But if humanity is to have a long-term future, the old political borders must disappear and power must be wrenched away from the grip of centralised state authority. Our great hope lies in becoming citizens of a twenty-first century polis.

Political Power and the Overton Window

These four approaches to deep democracy are not the only options available for enhancing long thinking and promoting intergenerational justice in political life. Some alternative strategies, found in a range of countries, include:

> Establishing parliamentary 'youth quotas' like those in Tunisia: since 2014, at least one of the top four candidates in a party's list for parliamentary elections must be under 35.

Lowering the voting age from 18 to 16, as has happened in Austria and Brazil, on the grounds that longer-living populations in many nations mean that the interests of older voters systematically outweigh those of disenfranchised youth.

Monitoring and rating the 'intergenerational impact' of government budgets, which has occurred in Canadian federal budgets since 2019, as a result of campaigning from youth pressure groups.

Creating 'commitment devices', such as the British government enshrining in law a commitment to reach net-zero carbon emissions by 2050, as recommended by the statutory Committee on Climate Change.

Insulating key policy areas from short-term political meddling, such as the Bank of England's Monetary Policy Committee, which has set the UK's official interest rate since 1997.

Developing better foresight capabilities, like Singapore's Centre for Strategic Futures, which acts as a high-profile think tank within the Prime Minister's Office.[53]

The problem with many of these strategies is that they lack a radical edge and do little to challenge entrenched structures of power. Do unaccountable institutions like the UK's Monetary Policy Committee really serve the interests of future citizens when four of its nine current members have worked for major investment banks? Will introducing parliamentary youth quotas prevent tech firms and oil companies from using their financial lobbying power to secure laws and policies to their advantage?

In each case the answer is 'probably not'. That is why we need the four design innovations of deep democracy, which are profound structural changes that do far more to dismantle the short-termism rooted into the political system.

The difficulty, however, is that fundamental political change is a rare phenomenon and typically requires a confluence of disparate factors to merge into a winning formula for transformation.[54] It is vital to have powerful and visionary ideas to supersede the old system, such as self-governing city-states, intergenerational rights, citizens' assemblies and guardians of the future. But that is just the beginning. These ideas need to be backed up by highly motivated and effective social movements supported by a critical mass of the population. It is also helpful to have a crisis that threatens those who dominate the system and undermines their power and authority, which could be anything from a war to a financial crash. Then throw in some technological change, economic transformation, clever strategy and a bit of good luck, and you might get the change you hoped for.

Despite such obstacles, the struggle for deep democracy is already creating a new public conversation that is shifting the 'Overton window' – the range of policies that are acceptable in mainstream politics at any given time. Just think how much pressure governments are now under to decarbonise their economies since the rise of rebel movements such as the youth climate strikes. Net-zero by 2050 is starting to sound like a feeble and conservative target, whereas dates that previously appeared extreme like the 2030s have become normalised. The Overton window has moved a sizable distance. This might not only help transform domestic politics in many countries, but also encourage national governments to make bolder commitments at the international negotiating table, securing the global mechanisms required to tackle the planetary crises we face.

In many countries, the time rebels will struggle against political inertia and powerful vested interests, but in others they will gradually secure a patchwork of gains that begins to alter the democratic landscape. Let's leave behind the myth of the benign dictator who will come galloping to our rescue and put our faith in the pioneering spirit of the political time rebels.

10

Ecological Civilisation

From Speculative Capitalism to Regenerative Economy

In a mountain retreat three hours west of Tokyo, there is an isolated hot spring hotel called Nishiyama Onsen Keiunkan. This is the world's oldest hotel, having welcomed guests to its tatami-floor rooms since the year 705. Japan is legendary for such ancient businesses, including breweries, robe makers and shrine builders that have been operating for over a thousand years. The country is home to more than 3,000 companies that have existed for at least two centuries, a large portion of them family firms, where not only ownership but traditional skills have been passed down from generation to generation, ensuring their long-term survival.[1]

Long-term vision is also visible among some of Japan's major corporate players, such as the tech giant SoftBank. 'We will create a company that can grow 300 years down the road,' says its founder Masayoshi Son. His flagship $100 billion Vision Fund has made far-sighted investments in sectors such as robotics, autonomous vehicles, satellite technology and genomics. Son is a big fan of AI, believing that 'the gold rush in artificial intelligence is coming for real' and that before long 'the Earth will become one big computer'.[2]

Like investors such as Warren Buffett, Son is considered living proof of a growing trend in corporate thinking that recognises the virtues of taking the long view. 'Long-term companies exhibit stronger financial performance over time,' concludes a report from the management consulting firm McKinsey. Companies that focus on long-range growth objectives and invest in research and development outperform those obsessed with meeting quarterly targets and keeping their share price buoyant. Between 2001 and 2014, they had 47 per cent higher revenues, 81 per cent higher profits and were better at surviving financial crises than their myopic competitors. Long-termism is apparently good for the economy too: McKinsey estimates that US GDP would be boosted by 0.8 per cent annually if all publicly listed companies adopted this strategic approach.[3]

It's time to press the pause button for a moment.

The problem with such statistics is that they assume that the goal of long-term economic thinking is all about financial returns and economic growth. This chapter takes an alternative view, arguing for a radically different guiding purpose: to create a global economy that meets human needs within the biophysical means of the planet, generation after generation. It is about aspiring to an 'ecological civi-lisation', described by visionary economic thinker David Korten as one that 'secures material sufficiency and spiritual abundance for all in balance with the regenerative systems of a living Earth'.[4]

Is it really possible to wean ourselves off our addiction to financial gain, GDP growth and consumer culture, and pursue an economic vision that respects the living world? This is precisely what a new breed of economic time rebels are attempting. They are not high-profile investors like Son or Buffett, but a growing band of ecological economists, urban designers and pioneering social entrepreneurs from Brazil to Bangladesh to Belgium. Their success is by no means guaranteed: they lead a fragile, embryonic rebellion that could easily fail in the face of the existing system. In fact, the historical odds are against them. But their struggle offers hope to all those seeking a world fit for posterity. So what challenges are they up against, how are they thinking and what are they doing to forge a path towards a long-term regenerative economy?

Speculative Finance and the Big Short

Here's the problem in a nutshell: short-termism is built into the genetic code of the neoliberal paradigm that has come to dominate economic thought since it was unleashed on the world in the 1980s by the free-market ideology of Margaret Thatcher and Ronald Reagan.

Its fullest expression has been the birth of a new era of speculative capitalism. The financial deregulation promoted by neoliberal economists such as Milton Friedman offered opportunities to make a quick killing in the markets, but was accompanied by a catastrophic series of booms and busts such as Black Monday in 1987, the 1997 Asian financial crisis, the bursting of the dot-com bubble in 2000 and the 2008 global financial crisis, in which millions of people lost their livelihoods and homes. From 1970 to 2016, the average period of stock holdings on the New York Stock Exchange fell from five years to just four months.[5] Digital technology has fuelled this shrinking of financial time horizons: the Rothschilds used carrier pigeons to trade on the outcome of the Battle of Waterloo in 1815, while today's fibre optic and microwave networks mean that share trades can take less than one millisecond (300 times faster than the blink of an eye). This is the age of the 'Big Short', the quick buck and the split-second algorithm.[6]

Short-termism was just as visible in the neoliberal desire to roll back the state through privatisation. Especially from the 1990s, state assets worth billions, including railway networks, water utilities and power stations, were sold into private hands in both rich and poor countries, often under pressure from the International Monetary Fund. This might have been a useful instant fix to deal with public debt, but it represented a long-term loss of public assets that were set to be the shared inheritance of future generations.

The growing influence of the financial sector also fuelled the drive towards short-termism. By 2011, 45 of the world's 50 largest multinational corporations were banks or insurance companies. As they gradually became the dominant shareholders of major manufacturing, mining and service corporations, they sought to exert short-term pressure on them via the two golden measures of financial extraction: shareholder value and return on investment (RoI). Big investors began ratcheting up their RoI targets for the companies they controlled, keeping them focused on hitting financial goals that were just a few months or even weeks into the future.[7]

Neoliberalism offered the world an economic model that denied the reality of the future. Yet it would be unfair to place all the blame for this myopia on the free marketeers and the greed-is-good traders on Wall Street. The three major models of economic development that have prevailed since the end of the Second World War – neoliberalism, its predecessor Keynesianism and Marxism – all have in common the belief in endless economic growth as the means to human progress.[8] It is this underlying faith in growth that poses the greatest challenge to securing a long future for humankind. As the economist Kenneth Boulding put it in the early 1970s, 'Anyone who believes that exponential growth can go on forever in a finite world is either a madman or an economist.'[9]

Boulding's quip may have infuriated mainstream economists, but it signalled the rise of a new model of economic thought that put the long-term interests of people and planet at its heart.

The Lorax, the Doughnut and the Rise of Ecological Economics

Boulding's critique of growth is best explained not by an economist but by the children's author Dr Seuss in his 1971 classic *The Lorax*. Described by the science journal *Nature* as 'a kind of *Silent Spring* for the playground set', it tells the tale of a creature, the Once-ler, who arrives in a beautiful land of plenty.[10] The Once-ler starts a business selling a strange but popular garment called a thneed, made from the silky leaves of the local truffula trees. The guardian of the trees, the Lorax, tries to stop him chopping them down, but to no avail. The Once-ler is bent on 'biggering' his smog-spewing thneed factory, biggering his wagons and biggering his money – 'I had to grow bigger. So bigger I got', he recounts. Soon the trees are all gone, the wildlife dead, the water polluted and the Once-ler out of business. The only consolation in this environmental fable appears at the end, when a boy is given the last surviving truffula seed to regenerate the ravaged land.

The story contains a stark warning for today's global consumer economy that is geared towards biggering and biggering despite the destructive long-term consequences: the goal of perpetual economic growth will eventually succumb to the logic of *The Lorax*.

Dr Seuss may have been an early economic time rebel, but he was not alone. Just as *The Lorax* was starting to be read at bedtime in homes across North America and Europe, a new branch of economics with an equally radical agenda was beginning to emerge. This was the field now known as ecological economics. For many years it languished in obscurity. When I was studying economics in the early 1990s, and then pursuing a short-lived career as a financial journalist, I had certainly never heard of it. But today it is starting to nudge at the mainstream, which is good news because it offers the core long-term economic vision for aspiring good ancestors.

An iconic moment in the origin story of ecological economics is the publication of *The Limits to Growth* report in 1972, in which a group of systems thinkers at MIT led by Donella Meadows and Dennis Meadows used computer modelling to show that, 'If the present growth trends in world population, industrialisation, pollution, food production, and resource depletion continue unchanged, the limits to growth on this planet will be reached sometime within the next hundred years.' It concluded that the most likely result would be civilisational collapse and a fundamental decline in human welfare, although major policy changes could enable a smooth transition to a post-growth economy.[11]

Their study was greeted by the majority of economists with incredulity and ridicule, but is now recognised by many as prophetic. One of its leading popularisers has been the ecological economist Herman Daly. His crucial insight – one that is both deceptively simple and absolutely perspective-changing – is that the economy is a subsystem of the larger biosphere that is finite and not growing in size, which means that the economy's material throughput cannot keep growing forever. 'Humankind,' says Daly, 'must make the transition to a sustainable economy – one that takes heed of the inherent biophysical limits of the global ecosystem so that it can continue to operate into the long future.'[12] In effect, this means not using earth's resources faster than they can be naturally regenerated and not creating waste faster than it can be naturally absorbed.

This all sounds like common sense, and reflects the vision of one-planet thriving discussed in Chapter 8. But you are unlikely to find this approach mentioned anywhere in standard economics textbooks, where the ecological impacts of resource use are typically considered 'externalities' – a kind of collateral damage that falls outside the price signals of the market – while core diagrams such as the circular flow of income show the economy set against a white background rather than embedded in the biosphere.[13] Daly tells a revealing story about his time working at the World Bank on its influential 1992 World Development Report entitled 'Development and the Environment'. An early draft of the report contained a diagram with a square labelled 'Economy' on the familiar blank background. In his comments, Daly suggested drawing another square around it labelled 'Environment', to show that one was a subset of the other and subject to its limits. When he received the next draft, the new box was there like a picture frame around the Economy, but without any descriptive label. Then in the final version the environment box was completely removed. Back to square one.[14]

Thankfully, times have changed and an economics rebellion is now in full flow. New models are appearing that question the old ecologically blind paradigm and what Daly calls 'growthmania', ranging from the circular economy and pluralist economics to Economy for the Common Good and the degrowth movement. Prominent among these alternatives is Doughnut Economics, created by the economist Kate Raworth (disclaimer: we're married). Raworth's Doughnut model (see below), which has been adopted by ambitious cities, governments, progressive businesses and activists worldwide, consists of two rings.[15] The outer ring of the Doughnut is an 'ecological ceiling' comprising the nine Planetary Boundaries developed by earth system scientists including Johan Rockström and Will Steffen: overshooting key boundaries such as on climate change or biodiversity loss threatens to throw our finely balanced, life-giving planetary system out of kilter. Below the Doughnut's inner ring, called the 'social foundation', lies a shortfall in basic human well-being, where people lack life's essentials such as food, housing and education.[16]

Raworth argues that the fundamental goal of economic systems should not be the endless GDP growth pursued by most governments, but to bring ourselves into the 'safe and just space for humanity' that lies between the two rings: in other words, meeting people's needs by raising them above the social foundation (so nobody is left in the Doughnut's hole) without overshooting the critical ecological ceiling. So where are we right now? At the global level we are failing significantly on both counts, with a shortfall on all 12 social dimensions, and overshooting four of the planetary boundaries for which data exist. This is a devastating portrait of twenty-first-century humanity, a shocking collective selfie for our times.

Can we live within the Doughnut?

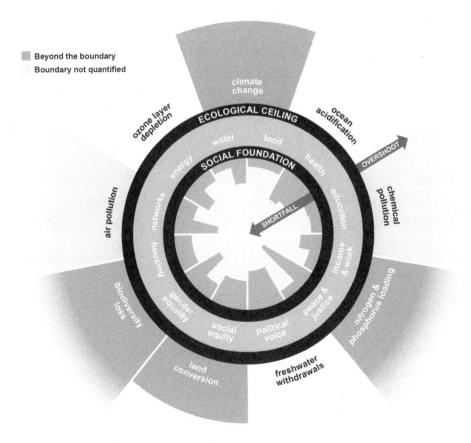

Kate Raworth's Doughnut of Social and Planetary Boundaries.
The area between the Social Foundation and the Ecological Ceiling is
'the safe and just space for humanity'. The dark grey segments show
the current extent of humanity's shortfall and overshoot.

Good ancestors will recognise that the ambition to get into the Doughnut embodies the transcendent goal of one-planet thriving, where we meet the needs of current and future generations within the means of earth's crucial life-supporting systems. It is a goal entirely aligned with the idea that if we wish to ensure our longevity as a species thousands of generations into the future, our first task is to learn from nature and take care of the living world that will take care of our offspring. The Doughnut offers a way of winning the tug of war against short-termism by caring about place – our one and only planetary home – rather than simply focusing on extending our sense of time. By doing so, it provides a powerful compass for ensuring human well-being into the coming centuries. As Raworth remarks, 'it turns out to be the only doughnut that is actually good for our long-term health.'

So having shifted from an unsustainable goal of endless GDP growth to thriving in balance between social and planetary boundaries, what are the time rebels doing to achieve it in practice?

Extending Time Horizons in the Corporate Economy

He originally wanted to be a priest. But he ended up becoming CEO of the Anglo-Dutch conglomerate Unilever, owner of household products from Dove soap to Hellmann's mayonnaise. The day Paul Polman took on the job in 2009, he stunned his shareholders by abolishing quarterly reporting, in a move designed to challenge the constant pressure every three months to prove that the company had achieved the holy trinity of growing sales, growing profits and growing market share. 'I figured I couldn't be fired on my first day,' he said. Until stepping down in 2019, Polman led a decade-long sustainability crusade across Unilever, boosting sustainable sourcing of raw materials like palm oil and soya beans from 10 per cent to 56 per cent. It was all part of his plan to create a business where values and purpose mattered as much as the financial bottom line. As he put it, 'Ethics, doing the right thing for the long term, taking care of your community, is really the way you want a responsible business to be run.'[17]

Although Polman's sustainability drive was sometimes criticised for lacking ambition and follow through, his commitment to the livelihoods of future generations is more genuine than most CEOs.[18] A growing number of business leaders are not only experts at 'greenwashing' (making unsubstantiated environmental claims for their companies) but also in what I think of as 'longwashing' (forging a long-term strategy primarily for the benefit of the firm's financial performance rather than for the welfare of tomorrow's world).

If we hope to steer economies as a whole towards longer thinking that brings us into the Doughnut, we cannot rely on the voluntary actions of progressive business people like Polman. They are simply too few and far between and remain embedded in companies that are still locked into the straitjacket of maximising shareholder returns (Unilever among them). An initial solution is for governments to change the rules of the game through regulations that extend time horizons in the corporate economy.

One possibility would be to limit the reckless short-termism of speculative capitalism by taxing stock trades based on the amount of time they are held for. Cultural thinker and former Silicon Valley tech CEO Jeremy Lent suggests the following tax rates: 10 per cent if the stock is held for less than a day, 5 per cent if less than a year, 3 per cent if less than 10 years, 1 per cent if less than 20 years, and 0 per cent for more than 20 years. 'The financial services industry would be transformed overnight,' he says. 'High-frequency stock trading and same-day traders would disappear, and the short-term orientation of the stock market would be replaced by carefully considered long-term investment decisions.' In particular, it would attract far more investment in sectors with longer-term payoff periods, such as renewable energy.[19] The French government is already leading the way in this form of 'time regulation', having introduced a tax on algorithmic high-frequency trading executed in under half a second.[20]

A second option would be to challenge the de facto duty of companies to maximise shareholder value. Corporations constantly claim that they couldn't prioritise long-term environmental targets even if they wanted to because of pressure from shareholders to maximise their earnings and the threat of being sued if they don't. But that would all change if company charters legally obliged them to do otherwise. While few national governments are likely to contemplate such a regulatory change in the near term, the 'B Corps' movement is showing them how it can be done. A certified Benefit Corporation is an innovative business model that is designed to balance purpose and profit, where companies are legally required to consider the impact of their decisions on their workers, customers, suppliers, community and the environment. So far over 2,500 firms from more than 50 countries have voluntarily signed up, writing these requirements into their articles of association. Most are small businesses, but there are some big players among them, including Patagonia, Ben & Jerry's, Kickstarter, the Brazilian cosmetics giant Natura and the green cleaning product company Seventh Generation.[21]

Would these kinds of regulatory changes, as well as others such as abolishing quarterly reporting or delinking CEO pay from short-term financial performance, really bring us into the Doughnut?[22] Unfortunately not. They may help extend economic time horizons but they will not stop all the material waste, all the ecological damage, and all the luxury consumption that has driven us to use natural resources at a rate far beyond the earth's biocapacity.[23] 'They represent mere tweaks in a system that ultimately needs to be completely transformed,' admits Jeremy Lent, 'but like a modest trim tab that helps redirect an ocean liner, perhaps they could begin to curb the destructive force of transnationals and redirect their enormous power toward a more sustainable path'.[24]

So what would a deeper economic transformation – one that went further than simply regulating the capitalist model – actually look like? Just ask the time rebels leading the regenerative design movement.

How to Start a Regenerative Rebellion

Most attempts to challenge dominant economic systems in the past have failed. The planned economies of state socialism survived for half a century but are now almost nowhere to be seen. The great hopes of the cooperative movement in the nineteenth century gradually faded away, only surviving in pockets such as Mondragón in Spain. Today we are witnessing another valiant effort to challenge the hegemony of the market system: regenerative design. It is an emerging movement in its earliest stages of life and its chances of success are admittedly slim. But if we ever hope to have an economic model that replaces the addiction to growth with a more sustainable vision, it will have regenerative thinking at its core.

Regenerative design is a holistic approach to design that asks us to consider how the way we shop, eat, work and live can take place within the biophysical limits of the planet, without running down the ecological systems on which all life depends or sending us over a cliff-edge of global heating. It is about processes that are able to restore, renew and revitalise their own sources of energy and materials, making them sustainable and resilient over the very long term – decades and centuries rather than months and years.[25] Today's regenerative rebels have taken their struggle into four crucial areas: the circular economy, cosmo-local production, democratic energy and rewilding.

Imagine walking into your local shopping centre. Most of the products you will see – from socks to smartphones to cotton buds to deodorant – are made through an old-fashioned linear model of industrial design that Kate Raworth sums up as 'take, make, use, lose'. We take earth's materials, make them into things we want, use them for a while – sometimes only once – and then throw them away. And it is this linear degenerative economic model that pushes us over the brink of planetary boundaries.[26]

An alternative model of regenerative design known as 'the circular economy' is gaining traction. This is where products are continually being transformed into new ones, through circular processes that minimise waste. A biological material such as coffee grounds might be first used to make your morning brew, then turned into compost to grow mushrooms, then sent to a farm to become cattle feed and finally returned to the soil as manure. For manufactured materials such as steel or plastics, the process is similar, with the material being used again and again through repairing, refurbishing, repurposing and recycling. In a circular system there really is no such thing as waste: it's just a resource in the wrong place. This is the manufacturing equivalent of shifting from a linear to a circular concept of time, generating a long-term 'eternal return' of planetary resources.

Thousands of businesses and social enterprises are getting into the circular mindset. The Canadian waste company Enerkem extracts carbon from household rubbish that can't be recycled and turns it into a gas to make green biofuels, a process that has helped the city of Edmonton re-use 90 per cent of its waste and reduce landfill by 100,000 tonnes annually.[27] To prove their circular credentials, in 2018 the Swedish sportswear company Houdini opened the world's first clothing compost facility, where customers can take their used organic wool garments, pop them into compost bins and then use the soil produced to grow vegetables and have a tasty meal made from their old hiking jacket.

It sounds great, but where's the catch? In the circular economy, closing the loop and eliminating environmental waste can be costly.

One result is that Houdini sportswear is expensive. Of course, says the company – that's because we're covering the full environmental costs of production, unlike our competitors. But the reality is that without major behavioural shifts, most people will continue to seek bargains at Primark or H&M, and Houdini gear will remain niche. What's really needed is to spread the circular model to the economy as a whole.

The Fab City movement is focused on this very task. Its origins go back to 2014, when the mayor of Barcelona challenged the world's cities to 'produce everything they consume' by 2054.[28] Since then, the movement has sprung up in over 30 cities, from Santiago to Shenzhen, not only promoting the creation of a zero-emission circular economy, but putting into practice an innovative manufacturing philosophy known as 'cosmo-local production'.

The basic idea of this second approach to regenerative design is that 'atoms are heavy and bits are light': it makes sense to manufacture products (made of atoms) locally to reduce transport costs and energy use, and base them on designs (made of bits of information) that are freely available globally through open-source digital platforms. We often hear about open-source software such as Linux, Drupal or Firefox, but the Fab City movement is also looking to open-source hardware. The Polish-American inventor Marcin Jakubowski, for example, has created what he calls the Global Village Construction Set, comprising free communally developed designs that can be downloaded to build 50 key machines from tractors to 3D printers, at a fraction of the regular commercial cost. 'Our goal,' he says, 'is a repository of published designs so clear, so complete that a single burned DVD is effectively a civilisation starter kit'.[29] His work has inspired others such as the Open Building Institute and WikiHouse, which offer designs for modular low-cost eco housing that can be manufactured and built locally. Many of these organisations can now be found in the makerspaces springing up across Africa, from Benin to Nigeria.[30]

Like many transformative ideas, cosmo-localism is struggling against an existing economic system that could easily stifle it. It would be great to live in a bargain-priced, low-carbon house that arrived like an IKEA flatpack and took only a few months to build, but given high urban property prices, how are you going to afford the land on which to build it unless you are willing to live miles away from anywhere? While we should be realistic about its prospects, the Belgian peer-to-peer economy guru Michel Bauwens believes that cosmo-local production has a game-changing potential to 'radically diminish the human footprint on natural resources, which need to be preserved for future generations and all beings of the planet'.[31] Moreover, it also possesses a built-in adaptability and flexibility, creating economies that are responsive to local needs and resilient to change: every city based on cosmo-local production will look different, drawing on the innovation of its tech-savvy local producers.

It goes without saying that a fully regenerative economy would be 100 per cent powered by sunlight, wind, waves and other renewable sources. If we want to keep below 1.5°C of planetary heating, we have no choice but to fully decarbonise our energy systems within two decades, at the very latest. Enormous strides are being made in this area: over 100 cities now generate more than 70 per cent of their electricity from renewable sources, from Dar es Salaam in Tanzania to Curitiba in Brazil.[32] But the really exciting development is what social theorist Jeremy Rifkin calls the 'democratisation of energy'.[33] This refers to the growth of renewable energy microgrids that allow households not only to produce their own solar electricity but to sell their surplus to their neighbours, through horizontal peer-to-peer networks. It isn't just happening in wealthy countries like Germany either. In Bangladesh, tens of thousands of people – many of them poor rural women – have been trained to become solar engineers in their own villages, installing solar systems in over four million homes under a government 'swarm electrification' programme. By 2030,

Women in villages such as Buri Goalini are at the forefront of the energy
revolution in rural Bangladesh, installing and maintaining solar panels.

over 10,000 microgrid systems will be connecting solar-generating
households across the country as part of the fastest growing solar
revolution in the world.[34]

The virtue of this model is that it is distributive as well as regenerative: it helps bring people above the Doughnut's social foundation
by distributing the capacity to produce electricity far more equitably
than if households were dependent on big private energy companies
geared to generate profit.[35] This democratisation of energy may have
profound political implications too. Microgrid networks tend to
strengthen community cohesion. With energy production, ownership and distribution becoming local, people may well want other
things to be local too, including political decision-making. Throughout human history, energy systems have shaped political systems. Just
as the development of the mining industry in the nineteenth century
strengthened the union movement and demands for workers' rights,

the community-led solar revolution of the twenty-first century could become a force for the radical decentralisation of power, which fosters long-term thinking.[36] If, on the other hand, householders opt for private battery storage and hoard their energy rather than share it, or if renewable energy production becomes dominated by large corporations – as is starting to happen in many countries – then its democratising potential may never be fully realised.

A fourth form of regenerative design is being championed by the rewilding movement that has sprung up over the last decade everywhere from Scotland to South Africa and Romania. Its origins are partly a response to the failures of traditional conservation organisations. For more than a century, conservationists argued that our great task is to preserve the earth so it can be passed on to future generations in pristine condition. While this might sound like an admirable aspiration in tune with the good ancestor's transcendent goal of thriving within nature's boundaries, critics point out that many conservation organisations have unintentionally succumbed to what is known as 'shifting baseline syndrome'.

As ecologist George Monbiot explains, 'the people of every generation perceive the state of the ecosystems they encountered in their childhoods as normal.' As a result, conservationists often call for the restoration of fish, animals or plants to the ecological baseline of their youth, unaware that this may already have been a state of extreme depletion. In Britain, for instance, many people campaign to preserve the country's open moorlands, but in fact these were previously rich woodlands teeming with wildlife that have been ravaged by centuries of sheep farming. 'The conservation movement, while well intentioned, has sought to freeze living systems in time,' argues Monbiot. Hence he and many others favour 'rewilding' rather than 'conservation', which is not about trying to restore nature to some remembered prior state but about enabling ecological processes to resume by reintroducing plants and animals that can kickstart the recovery of wilderness and wildness. The classic case is Yellowstone Park, where the reintroduction of wolves in 1995 resulted in a 'trophic cascade' of ecological regeneration: the wolves kept ravenous deer away from eating saplings, which allowed trees to grow back, which in turn brought back songbirds, beavers and other creatures down the food chain.[37]

The aim of the rewilding movement is not simply to regenerate landscapes and prevent biodiversity loss, but to provide a 'natural carbon solution' for the planetary climate emergency. The solution on offer is not a high-tech option like carbon capture and storage, but a far more ancient and effective technology for sucking up carbon dioxide: trees. The potential of rewilding for carbon sequestration is enormous. Together with other nature-based approaches like regenerative agriculture, rewilding areas such as peatlands and heathlands could provide over one-third of the global greenhouse gas mitigation required by 2030 to keep below dangerous levels of heating – and yet it has so far attracted only 2.5 per cent of mitigation funding. A study by the campaigning organisation Rewilding Britain reveals that diverting two-thirds of current agricultural subsidies to rewilding projects would sequester 47 million tonnes of carbon dioxide a year, more than a tenth of the UK's current emissions.[38] Of course, rewilding isn't the only solution – switching to plant-based diets, ending fossil fuel transport and insulating our homes will all make a big difference – but the regenerative potential of trees is a reminder that a long future for humanity might emerge from rediscovering the deep wonders of 'tree time'.

These four regenerative practices are innovative and inspiring. But let's face the disenchanting reality: the time rebels are up against formidable forces of economic and political power. They are battling the short-termism of entrenched corporate behaviour and financial speculation, intransigent governments wedded to quarterly growth targets, and a throwaway consumer culture. With such barriers to overcome, will people really look back in a century from today and see the emergence of a regenerative economic revolution as clearly as we can now see the Industrial Revolution?

Probably not. But possibly yes. Because the embryonic regenerative practices appearing around the world are precisely what an early-stage economic transformation looks like. It is fragile, fragmented and contingent. This is just how it was during the early days of industrialisation in the eighteenth century. Luminaries such as Adam Smith didn't even realise there was an Industrial Revolution happening before their very eyes.[39]

Hopes for a regenerative revolution are now being bolstered by governments that are beginning to think differently. The Netherlands has adopted a pathbreaking programme to create a circular economy by 2050, including a 50 per cent reduction in the consumption of raw materials by 2030.[40] Sweden has an ambitious 'generational goal' to solve the country's major environmental problems within a single generation. Finland has committed to becoming carbon neutral by 2035. A group of Well-Being Economy Governments including New Zealand, Scotland and Iceland are looking to develop new metrics of development that are based on collective well-being rather than economic growth. Some like Bhutan are starting to measure Gross National Happiness, while others are moving towards adopting Green New Deals.

The biggest challenge, however, is resolving the central tension at the heart of economics in the twenty-first century: whether it is possible to simultaneously pursue economic growth while keeping within the ecological boundaries of the planet. It is an inescapable dilemma facing governments across the globe. One country determined to resolve it is China, a nation often held up for its long-term vision, which has set its sights on creating the world's first ecological civilisation. What lessons might it offer?

Can China Create an Ecological Civilisation?

There is a traditional Chinese folk tale, much loved by Chairman Mao, called 'The Foolish Old Man Removes the Mountains'. A 90-year-old man was so annoyed by a pair of mountains obstructing the journey from his home that he decided to level them using just his hoe to remove the earth and rocks. When he was mocked for embarking on this seemingly impossible task, he replied that through his own hard work and that of his many generations of descendants, the mountains would eventually disappear. The gods were so impressed by his perseverance that they ordered the mountains to be separated.[41]

Chinese culture is full of similar fables and proverbs about the virtues of taking the long view. They help paint a picture of China as an ancient civilisation where time horizons stretch hundreds or even thousands of years back into the past and forward into the future, in contrast to the Western obsession with the now. When Chinese leader Zhou Enlai was asked, in 1972, about the impact of the French Revolution, his legendary reply was that it was 'too soon to say'. It later emerged that he had thought he was being asked about the student revolts in Paris in 1968, but still this anecdote adds to the idea that the Chinese think in terms of centuries, while the rest of the world watches the second hand. In contrast, the frenzied pace of urban development in China today displays little of this long-term mentality: many new buildings barely last 20 years before they are torn down and replaced, while city planners have completely razed historic districts such as the old city of Kashgar or Shanghai's Laoximen neighbourhood.

There is no doubt, however, that the country deserves its reputation for long-range thinking and planning, especially in the areas of infrastructure and industrial policy. Its leadership believes that China's success is largely due to the ability of its political system to 'concentrate forces' on long-term development projects and priorities, unlike democracies where there are constant elections and changes of government.[42] According to President Xi Jinping, 'our biggest advantage is that our country's socialist system can concentrate on doing big things'.[43]

Such long-term projects range from the Three Gorges Dam to the colossal South–North Water Transfer Project, a canal scheme begun in 2002 to move water from the wet south to the dry north of the country, with an expected completion date of 2050. It also includes a range of infrastructure and power projects under the Belt and Road Initiative, which aims to extend China's economic influence into Central Asia, Africa and Europe. The government's latest five-year science and technology plan reveals that traditional engineering megaprojects are now being joined by digital megaprojects: by 2030 China intends to be a dominant global force in Big Data, cybersecurity, artificial intelligence, smart cities and beyond.[44]

Alongside such initiatives, President Xi has announced that China aims to become an 'ecological civilisation' over the next three decades, which will ensure 'harmony between humans and nature' and 'benefit generations to come'.[45] Few governments in the Western world can claim such an ambitious vision. In practice it means policies such as major investment in renewable energy, action on air and water pollution and large-scale reforestation. One recent project is the world's largest floating solar farm, which sits on top of a lake above an old coal mine in the eastern city of Huainan, and has the capacity to supply electricity to nearly 100,000 homes.[46] The pace of change is remarkable: according to Greenpeace, China covers the equivalent of one football field every hour with solar panels, and installs more than one wind turbine every hour.[47] And China knows it has to act fast: its own climate scientists warn that it will face higher-than-average sea-level rises, flooding, drought and food insecurity in coming years.[48]

The goal of an ecological civilisation signals a move towards a more regenerative economy in tune with the natural systems of the living world. But it sits uneasily with the government's continued commitment to economic growth as a top policy priority.[49] One of President Xi's flagship policies is known as the two 'hundred-years goals'. The first goal is to build a moderately prosperous society by 2021 (the hundredth anniversary of the Chinese Communist Party) and the second is to create a highly developed economic powerhouse by 2049 (the centenary of the founding of the People's Republic of China). The latter goal is an admirable example of long-term cathedral thinking. Yet it is absolutely dependent on China sustaining a high growth rate of around 6 per cent a year until the middle of the century.[50]

Therein lies the problem, for there is little evidence that such momentous, exponential growth can be achieved without putting the whole vision of an ecological civilisation at risk. China may have floating solar farms, but it still uses half the world's coal, a third of the world's oil and 60 per cent of the world's cement.[51] It also produces more steel and uses more pesticides, artificial fertilisers and timber than any other country in the world. This is not only because China is big – it's also because the industrial model remains largely dependent on fossil fuels and toxic chemicals. Even under optimistic scenarios, coal will still provide 47 per cent of the country's electricity in 2040 (down from around 70 per cent today).[52] At the same time, China has outsourced much of its fossil fuel dependency: between 2001 and 2016 it participated in the development of 240 coal-fired power stations in 25 countries as part of its Belt and Road programme. As the population becomes wealthier, people will want more cars, more heating, more meat, more consumer appliances – and all this adds up to more energy use and environmental degradation.[53] As economist Richard Smith puts it, 'Xi Jinping can create an ecological civilisation or he can build a rich superpower. He can't do both.'[54]

Believers in 'green growth' claim that these two goals are compatible. Yet no country in the world has so far managed to pursue growth while simultaneously reducing its greenhouse gas emissions on anything like the scale required to avoid dangerous climate change. For all our technological ingenuity, we have not yet found a way to 'decouple' economic growth from levels of resource use that drive us far beyond planetary boundaries. The minimal 'absolute decoupling' that has been achieved in some countries is incremental and nowhere close to what is needed to halve global carbon dioxide emissions within a decade.[55] 'The economists will tell you we can decouple growth from material consumption,' says energy scientist Václav Smil, 'but that is total nonsense.'[56]

China is not alone in grappling with this dilemma: it's one that confronts all high and middle-income countries. The emerging truth that the Chinese leadership faces is that the twin goals of economic growth and an ecological civilisation may be profoundly incompatible with one another. They seem to defy the ancient Daoist philosophy of yin and yang, in which apparently contrary forces may coexist in harmony and balance as part of an integrated whole. Perhaps China will be the exception to the rule and President Xi will be remembered as the leader who brought the two goals into union. Yet even with all the powers of the Chinese state at his disposal, he may still need help from the gods who move mountains.

Beyond Climate Apartheid

The time rebels behind the circular economy and other regenerative economic designs may rescue us from our civilisational quandary, enabling a transition from an economy driven by the goal of endless GDP growth to one that – returning to the words of David Korten – 'secures material sufficiency and spiritual abundance for all, in balance with the regenerative systems of a living Earth'. But they are engaged in a classic David versus Goliath struggle that could easily end in victory for the existing growth-addicted system.

If that happens, and we continue with business as usual, we must ready ourselves for the consequences. And we already know what they might look like. When Hurricane Sandy hit New York City in 2012, hundreds of thousands of low-income and vulnerable families were left without access to power and health care, while the head-quarters of Goldman Sachs was protected by tens of thousands of its own sandbags and power from its own generator. For Philip Alston, UN Special Rapporteur on Extreme Poverty and Human Rights, it signalled the dangers of 'climate apartheid', in which 'the wealthy pay to escape overheating, hunger and conflict, while the rest of the world is left to suffer'.[57] Think Soylent Green, Elysium, The Wall, or any number of sci-fi dystopias.

Although the richest 1 per cent, who own half the world's wealth, might be able to insulate themselves from the ravages of the global ecological emergency, most people will not, especially those living in poverty in both high and low-income countries.[58] That is why it is so essential that we strive to create a regenerative economy that not only keeps us within the critical ring of planetary boundaries, but also brings people above the Doughnut's social foundation. This is not simply a matter of economic and social justice for today but of inter-generational justice for tomorrow, ensuring that both current and future populations possess the means and resilience to face possible climate calamites.

Some low-income countries argue that they cannot afford to create a regenerative economy and that they need economic growth now to lift their citizens out of acute deprivation. Moreover, why shouldn't they enjoy their fair share of fossil fuel emissions, when developed countries have been enjoying them for the last two centuries?

It is true that the burden of cutting emissions should fall most on those countries historically most responsible for them: a long-term perspective demands nothing less. But the shift to a regenerative economy is not a luxury only for the enjoyment of wealthy nations.

As the success of Bangladesh's decentralised solar industry demonstrates, it also offers a way for low-income countries to promote economic well-being within the ecological limits of the living world. Regenerative design could enable them to leapfrog the old model of industrial capitalism and create a different kind of economy: one that is cleaner, fairer and based on a vision of a longer now. That economy is already here, attempting to flower in the cracks and crevices. It may get trampled underfoot. But if we make the effort to nurture it, it might just bloom.

11

Cultural Evolution

Storytelling, Design and the Rise of Virtual Futures

The survival of our species depends on the biosphere surrounding us, which provides oxygen and other essentials of life. But according to anthropologist Wade Davis, we are also surrounded by an 'ethnosphere' that provides the cultural air in which we breathe. It contains the swirl of ideas, beliefs, myths and attitudes that are prevalent in society, and that constitute the worldviews shaping how we think and act.[1]

The ethnosphere is in a state of constant flux and changes through a process of 'cultural evolution', another useful concept for our long-term lexicon. At any one moment certain ways of thinking may be dominant in the ethnosphere, but then new ones come along to displace the old. For instance, in the late twentieth century, the belief in collective values (like social justice) gradually gave way to an ideology of individualism that came to permeate the ethnosphere of the Western world, thanks to the rise of neoliberalism and consumer capitalism. Similarly, secular values began to compete for dominance with religious belief systems.

Cultural evolution differs from biological evolution in three principal ways. Firstly, it can be a matter of conscious choice: we can potentially shape the direction in which the ethnosphere develops. Secondly, it can happen far more rapidly than its biological counterpart, enabling us to adapt to our changing environment, such as the challenges of the climate crisis or growing wealth inequality. Thirdly, unlike biological evolution, where natural selection embeds new traits in our DNA that can be inherited over generations, cultural evolution needs to be reproduced again and again in each successive generation by education systems and other institutions and movements that inculcate values and ideas.[2]

What has this all got to do with the tug of war between short-term and long-term thinking? We are in the midst of a momentous period of cultural evolution, with time rebels seeding new ideas and practices into the ethnosphere in a range of cultural habitats, from the visual arts to organised religion. If a time traveller from 1820 arrived in the world of 2020, they would no doubt be shocked by the quick tempo of daily life and our state of constant digital distraction, but they would also be amazed by the amount of time we spend imagining and thinking about the future, decades and even centuries from today. They would find evidence of it in cinemas, school classrooms, news articles, church sermons, video games and in the mindscapes of virtual reality. And we have the cultural time rebels to thank for it.

The result is that in parallel to the short-now mentality that occupies our minds, a longer now is beginning to emerge: never before in human history have we been so concerned with the world to come. Whether this is out of hope or fear, a profound shift is taking place in our mental landscapes. We are beginning to breathe the air of long-term thinking.

Who are the rebel figures behind this cultural transformation? What are their strategies? And what hope do they have of tapping into the unrealised potential of our acorn brains? This chapter takes us on a journey into the most creative and disruptive cultural zones of long-term thinking today, starting with one of the oldest human acts: storytelling.

Science Fiction and the Power of Storytelling

While the time rebellion in politics and economics has only developed since the 1970s, novelists and film makers have been extending our imaginations into the future for over a century. One early exponent was Charles Dickens; in *A Christmas Carol*, the Ghost of Christmas Yet to Come shows the miserly Ebenezer Scrooge the death of Tiny Tim and his own neglected grave. Yet the real leap into the future came in the late nineteenth century with the writings of Jules Verne and H.G. Wells, founders of science fiction, a genre now often known as 'speculative fiction'. Time machines, men in the moon and being lost in space soon became part of our everyday vocabulary.

Today it can almost feel like we are overdosing on it, with Hollywood pumping out a succession of apocalyptic sci-fi blockbusters like *The Day After Tomorrow*, in which climate change creates a giant superstorm that brings about a new ice age. It is easy to be disparaging of this 'apoco-tainment' industry, which gives us plenty of emotional and high-tech thrills yet often fails to forge a deep sense of connection with the fate of future people. Yet there are just as many serious and thoughtful attempts to explore possible futures, from novels such as *The Handmaid's Tale* by Margaret Atwood and its sequel *The Testaments*, to films like *Children of Men*, based on P.D. James's novel, which is set in a world where two decades of human infertility has left society on the brink of collapse and our species facing extinction.

In one of the first systematic attempts to study the genre, scholars at the University of Lisbon analysed the dominant themes in 64 of the most influential science fiction films and novels over the last 150 years, ranging from Yevgeny Zamyatin's *We* and Fritz Lang's *Metropolis* to Ursula Le Guin's *The Lathe of Heaven* and James Cameron's *Avatar*. By coding their content into over 200 thematic categories, clear patterns began to appear. In 27 per cent of the sample, technology had become a tool for manipulation and social control. The destruction of the living world appeared in 39 per cent of the books and films, and acute food scarcity was a theme in 28 per cent, while 31 per cent contained resistance movements to fight oppressive political systems and extreme inequality. One of the study's main conclusions was that speculative fiction and film don't simply help us visualise and connect with the abstract notion of 'the future', but also operate as an early warning system that actively engages us with the risks of technology or resource exploitation far more effectively than the dispassionate analyses of scientists or long government reports. It can politicise us, socialise us and alter us. According to the authors, sci-fi has a capacity to 'speak its truth to power' and promotes 'an ethics of precaution and responsibility'.[3]

So it might be fictional, it might be entertainment, but it might also be a message. Kim Stanley Robinson, who has tackled the impacts of global warming and the challenges of colonising other worlds in a series of politically savvy bestselling novels such as *New York 2140* and *Aurora*, says the purpose of his writing is to tell 'the story of the next century'. All his science fiction is intensely grounded in the latest climate and technology research, and although it might explore human foibles as much as any literary novel, its larger purpose is to help us understand the crises that are coming our way and inspire us to act now to prevent or minimise them. They are a wake-up call. Robinson describes his books as 'realism about our time'.[4]

If I were to highlight a single example to illustrate the 'early warning' power of science fiction, it would be Olaf Stapledon's prophetic masterpiece *Star Maker*, published in 1937. The novel describes a distant planet very much like ours known as the Other Earth, which is similarly populated by humans. One day, a geologist among them discovers a ten-million-year-old lithographic plate etched with a diagram of a radio resembling those in their own society.

The inhabitants of this planet cannot believe that there was once a human civilisation as technologically advanced as their own that had collapsed and disappeared, and comfort themselves with the belief that the diagram must have been left by some other intelligent but less hardy species that had experienced a brief flicker of civilisation. According to Stapledon, 'It was agreed that man, once he had reached such a height of culture, would never have fallen from it.'

What was the eventual fate of the people of the Other Earth? Theirs was a curious society, where radio technology became so advanced that most of the inhabitants carried a radio receiver in their pockets that stimulated their brains merely by touching it. Through this 'radio–brain–stimulation', people could experience the sensory pleasures of a banquet without eating, take part in a thrilling motorbike race without any danger, travel to wherever they pleased and even enjoy radio-induced sex. 'Such was the power of this kind of entertainment that both men and women were nearly always seen with one hand in a pocket,' Stapledon tells us. Eventually 'a system was invented by which a man could retire to bed for life and spend all his time receiving radio programmes'.

Governments on the Other Earth soon realised that they could manipulate this virtual world of 'radio bliss', using the receivers to broadcast nationalist propaganda messages that demonised their enemies. The result was the outbreak of devastating wars. Not long after, scientists discovered that the planet's weak gravitational field was causing the gradual loss of the precious oxygen that sustained life. Although they had always possessed a self-confident belief that their civilisation could overcome any challenge 'by means of its unique scientific knowledge', one of the unintended consequences of the radio-induced wars was that scientific advancement had been set back by at least a century, leaving the people of the Other Earth insufficient time to solve the problem of their deteriorating atmosphere. Their fate was settled. They were destined for extinction.[5]

Stapledon may have written all this over 80 years ago, but there could hardly be a better parable for our times. As we fiddle distractedly with our own digital versions of radio bliss in our pockets, might we become yet another lost civilisation to be discovered in the rock strata by the geologists of tomorrow?

The Creative Gateway to Mental Time Travel:
Art, Music and Design

Walk through the Renaissance galleries of the Louvre or the Uffizi and you will see very few attempts to represent future imagined worlds. Yet wander into a museum of conceptual art today, and you will find a whole genre of time-related works dedicated to exploring our many possible relationships with the future, and extending our time horizons far beyond the here and now. A time rebellion is shaking the very foundations of the art world, representing a turn towards temporal expressionism. Here are a few examples:

> Arthur Ganson has built *Machine with Concrete*, containing a gear turning at 200 revolutions per minute at one end that is connected to 11 further gears, each running at one-fiftieth the speed of the preceding gear, the last of which is embedded in solid concrete and completes a single revolution every two trillion years.
>
> Cathy Haynes has created *Stereochron Island*, a campaign to found a new state without clocks in a London park, which endeavours to return its citizens to a cyclical relationship with solar time.
>
> John Cage's intergenerational composition *As Slow as Possible* is currently being played on an organ in the German city of Halberstadt, over a period of 639 years. One chord began sounding in January 2006 and lasted two-and-a-half years before the next note was struck. The final note will be played in 2640.
>
> Working with the World Wildlife Fund, Yoshiyuki Mikami created photos of disappearing species, where each pixel represented one remaining animal left in the wild: the image of the panda had only 1,600 pixels.

In April 2019, scientists in Iceland erected the first memorial plaque to a lost glacier – the OK Glacier – recognising that all the country's glaciers are likely to disappear within 200 years.

Scottish artist Katie Paterson ranks among the greatest exponents of this temporal expressionism, having created a series of breathtaking works using time itself as her raw material.[6] In *Vatnajökull (the sound of)*, members of the public could call a phone number and listen live to the sound of a melting Icelandic glacier through an underwater microphone. The beads of *Fossil Necklace* were made from fossils across the expanses of deep time: a starfish from the Sahara, a giant lizard's tooth from the Atlas Mountains, a toe-bone from a long-extinct English woolly rhino. None of Paterson's works has done more to capture the public imagination than the 100-year art project *Future Library*. Starting in 2014, every year for a century a well-known writer is donating a new work that will be held in trust, unread, as a gift for future generations. In 2114, the 100 books will be printed on paper supplied from a forest of 1,000 trees that have been especially planted outside Oslo. 'There is something magical about it,' says Margaret Atwood, one of the contributing writers. 'It's like *Sleeping Beauty*. The texts are going to slumber for 100 years and then they'll wake up, come to life again.'[7]

Future Library perfectly distils the ideal of a transcendent legacy, one that will be enjoyed by the readers of the twenty-second century when most of the authors involved in the project will be long dead. It raises questions that help forge a sense of intergenerational connection. Who will these readers be? What kind of world will they live in – will physical books even exist then? And how will they judge us and the legacies we have left them? Like the 10,000 Year Clock in the Texas desert, the forest of *Future Library* is destined to become a site of pilgrimage. When I suggested to Paterson that she was a time rebel leading a global struggle for intergenerational justice to decolonise the future, she looked a little startled. But within a few moments she was talking passionately about the global climate protests and how looking into deep time can help give us the perspective we need to recognise everything that we're putting at risk through our ecologically destructive actions. Her art, in all its temporal subtlety and originality, carries a profound political message for our times.[8]

A very different creative approach to long-term thinking can be found in the work of Brian Eno. His influential 77 *Million Paintings*, which has been projected onto structures including the Sydney Opera House, randomly combines 296 original artworks on a screen in groups of four, and overlays them with randomly generated music, producing an almost infinite number of variations. It reflects his long interest in 'generative music', the term he coined to describe compositions – including his classic 1970s albums *Discreet Music* and *Music for Airports* – that introduce random elements within a set of basic rules to create a kind of endless music that is not eternally repetitive but eternally changing. For Eno, such generative works expand our minds into a longer now in much the same way as regenerative economics, which is similarly based on the idea of creating self-sustaining 'complex adaptive systems' that ensure their longevity by adapting and changing through time within a set of basic parameters. He looks to Terry Riley's 1964 composition *In C* for inspiration, a piece of no set duration that was written for any number of performers, where the musicians play 53 short melodic phrases in order, but with each player repeating them as many times as they wish before moving on to the next one. 'To my way of thinking,' Eno told me, 'Terry Riley's *In C* is the dynamic complexity to Bach's very mechanical fugues.'[9]

While art and music can take us on imaginative journeys through time, a new generation of designers have begun creating immersive 'experiential futures' that enable us not only to visualise but to feel, hear and even smell the future. Anab Jain, co-founder of the Anglo-Indian

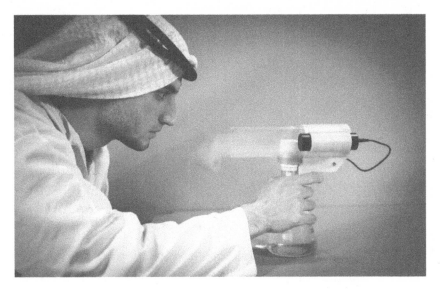

A government official from the United Arab Emirates breathes the
toxic air of 2034, courtesy of the design agency Superflux.

design studio Superflux, created the Future Energy Lab for the government of the United Arab Emirates. Among the exhibits was a 'pollution
machine' that allowed ministers to breathe in a noxious mixture of
carbon monoxide, sulphur dioxide and nitrogen dioxide, which represented the predicted air quality in the UAE in 2034 if they continue
polluting at current rates. According to Jain, sticking their noses into
the toxic fumes was among the factors that helped convince government officials of the need to invest heavily in renewable energy.[10]

If only we could all breathe the air that our children and grandchildren will be struggling to breathe in the future. If only we could
feel the heat, feel the hunger, feel the insecurity they might face.

This could just become possible with the help of virtual and aug-
mented reality, which have the potential to spread the experience of
Jain's pollution machine and other design innovations to a wider
public. Imagine popping on your Oculus headset (still expensive but
rapidly falling in price) and having a full-body sensory immersion in

worlds that are two, four or six degrees hotter than ours. At Stanford University's Virtual Human Interaction Lab you can scuba dive in a coral reef full of teeming life and then watch how it deteriorates into a biological dead zone by 2100, due to ocean acidification. 'We can't get everyone to read scientific papers about climate change, so this shortcuts all of that,' says its creator Jeremy Bailenson. 'We want people to walk out of there feeling empathy and wanting to act.' Visitors to the lab can also cut down a virtual tree by clutching a mechanical device that simulates a sawing motion. Studies show that individuals having this virtual experience use 20 per cent less paper during the next week than those who merely read or watch a video about tree cutting to encourage paper conservation.[11]

Unfortunately, much of this virtual technology remains at an early stage of development and is yet to leave the lab. Do we really have time to wait for it to reach *Matrix*-level quality? And how much faith should we really have in it as an elixir for long-term thinking anyway? Rather than cutting down a virtual tree, Stanford students might in the meantime go for a 20-minute walk to visit El Palo Alto, a thousand-year-old redwood on the edge of the campus, or hike in California's White Mountains in search of a bristlecone pine that has been growing for even longer. As they sit around the campfire, they might play The Thing from the Future, a visionary (and often hilarious) card game invented by designers Stuart Candy and Jeff Watson. There are three kinds of cards: one specifying a possible future world, one a cultural artifact from it, and one a theme that the artifact relates to. So the three cards you pick might say, 'In a feminist future – there is a law – related to money' or 'In a reactionary future – there is a machine – related to love'. The aim is to invent and describe the artifact using nothing more than the tools of imagination and conversation. In different combinations, the cards allow for tens of thousands of possible prompts. Candy refers to the game as a form of 'anticipatory anthropology'.[12]

We should not forget the virtues of such analogue experiences while we hanker for the virtual future. Nor should we forget the power of art, music and design to create far-reaching cultural disruption. In 1787, anti-slavery campaigners in Britain produced a poster called 'The Brookes Slave Ship', showing how 482 slaves could be squeezed on board in utterly inhumane conditions. The image went viral. Soon there were tens of thousands of copies pinned up in pubs, churches, coffee houses and homes around the country. It was one of the most influential pieces of graphic design in history, helping to publicise and galvanise the successful movement against slavery and the slave trade. We urgently need today's creative minds to produce works that electrify the struggle for intergenerational justice and a longer now.

Growing Imagined Communities Through Education and Religion

In the nineteenth century, political leaders in France embarked on one of the most ambitious cultural projects in European history: to invent the idea of being French. At the time of the French Revolution, what was nominally a single country was in fact a land severely divided by religion, customs, distance and, crucially, language: 50 per cent of the population didn't even speak French, and little more than 10 per cent spoke it well.[13] Their allegiances were local and regional rather than national. But this gradually changed through a series of reforms, such as a new education system to teach a shared language and history, the celebration of national holidays and the singing of the national anthem. It was a classic instance of forging what historian Benedict Anderson called an 'imagined community' – a sense of collective identity among people who could never possibly all know each other. This is how European nationalism developed into such a potent force: by the twentieth century, millions of people were willing to sacrifice their lives in wars for their fellow countrymen and women.[14]

A similar – or perhaps even greater – challenge faces us today. How do we create a sense of shared identity with the unborn generations of tomorrow's world, the future people who we can never meet but who we must endeavour to embrace as our kith and kin? The creative arts, film and literature will all play a crucial role. But they will never in themselves be potent enough to create and sustain a new imagined community based on intergenerational solidarity. It is vital to harness the power of two forces that have the potential to scale up and spread the values of the good ancestor: education and religion.

Education appears to suffer from an inherent time tension. On the one hand it embodies long-term thinking by providing investment in young people, the fruits of which may not fully emerge for at least a decade when they enter the workforce or become active citizens. On the other hand, what they need to learn is in a constant state of flux, perhaps now more so than ever due to rapid technological changes like automation. As Yuval Noah Harari argues: 'Since we do not know what the job market will look like in 2030 or 2040, today we have no idea what to teach our kids. Most of what they currently learn at school will probably be irrelevant by the time they are 40.'[15]

There are at least two core skills they should be learning that will stand the test of time. Firstly, relationship skills like empathy, where humans have a big advantage over the AI machines that threaten to take their jobs. Secondly, the skill of long-term thinking itself. This is something we will always need in a world undergoing rapid transformation and facing long-term threats. We need education systems that forge a bond with the future generations who will inherit the consequences of our actions. Education for everyone from pre-schoolers to lifelong learners should help create a new imagined community across the expanses of time, just like nineteenth-century education systems forged a nationalist community across space.

What should it look like? Just turn to the educational time rebels. Around the world, there are projects and movements for educational reform, which build on the environmental education that is already well established in many countries, by offering a more explicitly long-term perspective. Here is a taster of what is on offer for both young and old:

Roots of Empathy, an education programme that has reached nearly one million children in countries ranging from Costa Rica to South Korea, uses real babies to teach intergenerational empathy in the classroom. The Junior Curriculum for ages nine to eleven gets pupils to imagine the baby in the future and explore what their connection and responsibility is to them.[16]

FutureLab has produced a Futures Thinking Teachers Pack for schools in Scotland, including activities and games to explore possible, probable and preferred futures over the next 30 years, and introducing the methods of scenario planning for use in geography, English and citizenship education classes.[17]

In Canada, the David Suzuki Foundation has created classroom materials for high school students on intergenerational rights, drawing on indigenous ideas of seventh-generation thinking and including an activity to write new clauses focusing on future generations for the UN Universal Declaration of Human Rights.[18]

Futurist guru Jim Dator asks his students at the University of Hawaii to design an ideal governance system for a population of 50,000 people living on Mars in the mid-twenty-first century. Using video, images and words, they must address issues like the underlying values of the society, its constitution, resource allocation and obligations to future generations.[19]

The University of California at Berkeley has offered a design course on 'Thinking Like a Good Ancestor: Finding Meaning in the Technology We Build'. Its creator, Alan Cooper, gets students to shift from asking, 'How can I maximise my personal benefit now?' to 'How can I maximise the benefit to everyone, in perpetuity?'[20]

The growing discipline of systems thinking, pioneered by scholars such as Donella Meadows, is now taught in schools and universities worldwide. Deeply informed by long-term thinking, its insights can be explored through free massive open online courses, such as the Planetary Boundaries and Human Opportunities course offered by the Stockholm Resilience Centre.[21]

Educators can obtain ideas from a range of creative online sources to promote long-term thinking. At the DearTomorrow website, you can write a letter to someone in 2050 (for example, a child in your life or your future self), in which you pledge to take action on the climate crisis.

It is early days yet and this mosaic of fragmented approaches hardly constitutes a comprehensive educational revolution (and is currently concentrated in high-income countries). But together they have the potential to form the basis of Good Ancestor curriculums for different age groups and cultures around the globe. Progressive educational movements such as the International Baccalaureate – which reaches over one million children each day in 157 countries – might consider bringing the long term centre stage in its programmes. Some parents may worry about the dangers of raising possibly traumatic issues such as ecological collapse, especially with younger children. It's a legitimate concern that should be handled with sensitivity. But from the evidence of the growing global climate strike movement, it looks like schoolchildren are far ahead of most adults in recognising the threats. They want to learn about them – and to act on what they learn.

Any effort to bring future generations into our imagined community would be unwise to ignore the most powerful mechanism invented by humankind to create collective identities: religion. A Muslim, a Jew or a Christian can walk into a mosque, synagogue or church almost anywhere in the world and be welcomed as part of the community of believers. But what do we know about the long-term credentials of the major faiths? The picture is mixed. In Buddhism, for instance, concepts such as the interconnectedness of all living things, universal loving-kindness, karma and rebirth provide a link between current and future generations that cannot easily be found in Christianity, Islam or Judaism, as well as creating the basis for a strong conservation ethos.

Christianity offers believers the ultimate long-term gift of eternal life in Heaven, but has been accused of ecological short-sightedness. Since the Middle Ages, Christian thinkers have promoted the idea of human dominion over nature, with little consideration of the environmental consequences (despite some exceptions, such as the teachings of St Francis). In the 1960s, environmental historian Lynn White famously argued that by destroying pagan animism (in which every tree, river and animal had a guardian spirit), 'Christianity made it possible to exploit nature in a mood of indifference to the feelings of natural objects', making it 'the most anthropocentric religion the world has seen' and a ready accomplice of the Industrial Revolution.[22]

Christian ecologists have been defending themselves against such accusations ever since, stressing that human beings are stewards charged with respecting and preserving God's sacred creation. Such thinking appears prominently in Pope Francis's 2015 encyclical 'Laudato si'' which emphasises the importance of 'justice between generations' and 'intergenerational solidarity', and asks 'what kind of world do we want to leave to those who come after us?' It critiques 'the culture of consumerism, which prioritises short-term gain and private interest' and calls for a 'politics which is far-sighted'.[23] The Pope, it seems, has joined the brigade of time rebels. When I interviewed a representative of the Vatican in Rome, he not only highlighted the intergenerational outlook of *Laudato si'*, but pointed out the long-term credentials of Catholic institutions such as Einsiedeln Abbey, a Benedictine monastery in Switzerland that has been carefully maintaining its forest for over a thousand years.[24] Whether the Pope's time-rebel intentions will get played out in reality is another matter: despite public pressure, the Vatican Bank has still not divested from fossil fuels.[25]

The Catholic Church is clearly rewriting the story of what it means to be a Christian in the twenty-first century, just as evangelical Protestants are gradually raising their levels of ecological awareness and sense of intergenerational obligation (although there are still plenty of climate change deniers among them).[26] With their extensive global network of churches and community organisations, the world's two billion Christians have a greater potential to embed the values of long-term thinking in the ethnosphere than almost any other social movement on the planet.

What about the 16 per cent of the global population (including myself) who do not identify with any religion?[27] I had once thought that it would almost be necessary for someone to invent a new religion for them that could instil long-term values. But then, thanks to reading *Blessed Unrest* by Paul Hawken, I came to realise that the hundreds of thousands of environmental organisations around the world effectively operate as a massive decentralised religion, each worshipping the same deity that has been venerated by indigenous peoples for so long: Mother Earth. While it may not be written into their mission statements, they are all driven in their different ways by the quasi-religious belief that all life is sacred. There is no need to invent a new religion for it is already here, a product of the vibrant ecological activism that has emerged over the last half-century.[28] And with its decentralised form, it might even avoid some of the power-grabbing habits of traditional religions.

I put this idea to evolutionary biologist Richard Dawkins, perhaps the world's most famous atheist. In our age of ecological emergency, I asked him, isn't the worship of some version of Mother Earth the one religion that deserves our allegiance? I fully expected a characteristically strident rejection of this suggestion, but his reply surprised me:

> I would feel sorry if Mother Earth was considered a religion – I prefer to make the scientific arguments about why we should do something about climate change. But I can see that there might be a political argument to treat the earth as a goddess like Gaia, as a way of galvanising people and arousing them to protect it.[29]

Even among the most scientifically rational of people, there might be grounds – if only instrumental ones – for fostering a spiritual connection with the living planet and developing a set of beliefs and rituals that instil us with long-term values of preservation and regeneration. Whether we choose to worship a solstice dawn at Stonehenge, fight to protect species under threat, campaign to rewild degraded tracts of land or erect wind turbines out at sea, such acts bring us into communion with the ideals of the good ancestor. They remind us to take the perspective of deep time. They encourage us to consider our legacies to future generations. And they guide us towards the transcendent goal of thriving within the means of the planet.

The White Horse: 1,000 Years of Long-Term Ritual

Last summer, I found myself on an isolated hillside some 20 miles south of my home in Oxford, smashing chunks of chalk into the ground with a mallet. I was not alone: around a dozen of us were pounding away at the soft white rocks, pulverising them flat, taking part in an ancient ritual called 'chalking the horse', which has been going on for over a thousand years.

The horse in question is the Uffington White Horse, an iconic work of minimalist art that was cut into the chalk hill during the Bronze Age. Measuring over 100 metres in length, its prancing form can be seen from miles around. Nobody knows who made it, or why it is there. In a tradition stretching back at least to the Middle Ages and lasting until the nineteenth century, local villagers would climb the hill every seven years to clear the figure of weeds and replace the chalk that had washed away, preserving the horse for future generations. When the work was done, they headed back down and held a festival in the horse's honour.

Although the festival no longer takes place, it has been replaced

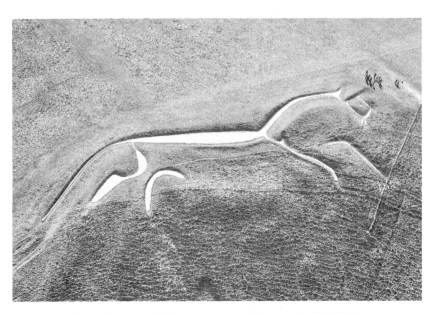

The Uffington White Horse, carved into a chalk hillside
in the Berkshire Downs.

by an annual pilgrimage of devotees who still re-chalk the horse, now under the watchful eye of the National Trust, which looks after the site. That's why I was there, along with colleagues from the London outpost of the Long Now Foundation. For all of us – a motley crew, including a software engineer, a graphic designer, a marketing professional, an eco-artist and a couple of kids who had bunked off school for the day with their dad – it was a chance to connect with a deeper sense of time. Our phones were turned off and our only timekeepers were the rhythmic beat of our hammers and the sun moving slowly across the sky.

The re-chalking ritual speaks to us of the value of maintenance. It is a reminder that preserving the things that matter to us – from our cultural inheritance to family relationships to the living planet itself – requires dedication, effort and cycles of care. Otherwise things fall apart, systems run down, cracks begin to appear.

As we pounded the stone into smaller and smaller pieces, making our modest contribution to a timeless work of communal art, I pictured the long chain of people who had done the very same thing for centuries stretching into the past, and might do so for centuries stretching into the future. An interconnected chain of human care, keeping the White Horse alive.

12

The Path of the Good Ancestor

November 02019. As I write, the country I grew up in is on fire: the east coast of Australia is burning. My 86-year-old father has had to flee, due to the flames threatening to engulf his Sydney home. Now he is choking on the ash that has filled the air and obscured the sun in a smoky haze, while tens of thousands of people gather in the city centre to demand immediate climate action from an intransigent, slumbering government.

In his book *The Uninhabitable Earth,* David Wallace-Wells predicted that the twenty-second century would be the 'century of hell'.[1] Perhaps it has already begun.

It is a world set to exacerbate the inequalities of the present. There are already a billion people who do not have enough food to eat and are living precarious lives, but now they are confronted by an ecological future rushing at them with more droughts, more floods, more hurricanes, more conflict. The era of climate apartheid is fast approaching, where the haves are able to protect themselves behind high walls, while the have-nots struggle to survive beyond them.

In 50 years, in 100 hundred years, in 500 years, there are still likely to be human beings living, working, loving and dreaming across the continents of planet earth. And the lives they lead will be profoundly influenced by how we act today, by the consequences of the history they will inherit. We are their ancestors, and the choices we make – political, environmental, cultural, technological – will inevitably shape their prospects.

We know what is at stake. So what is stopping us from shifting our gaze from the here and now to taking a longer view of the future of humanity? The easy answer is human nature: the inherent short-sightedness of our marshmallow brains. But this cannot be the whole story because our species, for all its shortcomings, has repeatedly demonstrated an aptitude for thinking and planning for posterity, drawing on the cognitive capacity of our acorn brains. In fact, there are four more fundamental barriers to change that have been recurring themes throughout this book:

Outdated Institutional Designs

Our political systems have little capacity to take the long view: both representative democracy and nation states are geared towards short time horizons and responding to near-term interests rather than long-term risks. There is an absence of institutional mechanisms that give voice to the interests of tomorrow's generations, who are effectively disenfranchised from the system. Politics enables the colonisation of the future.

The Power of Vested Interests

The future is being held to ransom by a whole economic ecosystem bent on short-term gains and instant gratification, from fossil fuel companies and financial speculators to online shopping emporiums. They are the lifeblood of a growth-based global economy that locks us into myopia. These interests increasingly exercise their power through social media channels, using smart algorithms and other tech tools to spread disinformation and influence political outcomes in their favour.[2]

Insecurity in the Here and Now

Long-term thinking will always be a challenge for those who are struggling to meet immediate needs in the present, due to factors such as job insecurity, hunger and the threat of violence. This is especially the case for the world's 230 million migrants and refugees – a number likely to increase to over 400 million by 2050 – most of whom understandably focus on dealing with their present context of uncertainty and dislocation, rather than on planning for a distant future.[3]

Insufficient Sense of Crisis

For all the ecological calamities and technological threats that we face, most people – especially those in positions of power – don't feel a genuine sense of crisis, urgency or fear that will spark them into radical action. We are a species slowly boiling in the pot and will need a sharp shock if we are to jump out of it. As Milton Friedman, one of the architects of neoliberalism, said, 'only a crisis – actual or perceived – produces real change'.[4]

Given such huge obstacles, what hope could there possibly be for long-term thinking? The answer comes back to the power of ideas. Ideas provide the mental playground in which human action takes place. They are the secret ingredient of the paradigms that shape our lives. Milton Friedman certainly recognised their transformative potential. After he and his like-minded colleagues worked for nearly half a century seeding free-market thinking in universities, think tanks, newspapers and political parties, neoliberalism finally overcame its arch-rival Keynesianism in the 1980s, and still reigns supreme decades later as one of the most dominant worldviews of our times. We must be equally ambitious in our hopes for long-term thinking, although its tug of war against short-termism needs to be won far more quickly. This is a struggle for the human mind. Decolonise our minds and we will decolonise the future, liberating it from domination by the present tense. And we have all the tools we need in the six ways to think long.

Transforming them into habits of mind and how we see the world requires time for reflection, exploration and conversation, so I have set out questions for contemplation that relate to each of the six ways below. These questions can be used as a spark for adventurous discussions with friends, family, colleagues or strangers. As the historian Theodore Zeldin said, 'A satisfying conversation is one which makes you say what you have never said before.'[5]

Underlying this set of questions is a larger one. We are poised at a moment in history where we face an existential choice, one that Jonas Salk recognised as the most critical of our time: do we want to remain a society driven by short-term thinking and individualistic values, or do we want to shift in the direction of long-term thinking for the common good?

Even if we make the choice to become good ancestors, we still face the seemingly insuperable challenge of overcoming the many barriers to long thinking. We are surrounded and suffocated by the short now of modernity that taps into our marshmallow brains. The daily peaks and troughs of the stock market, the airport queues for weekend flights, the frenzied rush of clearance sales, the pre-election deals of politicians and the twitch of people constantly checking their phones.

Yet there is also a more hopeful reality before us. Stand back and look at the time rebellion taking place across the cultural, economic and political landscape of the early twenty-first century – it is a remarkable constellation of commitment and action that is seeding long-term

Good ancestor conversations

 Deep-Time Humility
What have been your most profound experiences
of deep time, and how did they affect you?

 Intergenerational Justice
What, for you, are the most powerful reasons
for caring about future generations?

 Legacy Mindset
What legacy do you want to leave for your family,
your community and for the living world?

 Transcendent Goal
What do you think should be the ultimate goal
of the human species?

 Holistic Forecasting
Do you anticipate a future of civilisational breakdown,
radical transformation or a different pathway?

 Cathedral Thinking
What long-term projects could you pursue
with others that extend beyond your own lifetime?

values through the ethnosphere. Viewed as a whole, there is an emerging global movement dedicated to expanding our time horizons and forging a new imagined community with future people. We may be on the cusp of a long now civilisation. How might we best advance the cause and play a part in the struggle?

When it comes to being a good ancestor, the key question is not 'how can I make a difference?' but 'how can *we* make the difference?' A mere shift of pronoun has the power to change the world. The urgency of our current crises demands strategies of change based on collective action directed at those in power more than isolated personal actions. As David Wallace-Wells argues, 'the climate calculus is such that individual lifestyle choices do not add up to much, unless they are scaled by politics'.[6]

For those seeking to transform long-term thinking into long-term practice, the priority must be what we can do together. That could mean joining the time rebellions already under way: supporting the legal battles for intergenerational rights, taking part in citizens' assemblies or lobbying politicians to end fossil fuel subsidies and get into the Doughnut. It could mean looking at the organisations in which you are already embedded, such as schools, churches or workplaces, and asking what you can do to promote the long view – it might be a campaign to make its operations zero carbon, writing a strategic plan for 2100 or transforming it into a B Corp. It could also mean taking to the streets and blocking a new airport runway with your samba band, staging a sit-in to demand long-term investment in the public health system or joining your children on a climate strike. Remember the words of anthropologist James Scott: 'the great emancipatory gains for human freedom have not been the result of orderly, institutional procedures but of disorderly, unpredictable, spontaneous action cracking open the social order from below.'[7]

And the clock is ticking. We are enveloped in the paradox that we cannot wait patiently for long-term thinking to gradually emerge and make its presence felt: we need it urgently and immediately to tackle the multiple crises heading at speed towards us. As Martin Luther King Jr wrote, 'we are confronted with the fierce urgency of the now'.[8] Tomorrow has become today.

History tells us that collective action works. Yet drawing a strict line between individual and communal endeavours is a false dichotomy. Our personal actions are not a pointless drop in the ocean, for the simple reason that their ripple effects can turn into waves. Social contagion is a powerful force: one study showed that half of people who know someone who has given up flying because of climate change fly less themselves as a result of their example. Other research demonstrates that putting solar panels on your roof not only helps to drive down the market price of renewable energy but can also encourage friends and neighbours to do the same. The smart strategy is to consider actions that have the potential to be amplified.[9]

We must still, however, make space for the deeply personal.

To fall in love with a place – a mountain, a woodland, a river – can transform us into guardians of the future, instilling a desire to preserve its life-giving wonders for generations to come. Such landscapes provide an anchor in an age of dislocation and broken communities to which we can attach our temporal longings. They reconnect us with the transcendent goal of one-planet thriving, so we take care of the living world that will take care of our offspring.

To envision the lives of our younger loved ones stretching into the distance beyond our own can also be a bridge to a longer now. Who will they be when they are in old age? What kind of world will they inhabit? How will they look back on us, and what we did or didn't do when we had the chance? The power of *whakapapa* can become part of our imaginations, helping to shine light on the great chain of living, dead and unborn that extends unbroken through time itself.

Seeing ourselves as part of that chain can bring an unexpected gift: a sense of meaning in our lives. We can nurture our need for connection and relationship by creating an empathic bond with future generations across the timescape. We can derive purpose from striving to secure the flourishing of life, generation after generation. We can begin to liberate ourselves from the fear of death by seeing ourselves as part of a bigger picture. The quest to think long is full of existential sustenance.

As we reflect on our changing relationship with time, as we consider our own legacies, as we contemplate what it means for our lives to be just an eyeblink in the vast, 13.8-billion-year history of the universe, we begin our journey beyond the here and now. We begin to breathe new life into the evolution of human culture. We begin to walk the path of the good ancestor.

The Intergenerational Solidarity Index

The Intergenerational Solidarity Index has been developed by the interdisciplinary scientist Jamie McQuilkin. It was originally published in *Intergenerational Justice Review*, which contains a full discussion of its conceptual and methodological underpinnings.[1] The analysis in this book is based on an updated version of the index, which contains time series data for 122 countries each year from 2015 to 2019 (or the most recent years for which data are available), and includes adjustments to some of the component measures. Most indicators are based on data distribution not target values (with the exception of mortality-adjusted birth rate), and are calculated on the basis of five-year averages. The full dataset and detailed information about the construction of the index can be found at www.goodancestorproject.org.

The index contains ten indicators, which fall broadly into three dimensions: environmental, social and economic. They are summarised in the table below.

	INDICATOR	METRIC	SOURCE
Environmental	**Forest Depletion**	Annual forest cover change (%)	FAO
	Carbon Footprint	Carbon footprint intensity ($ GDP (PPP) per GHa)	Ecological Footprint Network
	Renewable Energy	Renewable and nuclear energy (% of energy consumption)	US EIA
Social	**Primary Education**	Primary pupil-to-teacher ratio	UNESCO; national statistical bodies.
	Child Mortality	Difference between expected and actual child mortality, based on GDP/capita regression	UNICEF; WHO; World Bank; UN DESA.
	Population Growth	Predicted birth rate per woman (adjusted for child mortality)	UNICEF; WHO; World Bank; UN DESA.
Economic	**Wealth Inequality**	Wealth inequality Gini coefficient	Crédit Suisse
	Current Account	Current account balance (% of GDP)	IMF
	Net Savings	Adjusted Net Savings (% of GNI)	World Bank
Penalty	**Fossil Fuel Production**	Fossil fuel hydrocarbon production (Gigajoules/capita)	US EIA

Scores on the index run from 0 (low intergenerational solidarity) to 100 (high intergenerational solidarity). To calculate the final index score, the indicators in the environmental, social and economic dimensions are given equal weighting and aggregated arithmetically within dimensions and then geometrically between them, following the method of the United Nations Development Programme's Human Development Index. A final indicator, Fossil Fuel Production, is applied as a penalty adjustment to the overall score, due to its effects on intergenerational welfare.

The following map shows the geographic distribution of country scores for the 2019 version of the index.

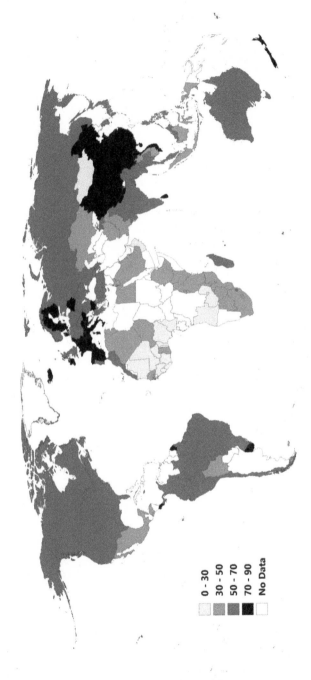

Scores for 122 countries on the Intergenerational Solidarity Index (2019).
A darker shade represents greater intergenerational solidarity

0 - 30
30 - 50
50 - 70
70 - 90
No Data

Acknowledgements

To my wonderful partner Kate Raworth, who not only helped me navigate fields such as systems thinking and earth system science – as well as the finer points of Doughnut Economics – but offered constant guidance, inspiration and support through my years of writing *The Good Ancestor*.

To my superb editors Drummond Moir and Suzanne Connelly, for their dedication, insight and wise advice; and to Patsy O'Neill, Jo Bennett, Andrew Goodfellow and everyone else at Ebury for giving the book such great support.

To my agent Maggie Hanbury, whose unwavering faith in my writing has continually raised my spirits and galvanised my determination, and without whom this book would not exist.

To Louisa Mann, Jen Hooke and Nikki Clegg from the Thirty Percy Foundation, for their invaluable and generous backing of the Good Ancestor Project.

To Jamie McQuilkin, for his brilliant work on the Intergenerational Solidarity Index, incisive critiques of the text and an enlightening 12-hour conversation on the possibilities and problems of long-term thinking.

To Brian Eno, for his intellectual generosity, comments on the manuscript and pathbreaking essay, 'The Big Here and Long Now', which I have returned to again and again.

To Nigel Hawtin, whose masterful graphic design work has given visual form to the ideas in the book.

To Sophia Blackwell, whose poetic eye and editorial scalpel did so much to improve the text, and to Ben Murphy for the magnificent index.

To Alicia Carey and Hawkwood College, for offering me a Changemaker Residency, where I wrote the chapter on intergenerational justice.

To Drew Dellinger, for the lines from his beautiful poem 'Hieroglyphic Stairway'.

To Tom Lee, for his fantastically inventive work on the video animations.

To the esteemed group of experts and friends who commented on the manuscript: Kevin Watkins, Lisa Gormley, Morten Kringelbach, Andrew Ray, Daan Roovers, Marc Jumelet, Kaj Lofgren, Christopher Daniel and Caspar Henderson.

To everyone who helped with their conversation, ideas and support: Caterina Ruggeri Laderchi, George Monbiot, Jonathan Salk, Mary Bennett, Samwel Nangiria, the Long Now Foundation and members of Long Now London, Stuart Candy, Svante Thunberg, Greta Thunberg, Richard Fisher, Jeremy Lent, Ari Wallach, Camilla Bustani, James Hill, Sophie Howe, Gijs van Hensbergen, Ella Saltmarshe and Beatrice Pembroke from the Long Time Project, Jonathan Smith, John Steele and the Sturmark team, everyone at the Empathy Museum, Rebecca Wrigley, Michael Bhaskar, Juliet Davenport, Mark Shorrock, David Kelly, Philippa Kelly, Luke Kemp, Toby Ord, Max Harris, Katie Paterson, Carlo Giardinetti, Nanaia Mahuta, Jane Riddiford and Rod Sugden from Global Generation, Anab Jain and Jon Ardern from Superflux, Sophie Howarth, Anthony Barnett, Judith Herrin, Tony Langtry, Jennifer Thorp, Tebaldo Vinciguerra, Pablo Suarez and Chris Jardine.

And finally to my children, Siri and Cas – futureholders whose ideas, advice and tolerance helped make this a better book and make me proud to be their father.

Endnotes

1: How Can We Be Good Ancestors?

1 Salk first mentioned the concept of the 'good ancestor' in 1977 (Jonas Salk, 'Are We Being Good Ancestors?', Acceptance Speech for the Jawaharlal Nehru Award for International Understanding, New Delhi, 10 January 1977. Reprinted in *World Affairs: The Journal of International Issues*, Vol. 1, No. 2 (December 1992)). Others who have since been inspired by the concept – which may have roots in indigenous cultures – include ecological campaigner David Suzuki, cultural critic Lewis Hyde, Dakota activist Winona LaDuke, futurists Bina Venkataraman and Ari Wallach, racial justice activist Layla Saad, design thinker Alan Cooper, leadership thinker James Kerr, nature writer Robert Macfarlane and tech strategist Tyler Emerson. For Salk's philosophy of long-term thinking, see Jonas Salk, *Anatomy of Reality: Merging of Intuition and Reason* (Columbia University Press, 1983), p. 8, p. 12, p. 105, p. 109, pp. 114–18, pp. 122–3), Jonathan Salk, 'Planetary Health: A New Perspective', *Challenges*, Vol. 10, No. 7 (2019): p. 5, and *A New Reality: Human Evolution for a Sustainable Future* by Jonas Salk and Jonathan Salk (City Point Press, 2018).

2 Mary Catherine Bateson, *Composing a Further Life: The Age of Active Wisdom* (Vintage, 2011), p. 22.

3 See Simon Caney, 'Democratic Reform, Intergenerational Justice and the Challenges of the Long-Term', Centre for the Understanding of Sustainability Prosperity, University of Surrey (2019), p. 4, on the concept of 'harmful short-termism'. For a comprehensive analysis of short-termism in politics, see Jonathan Boston, *Governing the Future: Designing Democratic Institutions for a Better Tomorrow* (Emerald, 2017).

4 Oxford University existential risk expert and philosopher Toby Ord puts the figure at one in six (with the biggest threat coming from AI), while a survey by the university's Future of Humanity Institute resulted in a slightly higher

figure of 19 per cent (Toby Ord, *The Precipice* (Bloomsbury, 2020), p. 167); https://thebulletin.org/2016/09/how-likely-is-an-existential-catastrophe/). When I asked existential risk researcher Anders Sandberg for his estimate, he replied that 'there's only a 12 per cent chance that we're doomed' (talk at The Hub, Oxford, 21 May 2018). Measuring the components of existential risk is, undoubtedly, an inexact and somewhat speculative science. On Nick Bostrom's fears about nanotechnology, see https://www.nickbostrom.com/existential/risks.html.

5 https://www.theguardian.com/society/2005/jan/13/environment.science; Jared Diamond, *Collapse: How Societies Choose to Fail or Survive* (Penguin, 2011), p. 522. See also Will Steffen and Johan Rockström et al., 'Trajectories of the Earth System in the Anthropocene', *PNAS*, Vol. 115. No. 33 (2019).

6 Quotes from Attenborough's speech to the UN COP24 climate talks in Poland on 3 December 2019, and his BBC TV programme, *Climate Change: The Facts*, broadcast 18 May 2019.

7 My use of the term *'terra nullius'* draws on the work of the historian of indigenous land rights in Australia, Henry Reynolds: https://www.themonthly.com.au/books-henry-reynolds-new-historical-landscape-responce-michael-connor039s-039the-invention-terra-nul. The idea of the future as a colonised territory was, to my knowledge, first hinted at in the writings of the pioneering Austrian futurist Robert Jungk, *Tomorrow is Already Here: Scenes from a Man-Made Word* (Rupert Hart-Davis, 1954), pp. 16–19. The metaphor appears more explicitly in the work of foresight scholar Jim Dator ('Decolonizing the Future', in Andrew Spekke (ed.), *The Next 25 Years: Challenges and Opportunities* (World Future Society, 1975)) and sociologist Barbara Adam (*Time* (Polity Press, 2004), pp. 136–43).

8 Martin Rees, *On the Future: Prospects for Humanity* (Princeton University Press, 2018), pp. 226–7. His comments on China were made at a talk about his latest book, *On the Future*, at Blackwell's Bookshop, Oxford, on 5 November 2018.

9 'The Short Long', speech by Andy Haldane, Brussels, May 2011. https://www.bankofengland.co.uk/-/media/boe/files/speech/2011/the-short-long-speech-by-andrew-haldane.

10 'Global Guardians: A Voice for the Future', Mary Robinson Foundation – Climate Justice Position Paper (April, 2017, p. 6); Pope Francis, 'Laudato Si", Encyclical Letter of the Holy Father Francis, Vatican City, Rome (2015). p. 118, p. 178.

11 Among the few exceptions to this intellectual vacuum is Ari Wallach's concept of 'longpath': https://www.longpath.org/. Thanks to Graham Leicester for the idea of a 'conceptual emergency': http://www.internationalfuturesforum.com/s/223.

12 For a review of these theories of social change, see my Oxfam report, 'How Change Happens: Interdisciplinary Perspectives for Human Development', an Oxfam Research Report (Oxfam, 2007).

13 Brian Eno, 'The Big Here and Long Now', Long Now Foundation, San Francisco (2000).

14 Charles D. Ellis, *The Partnership: The Making of Goldman Sachs* (Penguin, 2009), pp. 177–80.

15 John Dryzek, 'Institutions for the Anthropocene: Governance in a Changing Earth System', *British Journal of Political Studies*, Vol. 46 No. 4 (2014): pp. 937–41.

16 For a review of different time frames for envisioning the future, see Richard Slaughter, 'Long-Term Thinking and the Politics of Reconceptualization', *Futures*, Vol. 28, No. 1 (1996): pp. 75–86.

17 Stewart Brand, *The Clock of the Long Now: Time And Responsibility* (Phoenix, 1999), pp. 4–5.

18 Terry Eagleton, *Hope Without Optimism* (Yale University Press, 2015), pp. 1–38.

2: The Marshmallow and the Acorn

1 https://www.nytimes.com/interactive/2018/08/01/magazine/climate-change-losing-earth.html?hp&action=click&pgtype=Homepage&clickSource= story-heading&module=photo-spot-region&region=top-news&WT.nav= top-news. For a searing rebuke of Rich's view by Naomi Klein, see https://theintercept.com/2018/08/03/climate-change-new-york-times-magazine/.

2 Morten Kringelbach, *The Pleasure Centre: Trust Your Animal Instincts* (Oxford University Press, 2009), pp. 55–6; Kent Berridge and Morten Kringelbach, 'Affective Neuroscience of Pleasure: Reward in Humans and Animals', *Psychopharmacology*, Vol. 199, No.3 (2008); Morten Kringelbach and Helen Phillips, *Emotion: Pleasure and Pain in the Brain* (Oxford University Press, 2014), pp. 124–31.

3 Maureen O'Leary et al., 'The Placental Mammal Ancestor and the Post-K-Pg Radiation of Placentals', *Science*, Vol. 339 No. 6,120 (2013); https://www.nytimes.com/2013/02/08/science/common-ancestor-of-mammals-plucked-from-obscurity.html?_r=1&.

4 John Ratey, *A User's Guide to the Brain* (Abacus, 2013), p. 115.

5 Peter Whybrow, *The Well-Tuned Brain: A Remedy for a Manic Society* (Norton, 2016), p. 6; http://www.zocalopublicsquare.org/2015/09/18/low-interest-rates-are-bad-for-your-brain/ideas/nexus/.

6 Whybrow, pp. 112–13.

7 Walter Mischel, Yuichi Shoda and Monica Rodriguez, 'Delay of Gratification in Children', *Science*, Vol. 244, No. 4,907 (1989): pp. 933–98; http://behavioralscientist.org/try-to-resist-misinterpreting-the-marshmallow-test/; Kringelbach and Phillips, pp. 164–5; http://theconversation.com/its-not-a-lack-of-self-control-that-keeps-people-poor-47734.

8 Martin Seligman, Peter Railton, Roy Baumeister and Chandra Sripada, *Homo Prospectus* (Oxford University Press, 2016), p. ix.

9 Daniel Gilbert, *Stumbling on Happiness* (Harper Perennial, 2007), p. 9; Seligman et al., p. xi.

10 W. A. Roberts, 'Are Animals Stuck in Time?', *Psychological Bulletin*, Vol. 128, No. 3 (2002): pp. 481–6; Roland Ennos, 'Aping Our Ancestor', *Physics World* (May 2014).

11 https://www.nytimes.com/2017/05/19/opinion/sunday/why-the-future-is-always-on-your-mind.html.

12 Thomas Princen, 'Long-Term Decision-Making: Biological and Psychological Evidence', *Global Environmental Politics*, Vol. 9, No. 3 (2009): p. 12; David Passig,

'Future Time-Span as a Cognitive Skill in Future Studies', *Futures Research Quarterly* (Winter 2004): pp. 31–2; Jane Busby Grant and Thomas Suddendort, 'Recalling Yesterday and Predicting Tomorrow', *Cognitive Development*, Vol. 20 (2005).

13 Roy Baumeister et al, 'Everyday Thoughts in Time: Experience Sampling Studies of Mental Time Travel', *PsyArXiv* (2018), p. 22, p. 45.

14 Gilbert, pp. 10–15; Ricarda Schubotz, 'Long-Term Planning and Prediction: Visiting a Construction Site in the Human Brain', in W. Welsch et al. (eds), *Interdisciplinary Anthropology* (Springer-Verlag, 2011), p. 79.

15 Baumeister et al., p. 20.

16 http://www.randomhouse.com/kvpa/gilbert/blog/200607.html.

17 https://www.npr.org/templates/story/story.php?storyId=5530483.

18 Peter Railton, 'Introduction', in Martin Seligman, Peter Railton, Roy Baumeister and Chandra Sripada, *Homo Prospectus* (Oxford University Press, 2016), p. 4.

19 Princen, 'Long-Term Decision-Making', p. 13.

20 https://www.nytimes.com/2016/03/20/magazine/the-secrets-of-the-wave-pilots.html; Sander van der Leeuw, David Lane and Dwight Read, 'The Long-Term Evolution of Social Organization', in David Lane et al. (eds), *Complexity Perspectives in Innovation and Social Change* (Springer, 2009), p. 96; Jerome Barkow, Leda Cosmides and John Tooby, *The Adapted Mind: Evolutionary Psychology and the Generation of Culture* (Oxford University Press, 1996), pp. 584–5.

21 Princen, 'Long-Term Decision-Making', pp. 14–15; Kristen Hawkes, 'The Grandmother Effect', *Nature*, Vol. 428, No. 128 (2004): pp. 128–9.

22 http://longnow.org/seminars/02011/feb/09/live-longer-think-longer/; Bateson, pp. 14–15.

23 Roman Krznaric, *Empathy: Why It Matters, and How to Get It* (Rider Books, 2015), pp. 4–5.

24 Charles Darwin, *The Descent of Man* (Appleton and Company, 1889), p. 132.

25 https://www.romankrznaric.com/outrospection/2009/11/14/152; see also Chapter
    1 of my book *Empathy* (2015), which discusses the research on our empathic
    natures in evolutionary biology, neuroscience and developmental psychology.

26 Seligman et al., p. 5. See also Railton, pp. 25–6 and Roy Baumeister, 'Collective
    Prospection: The Social Construction of the Future', in Selegman et al., p. 143.

27 Van der Leeuw, Lane and Read, pp. 88–92; Sander van der Leeuw, 'The
    Archaeology of Innovation: Lessons for Our Times', in Carlson Curtis and Frank
    Moss (eds), *Innovation: Perspectives for the 21st Century* (BBVA, 2010), p. 38; David
    Christian, *Maps of Time: An Introduction to Big History* (University of California
    Press, 2005), p. 160.

28 Van der Leeuw, Lane and Read, p. 91.

29 Van der Leeuw, Lane and Read, p. 96.

30 Bruce E. Tonn, Angela Hemrick and Fred Conrad, 'Cognitive Representations of
    the Future: Survey Results', *Futures*, Vol. 38 (2006): p. 818.

3: Deep-Time Humility

 1 John G. Neihardt, *Black Elk Speaks* (Excelsior, 2008), pp. 155–6.

 2 Jacques Le Goff, *Time, Work, and Culture in the Middle Ages* (Chicago University
    Press, 1980), pp. 29–42; Jacques Le Goff, *Medieval Civilization 400–1500* (Folio
    Society, 2011), p. 171, p. 175, pp. 180–1, pp. 181–2; Jeremy Rifkin, *Time Wars: The
    Primary Conflict in Human History* (Touchstone, 1987), pp. 158–9; Barbara Adam
    and Chris Groves, *Future Matters: Marking, Making and Minding Futures for the 21st
    Century* (Brill, 2007), p. 7.

 3 E.P. Thompson, 'Time, Work Discipline and Industrial Capitalism', *Past &
    Present*, Vol. 38, No. 1 (1967): pp. 64–5.

 4 Lewis Mumford, *The Human Prospect* (Beacon Press, 1955), p. 4.

 5 https://www.theguardian.com/commentisfree/2018/may/27/
    world-distraction-demands-new-focus.

6 https://www.theguardian.com/technology/2018/mar/04/has-dopamine-got-us-hooked-on-tech-facebook-apps-addiction.

7 Rifkin, *Time Wars*, pp. 12–13, p. 226.

8 John McPhee, *Basin and Range* (Farrar, Straus and Giroux, 1980), pp. 91–108; Stephen Jay Gould, *Time's Arrow, Time's Cycle: Myth and Metaphor in the Discovery of Geological Time* (Harvard University Press, 1987), pp. 61–5; Bill Bryson, *A Short History of Nearly Everything* (Black Swan, 2004), pp. 90–108.

9 Gould, p. 62.

10 Bryson, pp. 104–5.

11 H.G. Wells, *The Discovery of the Future* (B.W. Huebsch, 1913), p. 18, p. 29, p. 32.

12 H.G. Wells, *The Conquest of Time* (Watts, 1942), p. 12.

13 James Gleick, *Time Travel: A History* (Fourth Estate, 2016), pp. 23–4.

14 Brand, *The Clock of the Long Now*, p. 2.

15 http://longnow.org/clock/.

16 Such critiques have been made by, among others, the philosopher Stefan Skrimshire, 'Deep Time and Secular Time: A Critique of the Environmental "Long View"', *Theory, Culture and Society*, Vol. 36, No. 1 (2018), pp. 6–8, and economist Mariana Mazzucato (in comments at the 'Planning for a Longer Now' seminar, British Library, London, 24 September 2018).

17 Quoted in Gould, p. 3; see also McPhee, p. 126.

18 https://www.theguardian.com/science/2005/apr/07/science.highereducation.

19 http://www.rachelsussman.com/portfolio/#/oltw/; https://www.mnn.com/earth-matters/wilderness-resources/photos/the-worlds-10-oldest-living-trees/olive-tree-of-vouves#top-desktop.

20 V. Bellassen and S. Luyssaert, 'Carbon Sequestration: Managing Forests in Uncertain Times', *Nature*, Vol. 13, No. 506 (2014).

21 https://www.theguardian.com/books/2019/may/11/richard-powers-interview-the-overstory-radicalised.

22 Thich Nhat Hanh, *Being Peace* (London, 1989), p. 109.

4: Legacy Mindset

1 The two sentences in this quote appear respectively on p. 3 and p. 4 of Jonas Salk's 1977 speech, 'Are We Being Good Ancestors?'.

2 The desire to leave a leave a legacy that nurtures and shapes future generations is known as 'generativity', and goes back to the work of psychologist Erik Erikson in the 1950s (John Kotre, *Make It Count: How to Generate a Legacy That Gives Meaning to Your Life* (The Free Press, 1995) p. 5, p. 11, p. 15; John Kotre, 'Generative Outcome', *Journal of Aging Studies*, Vol. 9, No. 1 (1995) p. 36; http://www.johnkotre.com/generativity.htm).

3 Michael Sanders, Sarah Smith, Bibi Groot and David Nolan, 'Legacy Giving and Behavioural Insights', Behavioural Insights Team, University of Bristol (2016), p. 2, p. 6; https://www.philanthropy.com/article/Donations-Grow-4-to-373/236790; https://givingusa.org/giving-usa-2019-americans-gave-427-71-billion-to-charity-in-2018-amid-complex-year-for-charitable-giving/.

4 Kimberley Wade-Benzoni et al., 'It's Only a Matter of Time: Death, Legacies, and Intergenerational Decisions', *Psychological Science*, Vol. 23, No. 7 (2012), pp. 705–6; Kimberley Wade-Benzoni, 'Legacy Motivations and the Psychology of Intergenerational Decisions', *Current Opinion in Psychology*, Vol. 26 (April 2019): p. 21.

5 Lisa Zaval, Ezra M. Markowitz and Elke U. Weber, 'How Will I Be Remembered? Conserving the Environment for the Sake of One's Legacy', *Psychological Science*, Vol. 26, No. 2 (2015): p. 235.

6 Michael Sanders and Sarah Smith, 'Can Simple Prompts Increase Bequest Giving? Field Evidence from a Legal Call Centre', *Journal of Economic Behaviour and Organization*, Vol. 125(C) (2016): p. 184.

7 See Chapter 2 of my book *Carpe Diem Regained* (Unbound, 2017).

8 Hal Hershfield et al., 'Increasing Saving Behavior Through Age-Progressed Renders of the Future Self', *Journal of Marketing Research*, Vol. 48 (2011); Hal Hershfield, 'The Self Over Time', *Current Opinion in Psychology*, Vol. 26 (2019): p. 73; Bina Venkataraman, *The Optimist's Telescope: Thinking Ahead in a Reckless Age* (Riverhead, 2019), pp. 20–1.

9 https://twitter.com/stewartbrand/status/1106102872372985856.

10 Lewis Hyde, *The Gift: How the Creative Spirit Transforms the World* (Canongate, 2006), pp. 11–16.

11 https://theanarchistlibrary.org/library/petr-kropotkin-the-conquest-of-bread.

12 Hunger Lovins, Stewart Wallis, Anders Wijkman, John Fullerton, *A Finer Future: Creating an Economy in Service to Life* (New Society Publishers, 2018), p. xiv.

13 Kris Jeter, 'Ancestor Worship as an Intergenerational Linkage in Perpetuity', *Marriage & Family Review*, Vol. 16, Nos 1–2 (1991), p. 196, p. 199.

14 In a speech at the Politics of Love Conference, All Souls College, Oxford University, 15 December 2018, and in the following interview: https://learnlawlife.co.nz/2017/10/30/2654/.

15 Lesley Kay Rameka , 'Kia whakatōmuri te haere whakamua: I walk backwards into the future with my eyes fixed on my past', *Contemporary Issues in Early Childhood*, Vol. 17, No. 4 (2017): pp. 387–9; Margaret Nicholls, 'What Motivates Intergenerational Practices in Aotearoa/New Zealand', *Journal of Intergenerational Relationships*, Vol. 1, No. 1 (2003), p. 180; https://teara.govt.nz/en/whakapapa-genealogy/print.

16 https://www.vice.com/en_us/article/9k95ey/its-transformative-maori-women-talk-about-their-sacred-chin-tattoos.

17 https://enablingcatalysts.com/legacy-our-first-responsibility-is-to-be-a-good-ancestor/.

18 Jeter, pp. 215–16.

5: Intergenerational Justice

1 https://quoteinvestigator.com/2018/05/09/posterity-ever/.

2 https://www.lifegate.com/people/news/greta-thunberg-speech-cop24.

3 Official government discount rates are sometimes structured to decline through time, and differ depending on expected project risk (Mark Freeman, Ben Groom and Michael Spackman, 'Social Discount Rates for Cost-Benefit Analysis: A Report for HM Treasury', HM Treasury, UK Government (2018), p. 5, p. 12, p. 15).

4 The UK Treasury's Green Book, used as the basis for cost-benefit analysis and discounting, sets the standard discount rate at 3.5 per cent. It is comprised of two components: a 'time preference' of 1.5 per cent, which reflects the preference for value now rather than later; and a 'wealth effect', which assumes annual economic growth of 2 per cent. Benefits that accrue after 60 years are not generally included in project appraisals, so in effect the discount rate rises to 100 per cent at this point (HM Treasury, *The Green Book: Central Government Guidance on Appraisal and Evaluation* (HM Treasury, UK Government, 2018), pp. 101–3). For details of the Swansea tidal lagoon ruling, see: http://www.tidallagoonpower.com/wp-content/uploads/2018/07/BEIS-statement-on-Swansea-Bay-Tidal-Lagoon.pdf; https://blackfishengineering.com/2018/07/27/analysis-swansea-bay-tidal-lagoon/; https://researchbriefings.parliament.uk/ResearchBriefing/Summary/CBP-7940.

5 Personal conversation, 26 May 2019.

6 Stern set the time preference component of the discount rate at 0.1 per cent (considerably less than the Treasury's usual 1.5 per cent), and the growth component at 1.3 per cent: Nicholas Stern, *The Economics of Climate Change: The Stern Review* (Cambridge University Press, 2014), p. i, p. ix, p. xii, p. 304, p. 629; Frank Ackerman, 'Debating Climate Economics: The Stern Review vs Its Critics', Report to Friends of the Earth UK (July 2007), p. 5.

7 United Nations Development Programme, Human Development Report 2007/8: Fighting Climate Change – Human Solidarity in a Divided World (UNDP, 2007), p. 29.

8 United Nations Development Programme, p. 63.

9 The architects of the UDHR may have wanted to prevent any repeat of the atrocities of the Second World War in the future – vowing 'never again' – but they showed no explicit concern for the possibility that people in the present might violate the rights of people in the future.

10 Gro Harlen Brundtland, *Report of the World Commission on Environment and Development: Our Common Future*, United Nations General Assembly document A/42/427 (1987). The phrase 'future generations' was recognised earlier, in the 1972 Declaration of the United Nations Conference on the Human Environment, but did not enter widespread usage until the Brundtland Report.

11 'A Case for Guardians of the Future', Mary Robinson Foundation – Climate Justice Position Paper (February 2017), p. 1, p. 6; Joerg Chet Tremmel (ed.), *Handbook of Intergenerational Justice* (Edward Elgar, 2006), pp. 192–6; Jamie McQuilkin, 'Doing Justice to the Future: A Global Index of Intergenerational Solidarity Derived from National Statistics', *Intergenerational Justice Review*, Vol. 4, No. 1 (2018), p. 5.

12 http://www.italiaclima.org/wp-content/uploads/2015/01/ITA_SFPM_Italian-Youth-Declaration-on-Intergenerational-Equity_Eng_Definitive.pdf.

13 https://www.medact.org/2019/blogs/fighting-for-intergenerational-justice-midwives-can-be-climate-champions/.

14 Mark O'Brien and Thomas Ryan, 'Rights and Representation of Future Generations in United Kingdom Policy', Centre for the Study of Existential Risk, University of Cambridge (2017), pp. 13–18.

15 Pope Francis.

16 https://globalnutritionreport.org/reports/global-nutrition-report-2018/burden-malnutrition/.

17 See, for instance, a report from Cambridge University's Centre for the Study of Existential Risk arguing for the creation of an All-Party Parliamentary Group for Future Generations in the UK (O'Brien and Ryan, p. 13).

18 Derek Parfit, *Reasons and Persons* (Clarendon Press, 1987), p. 357.

19 Nicholas Vroussalis, 'Intergenerational Justice: A Primer', in Iñigo González-Ricoy and Axel Grosseries (eds), *Institutions for Future Generations* (Oxford University Press, 2016), p. 59

20 Barry S. Gower, 'What Do We Owe Future Generations?', in David E. Cooper and Joy A. Palmer (eds), *Environment in Question: Ethics and Global Issues* (Routledge, 1992), p. 1.

21 This graphic is a revised and reconfigured version of a BBC Future graphic originally conceived by Richard Fisher, with design by Nigel Hawtin: http://www.bbc.com/future/story/20190109-the-perils-of-short-termism-civilisations-greatest-threat. The data for the future projection is based on the standard UN estimate that the average number of births per year in the twenty-first century will stabilise at around 135 million. See https://ourworldindata.org/future-population-growth.

22 The best known of these, the Difference Principle, states that social and economic inequalities are to be arranged so they offer the greatest benefit to the least advantaged members of society (John Rawls, *Political Liberalism* (Columbia University Press, 1993), p. 83).

23 Rawls's discussion of this issue referred to the need for a 'just savings principle' (Rawls, *Political Liberalism*, pp. 284–93; Bruce E. Tonn, 'Philosophical, Institutional, and Decision Making Frameworks for Meeting Obligations to Future Generations', *Futures*, Vol. 95 (2017): p. 46; O'Brien and Ryan, p. 14).

24 Rawls didn't consider that a healthy ecosystem was of any importance for a future just society. He was a philosopher of the Holocene, not the Anthropocene. For useful discussions see O'Brien and Ryan, p. 14, Tonn, 'Philosophical, Institutional, and Decision Making Frameworks', p. 44, and Mary Robinson Foundation, 'A Case for Guardians of the Future', p. 2.

25 Tonn, 'Philosophical, Institutional, and Decision Making Frameworks', p. 47; Rawls, *Political Liberalism*, p. 274.

26 https://www.sefaria.org/Taanit.23a?lang=bi.

27 Quoted in Princen, 'Long-Term Decision-Making', p. 11.

28 John Borrows, 'Earth-Bound: Indigenous Resurgence and Environmental Reconciliation', in Michael Asch, John Borrows and James Tully (eds), *Resurgence and Reconciliation: Indigenous–Settler Relations and Earth Teachings* (University of Toronto Press, 2018), p. 62.

29 Personal conversation with the author, Oxford, 14 November 2017.

30 Pope Francis, p. 118; Roman Krznaric, 'For God's Sake, Do Something! How Religions Can Find Unexpected Unity Around Climate Change', Human Development Occasional Papers, Human Development Report Office, United Nations Development Programme (2007).

31 https://therealnews.com/stories/dlascaris0504susuki.

32 David Suzuki, *The Legacy: An Elder's Vision for Our Sustainable Future* (Greystone Books, 2010), p. 55, pp. 71–5.

33 https://www.nas.org/articles/Seventh_Generation_Sustainability_-_A_New_Myth.

34 https://www.bbc.co.uk/ideas/videos/how-can-we-be-better-ancestors-to-future-generatio/p0818lnv?playlist=sustainable-thinking.

35 http://ecoactive.com/care-for-earth/earth-guardians; https://www.earthguardians.org/engage/2017/5/17.

36 http://www.souken.kochi-tech.ac.jp/seido/wp/SDES-2015-14.pdf; http://www.ceids.osaka-u.ac.jp/img/CEIDS_NL_NO.3(English).pdf.

37 https://workthatreconnects.org/the-seventh-generation/.

38 The Plantagon International holding company went bankrupt in 2019. The fate of its CityFarm in Kungsholmen, Sweden, and its multiple patents for vertical farming, were unknown at the time of writing.

39 https://www.aapss.org/news/crafting-rules-to-sustain-resources/.

6: Cathedral Thinking

1 http://www.gutenberg.org/files/35898/35898-h/35898-h.htm.

2 Personal correspondence, 14 May 2018. See also Jennifer Thorp, 'New College's Hall and Chapel Roofs', manuscript, New College, Oxford (2009).

3 Diamond, *Collapse*, p. 523.

4 Gijs Van Hensbergen, *The Sagrada Família: Gaudí's Heaven on Earth* (Bloomsbury, 2017), p. 4, p. 16, p. 28, p. 72.

5 When I met Thunberg in Rome a few days after the fire at Notre Dame in Paris in April 2019, she was incensed that the cathedral had already received funding pledges of hundreds of millions of euros to rebuild it, while governments were failing so dismally to finance the climate emergency. https://cathedralthinking.com/thinkers-cathedral-thinking/; https://www.theguardian.com/environment/2019/apr/16/greta-thunberg-urges-eu-leaders-wake-up-climate-change-school-strike-movement.

6 https://www.theguardian.com/science/2011/apr/06/templeton-prize-2011-martin-rees-speech.

7 Such projects, like the Svalbard Seed Vault, have been referred to as 'deep-time organisations' (Frederic Hanusch and Frank Biermann, 'Deep-Time Organizations: Learning Institutional Longevity from History', *The Anthropocene Review* (2019): pp. 1–3.

8 Robert Macfarlane, *Underland: A Deep Time Journey* (Hamish Hamilton, 2019), pp. 398–410.

9 Over time, the suffragette leadership developed more militant tactics due to their frustration with the slow pace of reform. https://www.bl.uk/votes-for-women/articles/suffragettes-violence-and-militancy.

10 https://www.nytimes.com/1982/01/15/world/soviet-food-shortages-grumbling-and-excuses.html.

11 https://theconversation.com/introducing-the-terrifying-mathematics-of-the-anthropocene-70749; https://web.archive.org/web/20070714085318/http://www.wbcsd.org/DocRoot/1IBetslPgkEie83rTa0J/cement-action-plan.pdf.

12 James Scott, *Seeing Like a State: How Certain Schemes to Improve the Human Condition Have Failed* (Yale University Press, 1998), p. 111.

13 Conrad Totman, *The Green Archipelago: Forestry in Pre-Industrial Japan* (Ohio University Press, 1989), p. 171.

14 Totman, *The Green Archipelago*, p. 79; Conrad Totman, *A History of Japan* (Blackwell, 2005), p. 255; Diamond, *Collapse*, p. 299.

15 Totman, *The Green Archipelago*, pp. 166–7.

16 Diamond, *Collapse*, pp. 304–5. For a more detailed analysis of the Tokugawa reforestation programme, see the report I wrote for the United Nations Development Programme on this topic (Roman Krznaric, 'Food Coupons and Bald Mountains: What the History of Resource Scarcity Can Teach Us About Tackling Climate Change', Human Development Occasional Papers, Human Development Report Office, United Nations Development Programme (2007)). There was a certain amount of grassroots community action alongside the top-down planning, for instance villages planted forests on communal lands to ensure an inheritance for future generations.

17 https://www.prospectmagazine.co.uk/magazine/if-i-ruled-the-world-martin-rees; https://www.theguardian.com/science/2010/mar/29/james-lovelock-climate-change.

18 Our exchange took place when Martin Rees was presenting his latest book, *On the Future*, at Blackwell's Bookshop, Oxford, on 5 November 2018.

19 https://yearbook.enerdata.net/renewables/renewable-in-electricity-production-share.html; https://www.tandfonline.com/doi/abs/10.1080/13569775.2013.773204.

20 Stephen Halliday, *The Great Stink of London: Sir Joseph Bazalgette and the Cleansing of the Victorian Metropolis* (Sutton Publishing, 2001), pp. 42–61, p. 124.

21 Quoted in Halliday, p. 74.

22 Quoted in Halliday, p. 3.

23 Natasha McCarthy, *Engineering: A Beginner's Guide* (Oneworld, 2009), p. 115.

24 Stewart Brand, *How Buildings Learn: What Happens After They're Built* (Phoenix, 1997), p. 181.

25 See the discussion on the importance of resilience and self-organisation for effective system functioning in Donella Meadows, *Thinking in Systems: A Primer* (Earthscan, 2009), pp. 75–81.

26 For my analysis of rationing policies in the Britain and the United States during the Second World War, see Krznaric, 'Food Coupons and Bald Mountains'.

27 https://www.weforum.org/agenda/2019/01/our-house-is-on-fire-16-year-old-greta-thunberg-speaks-truth-to-power/.

28 Milton Friedman, *Capitalism and Freedom* (Chicago University Press, 2002), p. xiv.

29 Diamond, *Collapse*, p. 519; Frank van Schoubroeck and Harm Kool, 'The Remarkable History of Polder Systems in the Netherlands', FAO, Rome (2010). For a fascinating study of communal water management in Bali, see Stephen Lansing, *Perfect Order: Recognizing Complexity in Bali* (Princeton University Press, 2006).

7: Holistic Forecasting

1 This story about the Nile priests was often told by Pierre Wack, one of the pioneers of scenario planning. Predictions were also made using measuring gauges called Nilometers, whose varying levels helped determine tax rates. Peter Schwartz, *The Art of the Long View: Planning the Future in an Uncertain World* (Currency, 1991), pp. 100–1, p. 109; Thomas Chermack, *The Foundations of Scenario Planning: The Story of Pierre Wack* (Routledge, 2017); https://news.nationalgeographic.com/2016/05/160517-nilometer-discovered-ancient-egypt-nile-river-archaeology/.

2 Jennifer M. Gidley, *The Future: A Very Short Introduction* (Oxford University Press, 2017), p. 2; Adam and Groves, pp. 2–3, p. 13; Bertrand de Jouvenel, *The Art of*

Conjecture (Weidenfeld & Nicolson, 1967), p. 89. For a classic account of forecasting as a scientific endeavour, see Alvin Toffler's *Future Shock* (Pan, 1971). Toffler was a champion of 'scientific futurism'.

3 It is sometimes also known as the 'cone of possibility' (Paul Saffo, 'Six Rules for Effective Forecasting', *Harvard Business Review* (July–August 2007)).

4 Nassim Nicholas Taleb, *The Black Swan: The Impact of the Highly Improbable* (Penguin, 2007), p. xii.

5 I have updated Harari's example, using 2020 as the base year instead of 2016 (Yuval Noah Harari, *Homo Deus: A Brief History of Tomorrow* (Vintage, 2017), p. 67).

6 Steven Johnson, *Farsighted: How We Make the Decisions That Matter Most* (Riverhead, 2018), pp. 82–3.

7 Charles Handy, *The Second Curve: Thoughts on Reinventing Society* (Random House Books, 2015), pp. 22–5.

8 Saffo. Tech forecasters frequently quote Moore's Law, which states that the number of transistors that would fit on a silicon wafer doubles around every two years, and present it as an ever-upswinging exponential J-curve. Yet even Singularity guru Ray Kurzweil admits that it will eventually turn into an S (Theodore Modis, 'Why the Singularity Cannot Happen', in A.H. Eden et al. (eds), *The Singularity Hypotheses, The Frontiers Collection* (Springer Verlag, 2012), pp. 314–17).

9 Fritjof Capra, *The Turning Point: Science, Society and the Rising Culture* (Flamingo, 1983), p. 8, p. 12.

10 Sigmoid curves are a key part of the analysis in the original *The Limits to Growth* report (Donella Meadows, Dennis Meadows, Jorgen Randers and William Behrens, *The Limits to Growth* (Universe Books, 1972), pp. 91–2, pp. 124–6), and also appear in *Limits to Growth: The 30-Year Update*, where they are discussed more explicitly (Donella Meadows, Jorgen Randers and Dennis Meadows (Chelsea Green, 2004), pp. 137–8).

11 Kate Raworth, *Doughnut Economics: Seven Ways to Think Like a 21st-Century Economist* (Random House Books, 2017) p. 251.

12 Ugo Bardi, *The Seneca Effect: Why Growth is Slow but Collapse is Rapid* (Springer, 2017).

13 Salk and Salk, p. 31.

14 Jonathan Salk.

15 Jonas Salk, *Anatomy of Reality*, pp. 24–5; Salk and Salk, pp. 68–73, 90; Jonathan Salk.

16 Steven Pinker, *Enlightenment Now: The Case for Reason, Science, Humanism and Progress* (Viking, 2018), p. 32, p. 153, p. 154, p. 306, p. 327. For powerful critiques of his claims – especially about environmental progress – see Jeremy Lent's essay at Open Democracy (https://www.opendemocracy.net/en/transformation/steven-pinker-s-ideas-are-fatally-flawed-these-eight-graphs-show-why/), the open letter from anthropologist Jason Hickell (https://www.jasonhickel.org/blog/2019/2/3/pinker-and-global-poverty) and the dismantling of his environmental argument by George Monbiot (https://www.theguardian.com/commentisfree/2018/mar/07/environmental-calamity-facts-steven-pinker).

17 Pinker, pp. 327–8.

18 https://quoteinvestigator.com/2013/10/20/no-predict/.

19 Gidley, pp. 42–5; Hyeonju Son, 'The History of Western Futures Studies: An Exploration of the Intellectual Traditions and Three-Phase Periodization', *Futures*, Vol. 66 (February 2015): pp. 123–4; Jenny Andersson, 'The Great Future Debate and the Struggle for the World', *The American Historical Review*, Vol. 117, No. 5 (2012), pp. 1413–15.

20 Herman Kahn, *On Thermonuclear War* (Princeton University Press, 1960), pp. 20–1, p. 98. As an illustration of his rational pragmatism, Kahn even suggested that the elderly should be fed with contaminated food, as their life expectancy would not exceed the time it would take to die as a consequence of it.

21 https://www.newyorker.com/magazine/2005/06/27/fat-man; https://www.nytimes.com/2004/10/10/movies/truth-stranger-than-strangelove.html.

22 Pierre Wack 'Scenarios: Unchartered Waters Ahead', *Harvard Business Review* (September 1985), p. 73.

23 Wack, 'Scenarios: Unchartered Waters Ahead', p. 76 ; Pierre Wack, 'Scenarios: Shooting the Rapids', *Harvard Business Review* (November 1985), p. 146; Schwartz, pp. 7–9; https://www.strategy-business.com/article/8220?gko=4447f.

24 Son, p. 127.

25 Son, p. 128; Gidley, pp. 56–7; Wack, 'Scenarios: Shooting the Rapids', p. 15.

26 Steffen and Rockström et al., p. 4; Intergovernmental Panel on Climate Change, *Climate Change 2014: Synthesis Report* (IPCC, 2014), p. 70, p. 74.

27 This graphic is a revised and reconfigured version of a BBC Future graphic, designed by Nigel Hawtin and based on Luke Kemp's data, which can be found at: https://www.bbc.com/future/article/20190218-are-we-on-the-road-to-civilisation-collapse.

28 Ronald Wright, *A Short History of Progress* (Canongate, 2004), pp. 78–9; Joseph Tainter, 'Problem Solving: Complexity, History, Sustainability', *Population and Environment: A Journal of Interdisciplinary Studies*, Vol. 22, No. 1 (2000), p. 12; Jeremy Lent, *The Patterning Instinct: A Cultural History of Humanity's Search for Meaning* (Prometheus, 2017), p. 411; Diamond, *Collapse*, pp. 168–70.

29 Diamond, *Collapse*, pp. 420–40; Jared Diamond, 'Easter Island Revisited', *Science*, Vol. 317, No. 5,845 (2007): pp. 1692–4; Tainter, pp. 6–9, pp. 20–3; Graeme Cumming and Garry Peterson, 'Unifying Research on Social-Ecological Resilience and Collapse', *Trends in Ecology and Evolution*, Vol. 32, No. 9 (2017): pp. 699–706; http://www.marklynas.org/2011/09/the-myths-of-easter-island-jared-diamond-responds/.

30 Yuval Noah Harari is among those who argue that global society has become so interdependent that there is, in effect, 'just one civilization in the world' (Noah Yuval Harari, *21 Lessons for the 21st Century* (Jonathan Cape, 2018), p. 93).

31 Steffen and Rockström et al.

32 https://thebulletin.org/2016/09/how-likely-is-an-existential-catastrophe/.

33 The diagram draws on the Three Horizons framework created by futures thinker
Bill Sharpe (not to be confused with a McKinsey growth model of the same
name), which he describes as a tool for developing 'future consciousness'
(Graham Leicester, *Transformative Innovation: A Guide to Practice and Policy*
(Triarchy Press, 2016), pp. 44–52). The various trajectories are largely based on the
research findings of Paul Raskin ('Journey to Earthland: The Great Transition to
Planetary Civilization', Tellus Institute, Boston (2016), p. 26), Cumming and
Peterson, Rupert Read and Samuel Alexander (*This Civilization Is Finished:
Conversations on the End of Empire – and What Lies Beyond* (Simplicity Institute,
2019), p. 7) and Seth Baum et al. ('Long-Term Trajectories of Human Civilization',
Foresight, Vol. 21, No. 1 (2019): pp. 53–83). For a good summary of current debates
around collapse pathways, see the analysis by systems theorist Nafeez Ahmed.

34 David Wallace-Wells, *The Unhabitable Earth: A Story of the Future* (Allen Lane,
2019), p. 28.

35 Raskin, pp. 71–91.

8: Transcendent Goal

1 Princen, 'Long-Term Decision-Making, p. vii; Viktor Frankl, *Man's Search for
Meaning: An Introduction to Logotherapy* (Hodder & Stoughton, 1987), p. 20.

2 Carl Sagan, *Pale Blue Dot: A Vision of the Human Future in Space* (Ballantine
Books, 1997), p. 51, p. 333. The importance of having a telos has been discussed
by other long-term thinkers such as Ari Wallach. My own focus on having a
transcendent goal or telos has been particularly influenced by the pioneering
systems thinker Donella Meadows, who argued that one of the most effective
ways to change any complex system is to change its ultimate goal (Meadows,
p. 161, p. 194).

3 The idea of the maintenance of privilege over the long term is particularly
evident in conservative thought, especially in the writings of the philosopher
Edmund Burke. In 1790, Burke wrote that society is 'a partnership not only
between those who are living, but between those who are living, those who are
dead, and those who are to be born.' He believed that we should respect the
'stupendous wisdom' of the past that we have inherited 'from a long line of
ancestors'. This all sounds like an admirable vision of long-term thinking and
one based on intergenerational continuity. But Burke's real target was radical

French revolutionaries who were bent on overthrowing the monarchy and aristocracy that he so deeply admired as a bulwark against the mob. Burke believed in conserving their power and privilege in the face of the winds of change. He valued tradition because it was a way of keeping the existing system intact (Burke, *Reflections on the Revolution in France* (J. Dodsley, 1790), paragraphs 55, 56, 165).

4 Pinker, p. 6.

5 Wright, pp. 37–9; Lawrence Guy Straus, 'Upper Paleolithic Hunting Tactics and Weapons in Western Europe', *Archeological Papers of the American Anthropological Association*, Vol. 4, No. 1 (1993): pp. 89–93; George Frison, 'Paleoindian large mammal hunters on the plains of North America', *PNAS*, Vol. 95, No. 24 (1998): pp. 14,576–83.

6 Diamond, *Collapse*, pp. 427–9; George Monbiot, *Feral: Searching for Enchantment on the Frontiers of Rewilding* (Allen Lane, 2013), pp. 90–1, pp. 137–8; Wright, p. 37; Tim Flannery, *The Future Eaters: An Ecological History of the Australian Lands and People* (Secker & Warburg, 1996), p. 143, p. 155, pp. 180–6, pp. 307–8.

7 By capitalism, I mean an economic system based on the self-interested pursuit of profit, the rule of the market, and private property ownership, and where even human labour is a commodity for sale (Ellen Meiksins Wood, *The Origin of Capitalism: A Longer View* (Verso, 2017), p. 2).

8 E.A. Wrigley, *Energy and the English Industrial Revolution* (Cambridge University Press, 2010), p. 2, pp. 242–9.

9 http://worldif.economist.com/article/12121/debate; Tim Jackson, *Prosperity Without Growth: Foundations for the Economy of Tomorrow* (Routledge, 2016), pp. 1–23; Raworth, *Doughnut Economics*, p. 246.

10 This graph is based on the data in Will Steffen et al. 'The Trajectory of the Anthropocene: The Great Acceleration', *The Anthropocene Review*, Vol. 2, No. 1 (2015).

11 https://www.marxists.org/reference/archive/wilde-oscar/soul-man/.

12 Rifkin, *Time Wars*, p. 154.

13 Krznaric, 'For God's Sake, Do Something!', pp. 5–11.

14 Jonathan Porritt, *The World We Made* (Phaidon, 2013), p. 1.

15 Quoted in Maria Alex Lopez, *Invisible Women* (Palibrio, 2013), p. 36.

16 Sagan, pp. 309–12.

17 https://www.vox.com/the-goods/2018/11/2/18053824/elon-musk-death-mars-spacex-kara-swisher-interview; https://www.theguardian.com/technology/2018/mar/11/elon-musk-colonise-mars-third-world-war.

18 https://www.newscientist.com/article/2175414-terraforming-mars-might-be-impossible-due-to-a-lack-of-carbon-dioxide/.

19 Rees, p. 150. A similar point is made by the geologist Marcia Bjornerud: http://longnow.org/seminars/02019/jul/22/timefulness/.

20 I've borrowed the concept of techno-split from the cultural historian Jeremy Lent, p. 432.

21 Mark O'Connell, *To Be a Machine: Adventures Among Cyborgs, Utopians, Hackers, and the Futurists Solving the Modest Problem of Death* (Granta, 2017), p. 6, p. 29, p. 51.

22 O'Connell, pp. 54–5.

23 https://aeon.co/essays/we-are-more-than-our-brains-on-neuroscience-and-being-human.

24 Harari, *Homo Deus*, p. 408.

25 Rees, p. 58; Lent, p. 418.

26 https://www.ncbi.nlm.nih.gov/pubmed/15968832.

27 Read and Alexander, p. 20.

28 Jem Bendell, 'Deep Adaptation: A Map for Navigating Climate Tragedy', IFLAS Occasional Paper 2, University of Cumbria (2018), p. 2, p. 6, p. 12; Roy Scranton, *Learning to Die in the Anthropocene*, (City Light Books, 2015), p. 16.

29 Bendell, p. 13, p. 23. Bendell argues that we need a tripartite approach to Deep Adaptation involving 'resilience, relinquishment and restoration'.

30 Even Bendell himself admits this possibility, sometimes describing collapse as 'likely' or 'possible', rather than simply 'inevitable' (Bendell, p. 13, p. 19).

31 Rebecca Solnit, *A Paradise Built in Hell: The Extraordinary Communities that Arise in Disasters* (Penguin, 2010), p. 2, p. 8.

32 https://www.opendemocracy.net/en/transformation/what-will-you-say-your-grandchildren/.

33 Read and Alexander, p. 12.

34 https://www.overshootday.org/newsroom/press-release-july-2019-english/.

35 https://www.youtube.com/watch?v=sf4oW8OtaPY&t=778s.

36 Such thinking resonates with what naturalist Aldo Leopold called the 'land ethic', the idea that 'a thing is right when it tends to preserve the integrity, the stability, and the beauty of the biotic community' (Aldo Leopold, *A Sand County Almanac* (Oxford University Press, 1968), pp. 224–5).

37 Quote from the film *Planetary* (http://weareplanetary.com/).

38 Eno, 'The Big Here and Long Now'.

39 Janine Benyus, *Biomimcry: Innovation Inspired by Nature* (Perennial, 2002), p. 297; Rifkin, *Time Wars*, pp. 277–81.

9: Deep Democracy

1 David Hume, *A Treatise of Human Nature* (John Noon, 1739), Book 3, Section 7.

2 Dennis Thompson, 'Representing Future Generations: Political Presentism and Democratic Trusteeship', *Critical Review of International Social and Political Philosophy*, Vol. 13, No. 1 (2010): p. 17; Boston, p. xxvii.

3 https://www.independent.co.uk/news/world/europe/climate-change-2050-eu-eastern-europe-carbon-neutral-summit-countries-a8968141.html.

4 Michael K. MacKenzie, 'Institutional Design and Sources of Short-Termism', in Iñigo González-Ricoy and Axel Grosseries (eds), *Institutions for Future Generations* (Oxford University Press, 2016), p. 27.

5 William Nordhaus, 'The Political Business Cycle', *Review of Economic Studies*, Vol. 42, No. 2 (1975): p. 177, p. 179, p. 184.

6 MacKenzie, pp. 28–9.

7 Quoted in Mark Green (ed.), *The Big Business Reader on Corporate America* (Pilgrim Press, 1983), p. 179.

8 https://www.oxfordmartin.ox.ac.uk/videos/view/317.

9 Diamond, *Collapse*, p. 430.

10 MacKenzie, pp. 29–30; Barbara Adam, *Time* (Polity Press, 2004), pp. 136–43; Sabine Pahl, Stephen Sheppard, Christine Boomsma and Christopher Groves, 'Perceptions of Time in Relation to Climate Change', *WIREs Climate Change*, Vol. 5 (May/June 2014): p. 378; Ivor Crewe and Anthony King, *The Blunders of our Government* (Oneworld, 2014), p. 356; Simon Caney, 'Political Institutions and the Future', in Iñigo González-Ricoy and Axel Grosseries (eds), *Institutions for Future Generations* (Oxford University Press, 2016), pp. 137–8.

11 https://yougov.co.uk/topics/politics/articles-reports/2016/06/27/how-britain-voted.

12 Oxford Martin Commission, 'Now for the Long-Term: The Report of the Oxford Martin Commission for Future Generations', Oxford Martin School, Oxford University (2013), pp. 45–6.

13 https://www.who.int/antimicrobial-resistance/interagency-coordination-group/IACG_final_report_EN.pdf?ua=1&utm_source=newsletter &utm_medium=email&utm_campaign=newsletter_axiosscience&stream=science.

14 Eric Hobsbawm, *The Age of Capital, 1848–1875* (Weidenfeld & Nicolson, 1995), pp. 82–97.

15 https://www.theguardian.com/world/commentisfree/2019/mar/20/eco-fascism-is-undergoing-a-revival-in-the-fetid-culture-of-the-extreme-right. This growing turn against democracy is more broadly visible in the declining legitimacy of traditional political parties across the Western world, falling levels of trust in government, and the rise of far-right populism. There is even data to show this trend among younger generations: one study found that while 60 per cent of Europeans and Americans born in the 1950s believe it is essential to live in a democracy, only 45 per cent of Europeans and just over 30 per cent of Americans born in the 1980s share the same view (Robert Stefan Foa and Yascha Mounk, 'The Signs of Deconsolidaiton', *Journal of Democracy*, Vol. 28, No. 1 (2017)).

16 Examples include the European Intergenerational Fairness Index produced by the Intergenerational Foundation, the World Economic Forum's measure of 'intergenerational equity' in their Inclusive Development Index, Pieter Vanhuysse's Intergenerational Justice Index, the Hoftstede Model of Long-Term Orientation, and Stefan Wurster's measure of Ecological Sustainability ('Comparing Ecological Sustainability in Autocracies and Democracies', *Contemporary Politics*, Vol. 19, No. 1 (2013)).

17 McQuilkin, 'Doing Justice to the Future'.

18 For the purposes of this book, McQuilkin has produced an updated version of the ISI, based on the latest available data and making minor adjustments to some of its components.

19 See, for example, Joe Foweraker and Roman Krznaric, 'Measuring Liberal Democratic Performance: An Empirical and Conceptual Critique', *Political Studies*, Vol. 48, No. 4 (2000).

20 In relation to patchy data, a country such as Cuba might have scored well on the ISI but had to be omitted due to a lack of data on four of the ten measures. Cuba is the highest-ranked country in the Sustainable Development Index (Jason Hickel, 'The Sustainable Development Index: Measuring the Ecological Efficiency of Human Development in the Anthropocene', *Ecological Economics*, Vol. 167 (2020)). https://www.sustainabledevelopmentindex.org/.

21 V-Dem Institute, 'Democracy Facing Global Challenges: V-Dem Annual Democracy Report 2019', V-Dem Institute, University of Gothenburg (2019),

p. 53. Alternative democracy indices that were considered but not selected for the analysis included Polity IV, Freedom House and the EIU democracy index. We also considered other V-DEM measures such as Polyarchy.

22 The category of 'autocracy' includes a range of governmental forms, from military dictatorships and one-party states to hereditary monarchies and electoral regimes with strong authoritarian tendencies. A country is classified as a 'autocracy' if it scores 0.45 or below on the V-Dem Liberal Democracy Index. There is scholarly debate about where this cut-off point should be located. Some argue for a lower cut off point of 0.42 when using V-Dem data, whereas others favour 0.50 (Yuko Kasuya and Kota Mori, 'Better Regime Cutoffs for Continuous Democracy Measures', *Users Working Paper Series 2019:25*, The Varieties of Democracy Institute, University of Gothenburg, (2019)). In this analysis, 0.45 was chosen as a fair compromise position. Brunei has been classified as an autocracy and Belize as a democracy, although they are not included in the V-Dem Liberal Democracy Index due to lack of data and hence do not appear on the scatterplot itself (only in the subsequent analysis). A 'short-term' regime is one that scores 50 or below on the Intergenerational Solidarity Index, which is the mean score for all countries.

23 Boston, p. 170.

24 O'Brien and Ryan, p. 27; Schlomo Shoham and Nira Lamay, 'Commission for Future Generations in the Knesset: Lessons Learnt', in Joerg Chet Tremmel (ed.), *Handbook of Intergenerational Justice* (Edward Elgar, 2006), p. 254; Graham Smith, 'Enhancing the Legitimacy of Offices for Future Generations', *Political Studies* (2019), p. 5.

25 The Hungarian Ombudsman had its powers reduced in 2011 under a change in the constitution (Graham Smith, p. 4).

26 https://www.bbc.co.uk/iplayer/episode/m0006bjz/longtermism-how-to-think-in-deep-time-bbc-future-at-hay-festival; https://futuregenerations.wales/wp-content/uploads/2017/02/150623-guide-to-the-fg-act-en.pdf; http://www.if.org.uk/2019/07/11/how-can-wales-invest-in-climate-action-today-for-future-generations/.

27 https://futuregenerations.wales/news/future-generations-commissioner-for-wales-welcomes-brave-decision-by-first-minister-on-the-m4-relief-road/; https://www.ft.com/content/86d32314-86ca-11e9-a028-86cea8523dc2; http://www.assembly.wales/laid%20documents/gen-ld11694/gen-ld11694-e.pdf.

28 https://hansard.parliament.uk/lords/2019-06-20/debates/E11B7D05-3E68-4D7F-BF09-81E9312918C0/Policy-MakingFutureGenerations%E2%80%99Interests.

29 https://www.theguardian.com/commentisfree/2019/mar/15/capitalism-destroying-earth-human-right-climate-strike-children; https://www.worldfuturecouncil.org/need-un-high-commissioner-future-generations/; https://www.mrfcj.org/wp-content/uploads/2018/02/Global-Guardians-A-Voice-for-Future-Generations-Position-Paper-2018.pdf.

30 Graham Smith, pp. 4–9.

31 https://www.nationalobserver.com/2018/03/05/news/david-suzuki-fires-death-zone-trudeau-weaver-and-broken-system.

32 https://www.thersa.org/discover/publications-and-articles/matthew-taylor-blog/2019/03/deliberation.

33 David Owen and Graham Smith, 'Sortition, Rotation and Mandate: Conditions for Political Equality and Deliberative Reasoning', *Politics and Society*, Vol. 46, No. 3 (2018).

34 Graham Smith, p. 13. See also Rupert Read, 'The Philosophical and Democratic Case for a Citizens' Super-Jury to Represent and Defend Future People', *Journal of International Relations Research*, No. 3 (December 2013): pp. 15–19); Simon Caney, 'Democratic Reform, Intergenerational Justice and the Challenges of the Long-Term', Centre for the Understanding of Sustainability Prosperity, University of Surrey (2019), p. 12; Marit Hammond and Graham Smith, 'Sustainable Prosperity and Democracy – A Research Agenda', Centre for the Understanding of Sustainability Prosperity, Working Paper No. 8, University of Surrey (2017), p. 15; Stuart White, 'Parliaments, Constitutional Conventions, and Popular Sovereignty', *British Journal of Politics and International Relations*, Vol. 19, No. 2 (2017).

35 https://www.japanpolicyforum.jp/backnumber/no51/pt20190109210522.html.

36 The Cambridge political theorist David Runciman has argued (somewhat playfully) that six-year-olds be given the vote. I suggest 12 as an appropriate age for membership of a citizens' assembly, on the grounds that this is the moment of 'coming of age' in many cultures, signalling a turning point in

maturity. It would also give the young participants the opportunity to have already potentially received several years of citizenship education in school. https://www.talkingpoliticspodcast.com/blog/2018/129-democracy-for-young-people?rq=age%206.

37 Such powers are similar to those suggested by philosopher and Extinction Rebellion activist Rupert Read in his proposals for a 'third legislative house' of guardians to protect future generations (Rupert Read, *Guardians of the Future: A Constitutional Case for Representing and Protecting Future People* (Green House, 2011), pp. 9–14).

38 https://phys.org/news/2019-12-climate-activists-victory-dutch-court.html.

39 http://ecoactive.com/care-for-earth/earth-guardians; https://www.earthguardians.org/engage/2017/5/17.

40 https://www.teenvogue.com/story/xiuhtezcatl-martinez-explains-why-hes-fighting-climate-change.

41 https://www.ourchildrenstrust.org/juliana-v-us.

42 Joel Bakan, *The Corporation: The Pathological Pursuit of Profit and Power* (Free Press, 2004), p. 16.

43 O'Brien and Ryan, p. 36; Read, 'Guardians of the Future', p. 11; https://www.parliament.nz/en/get-involved/features/innovative-bill-protects-whanganui-river-with-legal-personhood/.

44 https://www.youtube.com/watch?v=8EuxYzQ65H4; https://eradicatingecocide.com/; https://www.stopecocide.earth/; http://www.earthisland.org/journal/index.php/magazine/entry/ecocide_the_fifth_war_crime/.

45 Decentralisation and intergenerational solidarity appear to be closely related: the ISI shares 42 per cent of its variation with an index of political, fiscal and administrative decentralisation published by the World Bank (Maksym Ivanya and Anwar Shah, 'How Close Is Your Government to its People? Worldwide Indicators on Localization and Decentralization', World Bank Policy Research Working Paper 6138, East Asia and Pacific Region (2012)).

46 Elinor Ostrom, *A Polycentric Approach for Coping with Climate Change*, World Bank Policy Research Working Paper 5095 (2009); Keith Carlisle and Rebecca L. Gruby, 'Polycentric Systems of Governance: A Theoretical Model for the Commons', *Policy Studies Journal*, Vol. 47, No. 4 (2017): pp. 927–52. Ostrom argued that polycentric governance is an especially effective way of managing scarce environmental resources. It reflects one of her eight fundamental design principles for managing the commons: 'build responsibility for governing the common resource in nested tiers from the lowest level up to the entire interconnected system'. http://www.onthecommons.org/8-keys-successful-commons#sthash.rzGC85Nc.dpbs.

47 Parag Khanna, *Connectography: Mapping the Future of Global Civilization* (Random House, 2016), p. 49; https://www.un.org/development/desa/publications/2018-revision-of-world-urbanization-prospects.html.

48 Khanna, p. 6, pp. 58–60.

49 This depiction of Europe as city-states was inspired by a graphic by John Donald.

50 https://www.nytimes.com/2015/07/17/opinion/the-art-of-changing-a-city.html; https://www.power-technology.com/features/100-club-cities-going-renewables/; http://www.cycling-embassy.dk/2017/07/04/copenhagen-city-cyclists-facts-figures-2017/.

51 https://www.scientificamerican.com/article/building-more-sustainable-cities/.

52 https://media.nesta.org.uk/documents/digital_democracy.pdf; https://www.thersa.org/discover/publications-and-articles/rsa-blogs/2017/09/the-digital-city-the-next-wave-of-open-democracy; https://datasmart.ash.harvard.edu/news/article/how-smart-city-barcelona-brought-the-internet-of-things-to-life-789.

53 Jana Belschner, 'The Adoption of Youth Quotas after the Arab Uprisings', *Politics, Groups, and Identities* (2018); https://budget.fin.gc.ca/2019/docs/plan/chap-05-en.html?wbdisable=true; https://www.gensqueeze.ca/win_intergenerational_analysis_in_public_finance; https://www.intergenerationaljustice.org/wp-content/uploads/2019/02/PP_Newcomer-Quota_2019.pdf.

54 My approach to historical change and theories of power has been profoundly influenced by Tzvetan Todorov's book *The Fragility of Goodness* (Weidenfeld & Nicolson, 2001). See also my analysis of how change happens in Krznaric, 'How Change Happens: Interdisciplinary Perspectives for Human Development'.

10: Ecological Civilisation

1 https://slate.com/business/2014/10/worlds-oldest-companies-why-are-so-many-of-them-in-japan.html; https://en.wikipedia.org/wiki/List_of_oldest_companies.

2 https://journal.accj.or.jp/masayoshi-sons-300-year-plan/.

3 Dominic Barton et al., 'Measuring the Economic Impact of Short-Termism', McKinsey Global Institute Discussion Paper (2017), pp. 1–2.

4 Although Korten was not the first to coin the term 'ecological civilisation', he has been one of its main popularisers in the West. Korten was born, appropriately enough, in the town of Longview, Washington. https://davidkorten.org/living-earth-econ-for-eco-civ/.

5 https://www.politifact.com/virginia/statements/2016/jul/06/mark-warner/mark-warner-says-average-holding-time-stocks-has-f/.

6 IPPR, 'Prosperity and Justice: A Plan for the New Economic – The Report of the IPPR Commission on Economic Justice', Institute for Public Policy Research, London (2018), p. 37; https://www.ft.com/content/d81f96ea-d43c-11e7-a303-9060cb1e5f44; Oxford Martin Commission, p. 46.

7 Ernst Ulrich von Weizsäcker and Anders Wijkman, *Come On! Capitalism, Short-termism, Population and the Destruction of the Planet – A Report to the Club of Rome* (Springer, 2018), p. 71.

8 http://worldif.economist.com/article/12121/debate.

9 https://science.sciencemag.org/content/366/6468/950.full.

10 https://www.nature.com/articles/476148a.

11 Meadows, Randers and Meadows, p. i, p. xi.

12 Herman Daly, *Ecological Economics and Sustainable Development: Selected Essays of Herman Daly* (Edward Elgar, 2007), p. 12.

13 Raworth, *Doughnut Economics*, p. 66, p. 143.

14 Herman Daly, *Beyond Growth: The Economics of Sustainable Development* (Beacon Press, 1996), p. 6.

15 The Doughnut has, for instance, become a framework for city planning in Amsterdam and other cities that are part of the C40 alliance of cities that are committed to taking action on climate change. https://medium.com/circleeconomy/the-amsterdam-city-doughnut-how-to-create-a-thriving-city-for-a-thriving-planet-423afd6b2892.

16 For the latest version of the Doughnut, including full details of dimensions and data, see Kate Raworth, 'A Doughnut for the Anthropocene: Humanity's Compass in the 21st Century', *The Lancet Planetary Health*, Vol. 1, No. 2 (2017). See also Raworth, *Doughnut Economics*, pp. 43–53; Will Steffen et al., 'The Anthropocene: From Global Change to Planetary Stewardship', *Ambio*, Vol. 40, No. 7 (2011): pp. 753–4.

17 https://hbr.org/2012/06/captain-planet; https://www.unilever.co.uk/sustainable-living/; https://www-nytimes-com.cdn.ampproject.org/c/s/www.nytimes.com/2019/08/29/business/paul-polman-unilever-corner-office.amp.html.

18 https://newint.org/features/web-exclusive/2017/04/13/inside-unilever-sustainability-myth.

19 https://www.opendemocracy.net/en/transformation/five-ways-to-curb-power-of-corporations/. Such a proposal is a variant of the financial transaction taxes advocated by figures such as US senator Bernie Sanders.

20 The success of the French government's measure is, however, a subject of debate. https://www.epi.org/blog/lessons-french-time-tax-high-frequency-trading/; https://www.theguardian.com/business/economics-blog/2014/apr/04/high-frequency-trading-markets-tobin-tax-financial-transactions-algorithms.

21 https://bcorporation.net/; https://www.forbes.com/sites/billeehoward/2017/10/01/joey-bergstein-cause-brand-purpose/#81aa5d345939.

22 John Kay, 'The Kay Review of UK Equity Markets and Long-Term Decision Making', Department for Innovation, Business and Skills, UK Government (2012), p. 13.

23 https://www.overshootday.org/newsroom/press-release-july-2019-english/.

24 https://www.opendemocracy.net/en/transformation/five-ways-to-curb-power-of-corporations/.

25 Daniel Christian Wahl, *Designing Regenerative Cultures* (Triarchy Press, 2016); Von Weizsäcker and Wijkman, pp. 101–44.

26 Raworth, *Doughnut Economics*, p. 212.

27 https://www.weforum.org/agenda/2019/02/companies-leading-way-to-circular-economy/.

28 https://fab.city; Michael Blowfield and Leo Johnson, *The Turnaround Challenge: Business and the City of the Future* (Oxford University Press, 2013), pp. 193–5.

29 https://www.ted.com/talks/marcin_jakubowski?language=en.

30 https://theconversation.com/how-fab-labs-help-meet-digital-challenges-in-africa-99202.

31 Michel Bauwens and Vasilis Niaros, 'Changing Society Through Urban Commons Transitions', P2P Foundation, Amsterdam (2017) pp. 21–2; http://commonsfilm.com/2019/09/18/futures-of-production-through-cosmo-local-and-commons-based-design/; http://wiki.commonstransition.org/wiki/Cosmo-localism_and_the_futures_of_material_production; https://environmentjournal.online/articles/plymouth-pledge-to-produce-everything-they-consume-by-2054/.

32 https://www.cdp.net/en/cities/world-renewable-energy-cities.

33 Jeremy Rifkin, *The Third Industrial Revolution: How Lateral Power is Transforming Energy, the Economy and the World* (Palgrave Macmillan, 2013), p. 62.

34 http://microgridmedia.com/bangladesh-emerges-hotbed-solar-microgrids-p2p-energy-trading/; https://unfccc.int/climate-action/momentum-for-change/ict-solutions/solshare; https://www.worldbank.org/en/results/2013/04/15/bangladesh-lighting-up-rural-communities.

35 Raworth, *Doughnut Economics*, pp. 176–8, p. 226.

36 Timothy Mitchell, *Carbon Democracy: Political Power in the Age of Oil* (Verso, 2011), pp. 19–21.

37 Monbiot, p. 8, pp. 69–70, pp. 84–5. See also Diamond, *Collapse*, p. 425.

38 Rewilding Britain, 'Rewilding and Climate Breakdown: How Restoring Nature Can Help Decarbonise the UK', Rewilding Britain, Steyning, UK, 2019, p. 4, p. 6; Bronson W. Griscom et al., 'Natural Climate Solutions', *PNAS*, Vol. 114, No. 44 (2017).

39 Wrigley, p. 3.

40 https://www.government.nl/topics/circular-economy.

41 Ryu Jaeyun, *5 Keys to Understanding China: A Samsung Veteran Shares How to Succeed in China* (Seoul Selection, 2016), p. x.

42 Sebastian Heilmann (ed.), *China's Political System* (Rowman & Littlefield, 2016), p. 302.

43 http://www.cwzg.cn/politics/201605/28471.html; http://www.cqhri.com/lddy_mobile/jdzs/20170911/12505426402.html.

44 https://thediplomat.com/2018/02/chinas-ai-agenda-advances/; Fei Xu, *The Belt and Road: The Global Strategy of China High-Speed Railway* (Truth and Wisdom Press/Springer, 2018), p. 189.

45 See President Xi's address to the 19th National Congress of the Communist Party of China: http://www.chinadaily.com.cn/china/19thcpcnationalcongress/2017-11/04/content_34115212.htm; https://www.ecowatch.com/china-ecological-civilization-2532760301.html.

46 https://www.ecowatch.com/china-floating-solar-farm-2516880461.html.

47 https://www.nytimes.com/2017/01/05/world/asia/china-renewable-energy-investment.html.

48 Barbara Finamore, *Will China Save the Planet?* (Polity Press, 2018), p. 1.

49 Heilmann, p. 361.

50 Lu Ding, 'China's "Two Century Goals": Progress and Challenges', *EAI Background Brief No. 1072*, National University of Singapore (2015); https://www.ecowatch.com/china-ecological-civilization-2532760301.html.

51 https://patternsofmeaning.com/2018/02/08/what-does-chinas-ecological-civilization-mean-for-humanitys-future/; https://www.independent.co.uk/news/world/asia/how-did-china-use-more-cement-between-2011-and-2013-than-the-us-used-in-the-entire-20th-century-10134079.html.

52 https://www.eia.gov/todayinenergy/detail.php?id=33092.

53 https://www.iea.org/weo/china/; Global Environmental Institute, 'China's Involvement in Coal-Fired Projects Along the Belt and Road', Global Environmental Institute, Beijing (2017), p. 1; Diamond, *Collapse*, pp. 372–3.

54 Richard Smith, 'China's Drivers and Planetary Ecological Collapse', *Real World Economics Review*, No. 82 (2017): p. 27; Björn Conrad, 'Environmental Policy: Curtailing Urban Pollution', in Sebastian Heilmann (ed.), *China's Political System* (Rowman & Littlefield, 2016), pp. 356–7; https://cleantechnica.com/2014/10/06/chinas-21st-century-dilemma-development-carbon-emissions/.

55 This is what Raworth (*Doughnut Economics*, pp. 259–60) describes as 'sufficient absolute decoupling'. See also Tim Jackson and Peter Victor, 'Unraveling the Claims for (and Against) Green Growth', *Science*, Vol. 366, No. 6468 (2019).

56 https://www.theguardian.com/books/2019/sep/21/vaclav-smil-interview-growth-must-end-economists.

57 Philip Alston, 'Climate Change and Poverty: Report of the Special Rapporteur on Extreme Poverty and Human Rights', A/HRC/41/39, UN Human Rights Council, Geneva (2018).

58 https://www.theguardian.com/inequality/2017/nov/14/worlds-richest-wealth-credit-suisse.

11: Cultural Evolution

1 Davis describes the ethnosphere as 'the cultural web of life' and defines it as 'the sum total of all thoughts and dreams, myths, ideas, inspirations and intuitions brought into being by the human imagination since the dawn of consciousness': https://www.ted.com/talks/wade_davis_on_endangered_cultures/transcript?language=en. The concept of the ethnosphere has some similarities with Pierre Teilhard de Chardin's notion of the 'noosphere' (Teilhard de Chardin, *The Phenomenon of Man* (Collins, 1970), pp. 200–4) and the idea of 'collective consciousness', as originally used by Émile Durkheim. But I don't use it to refer to any kind of reified entity with an independent existence; it is simply a concept to describe ideas that are widely shared by a large number of people and that shape their *Weltanschauung*.

2 David Sloan Wilson, *This View of Life: Completing the Darwinian Revolution* (Pantheon, 2019), p. xiv. See also Salk (*Anatomy of Reality*, p. 32, p. 114), who described cultural evolution as 'metabiological evolution'. He believed that evolution itself has evolved and has now partly become a matter of human choice.

3 Olivia Bina, Sandra Mateus, Lavinia Pereira and Annalisa Caffa, 'The Future Imagined: Exploring Fiction as a Means of Reflecting on Today's Grand Societal Challenges and Tomorrow's Options', *Futures* (June 2016): p. 170, p. 178, p. 180.

4 http://www.bbc.com/culture/story/20190110-how-science-fiction-helps-readers-understand-climate-change; https://www.theguardian.com/books/2015/aug/07/science-fiction-realism-kim-stanley-robinson-alistair-reynolds-ann-leckie-interview.

5 Olaf Stapledon, *Star Maker* (Methuen, 1937).

6 James Attlee, 'A Place That Exists Only in Moonlight: Katie Paterson & JMW Turner', Turner Contemporary, Margate, UK (2019).

7 *Guardian* (27 May 2015).

8 Public conversation between Katie Paterson, Elif Shafak and the author at the British Library, 8 October 2019.

9 Personal correspondence, 6 September 2018; https://www.wired.com/2007/07/interview-brian-eno-on-full-transcript/.

10 Personal conversation, 15 January 2019; http://superflux.in/index.php/work/futureenergylab/#; https://www.thenational.ae/arts-culture/uturis-symposium-weimar-2019-international-cultural-event-opens-with-praise-for-the-uae-1.877009.

11 https://www.popsci.com/virtual-reality-coral-reef-environment/; http://vhil.stanford.edu/pubs/2014/short-and-long-term-effects-of-embodied-experiences-in-immersive-virtual-environments/.

12 https://www.popsci.com/virtual-reality-coral-reef-environment/; http://vhil.stanford.edu/pubs/2014/short-and-long-term-effects-of-embodied-experiences-in-immersive-virtual-environments/.

13 Eric Hobsbawm, *Nations and Nationalism Since 1780: Programme, Myth, Reality* (Cambridge University Press, 1990), pp. 80–1.

14 Benedict Anderson, *Imagined Communities: Reflections on the Origin and Spread of Nationalism* (Verso, 1991), pp. 5–7.

15 Harari, *Homo Deus*, p. 380.

16 Personal correspondence with Roots of Empathy founder, Mary Gordon, 11 October 2019; www.rootsofempathy.org.

17 https://www.nfer.ac.uk/publications/FUTL21/FUTL21.pdf.

18 http://www.bullfrogfilms.com/guides/foninternhiroshhrnextgenguide.pdf.

19 http://www.politicalscience.hawaii.edu/courses/syllabi/dator/pols342_dator_S13.pdf; Jake Dunagan et al., 'Strategic Foresight Studio: A First-Hand Account of an Experiential Futures Course', *Journal of Futures Studies*, Vol. 23, No. 3 (2019), p. 62.

20 https://medium.com/@MrAlanCooper/ancestry-thinking-52fd3ff8da17.

21 https://sdgacademy.org/course/planetary-boundaries-human-opportunities/.

22 Lynn White, 'The Historical Roots of Our Ecologic Crisis', *Science*, Vol. 155, No. 3,767 (1967): p. 1205; Krznaric, 'How Change Happens: Interdisciplinary Perspectives for Human Development'.

23 Pope Francis.

24 Interview with Dr Tebaldo Vinciguerra, Pontifical Council for Justice and Peace, Rome, 20 April 2018.

25 https://www.theguardian.com/commentisfree/2018/dec/16/divestment-fossil-fuel-industry-trillions-dollars-investments-carbon.

26 https://thehumanist.com/magazine/may-june-2019/features/whats-really-behind-evangelicals-climate-denial.

27 https://www.pewforum.org/2012/12/18/global-religious-landscape-exec/.

28 Hawken himself sees the environmental movement not so much as a decentralised religion than as a biological immune response to the threat to planetary health (Paul Hawken, *Blessed Unrest: How the Largest Social Movement in History is Restoring Grace, Justice and Beauty to the World* (Penguin, 2008), Chapter 1).

29 I asked him this question at a public event at the Sheldonian Theatre, Oxford, 2 October 2019.

12: The Path of the Good Ancestor

1 Wallace-Wells, p. 12.

2 https://www.ted.com/talks/carole_cadwalladr_facebook_s_role_in_brexit_and_the_threat_to_democracy?language=en.

3 https://publications.iom.int/system/files/pdf/wmr_2018_en.pdf.

4 Friedman, p. xiv.

5 Theodore Zeldin, *Conversation* (Harvill Press, 1998), p. 14.

6 Wallace-Wells, p. 34.

7 James Scott, *Two Cheers for Anarchism: Six Easy Pieces on Autonomy, Dignity, and Meaningful Work and Play* (Princeton University Press, 2012), p. 141.

8 http://inside.sfuhs.org/dept/history/US_History_reader/Chapter14/ MLKriverside.htm.

9 https://theconversation.com/climate-change-yes-your-individual-action-does-make-a-difference-115169; https://www.vox.com/2016/5/4/11590396/ solar-power-contagious-maps.

Appendix: The Intergenerational Solidarity Index

1 McQuilkin, 'Doing Justice to the Future'; see also Jamie McQuilkin, 'Intergenerational Solidarity, Human Values and Consideration of the Future', thesis submitted for degree of Magister Scientiarum, Faculty of Psychology, University of Iceland (2015).

List of Illustrations

Bibliography

Ackerman, Frank, 'Debating Climate Economics: The Stern Review vs Its Critics', Report to Friends of the Earth UK (July 2007).

Adam, Barbara, *Time* (Polity Press, 2004).

Adam, Barbara and Chris Groves, *Future Matters: Marking, Making and Minding Futures for the 21st Century*. Also published as *Future Matters: Action, Knowledge, Ethics* (Brill, 2007).

Alston, Philip, 'Climate Change and Poverty: Report of the Special Rapporteur on Extreme Poverty and Human Rights', A/HRC/41/39, UN Human Rights Council, Geneva (2018).

Anderson, Benedict, *Imagined Communities: Reflections on the Origin and Spread of Nationalism* (Verso, 1991).

Andersson, Jenny, 'The Great Future Debate and the Struggle for the World', *The American Historical Review*, Vol. 117, No. 5 (2012): pp. 1402–10.

Asimov, Isaac, *Foundation* (Panther, 1960).

Attlee, James, 'A Place That Exists Only in Moonlight: Katie Paterson & JMW Turner', Turner Contemporary, Margate, UK (2019).

Bakan, Joel, *The Corporation: The Pathological Pursuit of Profit and Power* (Free Press, 2004).

Bardi, Ugo, *The Seneca Effect: Why Growth is Slow but Collapse is Rapid* (Springer, 2017).

Barkow, Jerome, Leda Cosmides and John Tooby, *The Adapted Mind: Evolutionary Psychology and the Generation of Culture* (Oxford University Press, 1996).

Barton, Dominic et al, 'Measuring the Economic Impact of Short-Termism', McKinsey Global Institute Discussion Paper (2017).

Bateson, Mary Catherine, *Composing a Further Life: The Age of Active Wisdom* (Vintage, 2011).

Baum, Seth et al, 'Long-Term Trajectories of Human Civilization', *Foresight*, Vol. 21, No. 1 (2019): pp. 53–83.

Baumeister, Roy, 'Collective Prospection: The Social Construction of the Future', in Seligman, Martin, Peter Railton, Roy Baumeister and Chandra Sripada, *Homo Prospectus* (Oxford University Press, 2016).

Baumeister, Roy et al., 'Everyday Thoughts in Time: Experience Sampling Studies of Mental Time Travel', *PsyArXiv* (2018).

Bauwens, Michel and Vasilis Niaros, 'Changing Society Through Urban Commons Transitions', P2P Foundation, Amsterdam (2017).

Bellassen, V. and S. Luyssaert, 'Carbon Sequestration: Managing Forests in Uncertain Times', *Nature*, Vol. 13, No. 506 (2014): pp. 153–5.

Belschner, Jana, 'The Adoption of Youth Quotas after the Arab Uprisings', *Politics, Groups, and Identities* (2018).

Bendell, Jem, 'Deep Adaptation: A Map for Navigating Climate Tragedy', IFLAS Occasional Paper 2, University of Cumbria (2018).

Benyus, Janine, *Biomimcry: Innovation Inspired by Nature* (Perennial, 2002).

Berridge, Kent and Morten Kringelbach, 'Affective Neuroscience of Pleasure: Reward in Humans and Animals', *Psychopharmacology (Berl)*, Vol. 199, No. 3 (2008): pp. 457–80.

Bidadanure, Juliana, 'Youth Quotas, Diversity, and Long-Termism: Can Young People Act as Proxies for Future Generations' in Iñigo González-Ricoy and Axel Grosseries (eds) *Institutions for Future Generations* (Oxford University Press, 2016).

Bina, Olivia, Sandra Mateus, Lavinia Pereira and Annalisa Caffa, 'The Future Imagined: Exploring Fiction as a Means of Reflecting on Today's Grand Societal Challenges and Tomorrow's Options', *Futures* (June 2016): pp. 166–84.

Blowfield, Michael and Leo Johnson, *The Turnaround Challenge: Business and the City of the Future* (Oxford University Press, 2013).

Borrows, John, 'Earth-Bound: Indigenous Resurgence and Environmental Reconciliation', in Michael Asch, John Borrows and James Tully (eds), *Resurgence and Reconciliation: Indigenous–Settler Relations and Earth Teachings* (University of Toronto Press, 2018).

Boston, Jonathan, *Governing the Future: Designing Democratic Institutions for a Better Tomorrow* (Emerald, 2017).

Brand, Stewart, *How Buildings Learn: What Happens After They're Built* (Phoenix, 1997).

Brand, Stewart, *The Clock of the Long Now: Time And Responsibility* (Phoenix, 1999).

Brundtland, Gro Harlen, *Report of the World Commission on Environment and Development: Our Common Future*, United Nations General Assembly document A/42/427 (1987).

Burke, Edmund, *Reflections on the Revolution in France* (J. Dodsley, 1790).

Bryson, Bill, *A Short History of Nearly Everything* (Black Swan, 2004).

Busby Grant, Jane, and Thomas Suddendorf, 'Recalling Yesterday and Predicting Tomorrow', *Cognitive Development*, Vol. 20 (2005): pp. 362–72 .

Caney, Simon, 'Political Institutions and the Future', in Iñigo González-Ricoy and Axel Grosseries (eds), *Institutions for Future Generations* (Oxford University Press, 2016): pp. 135–55.

Caney, Simon, 'Democratic Reform, Intergenerational Justice and the Challenges of the Long-Term', Centre for the Understanding of Sustainability Prosperity, University of Surrey (2019).

Capra, Fritjof, *The Turning Point: Science, Society and the Rising Culture* (Flamingo, 1983).

Carlisle, Keith and Rebecca L. Gruby, 'Polycentric Systems of Governance: A Theoretical Model for the Commons', *Policy Studies Journal*, Vol. 47, No. 4 (2017): pp. 927–52.

Carse, James, *Finite and Infinite Games: A Vision of Life as Play and Possibility* (Free Press, 1986).

Chermack, Thomas, *The Foundations of Scenario Planning: The Story of Pierre Wack* (Routledge, 2017).

Christian, David, *Maps of Time: An Introduction to Big History* (University of California Press, 2005).

Conrad, Björn, 'Environmental Policy: Curtailing Urban Pollution', in Sebastian Heilmann (ed.), *China's Political System* (Rowman & Littlefield, 2016).

Crewe, Ivor and Anthony King, *The Blunders of Our Government* (Oneworld, 2014).

Cumming, Graeme and Garry Peterson, 'Unifying Research on Social-Ecological Resilience and Collapse', *Trends in Ecology and Evolution*, Vol. 32, No. 9 (2017): pp. 695–713.

Daly, Herman, *Beyond Growth: The Economics of Sustainable Development* (Beacon Press, 1996).

Daly, Herman, *Ecological Economics and Sustainable Development: Selected Essays of Herman Daly* (Edward Elgar, 2007).

Darwin, Charles, *The Descent of Man* (Appleton and Company, 1889).

Dator, Jim, 'Decolonizing the Future', in Andrew Spekke (ed.), *The Next 25 Years: Challenges and Opportunities* (World Future Society, 1975).

de Jouvenel, Bertrand, *The Art of Conjecture* (Weidenfeld & Nicolson, 1967).

Diamond, Jared, 'Easter Island Revisited', *Science*, Vol. 317, No. 5,845 (2007): pp. 1692–4.

Diamond, Jared, *Collapse: How Societies Choose to Fail or Survive* (Penguin, 2011).

Ding, Lu, 'China's "Two Century Goals": Progress and Challenges', *EAI Background Brief No. 1072*, National University of Singapore (2015).

Donella Meadows, Jorgen Randers and Dennis Meadows, *Limits to Growth: The 30-Year Update* (Chelsea Green Publishing, 2005).

Dryzek, John, 'Institutions for the Anthropocene: Governance in a Changing Earth System', *British Journal of Political Studies*, Vol. 46, No. 4 (2014): pp. 937–56.

Dunagan, Jake et al., 'Strategic Foresight Studio: A First-Hand Account of an Experiential Futures Course', *Journal of Futures Studies*, Vol. 23, No. 3 (2019): pp. 57–74.

Eagleton, Terry, *Hope Without Optimism* (Yale University Press, 2015).

Ellis, Charles D., *The Partnership: The Making of Goldman Sachs* (Penguin, 2009).

Ennos, Roland, 'Aping Our Ancestor', *Physics World* (May 2014): pp. 32–6.

Eno, Brian, 'The Big Here and Long Now', Long Now Foundation, San Francisco (2000).

Finamore, Barbara, *Will China Save the Planet?* (Polity Press, 2018).

Flannery, Tim, *The Future Eaters: An Ecological History of the Australian Lands and People* (Secker & Warburg, 1996).

Foa, Robert Stefan and Yascha Mounk, 'The Signs of Deconsolidaiton', *Journal of Democracy*, Vol. 28, No. 1 (2017): pp. 5–15.

Foweraker, Joe and Roman Krznaric, 'Measuring Liberal Democratic Performance: An Empirical and Conceptual Critique', *Political Studies*, Vol 48, No. 4 (2000): pp. 759–87.

Frankl, Viktor, *Man's Search for Meaning: An Introduction to Logotherapy* (Hodder & Stoughton, 1987).

Freeman, Mark, Ben Groom and Michael Spackman, 'Social Discount Rates for Cost-Benefit Analysis: A Report for HM Treasury', HM Treasury, UK Government (2018).

Friedman, Milton, *Capitalism and Freedom* (Chicago University Press, 2002).

Frison, George, 'Paleoindian large mammal hunters on the plains of North America', *PNAS*, Vol. 95, No. 24 (1998): pp. 14,576–83.

Gidley, Jennifer M., *The Future: A Very Short Introduction* (Oxford University Press, 2017).

Gilbert, Daniel, *Stumbling on Happiness* (Harper Perennial, 2007).

Giono, Jean, *The Man Who Planted Trees* (Chelsea Green, 1985).

Gleick, James, *Time Travel: A History* (Fourth Estate, 2016).

Global Environmental Institute, 'China's Involvement in Coal-Fired Projects Along the Belt and Road', Global Environmental Institute, Beijing (2017).

Gould, Stephen Jay, *Time's Arrow, Time's Cycle: Myth and Metaphor in the Discovery of Geological Time* (Harvard University Press, 1987).

Gower, Barry S., 'What Do We Owe Future Generations?', in David E. Cooper and Joy A. Palmer (eds), *Environment in Question: Ethics and Global Issues* (Routledge, 1992).

Green, Mark (ed.), *The Big Business Reader on Corporate America* (Pilgrim Press, 1983).

Griscom, Bronson W. et al., 'Natural Climate Solutions', *PNAS*, Vol. 114, No. 44 (2017): pp. 11,654–11,650.

Halliday, Stephen, *The Great Stink of London: Sir Joseph Bazalgette and the Cleansing of the Victorian Metropolis* (Sutton Publishing, 2001).

Hammond, Marit and Graham Smith, 'Sustainable Prosperity and Democracy – A Research Agenda', Centre for the Understanding of Sustainability Prosperity, Working Paper No. 8, University of Surrey (2017).

Handy, Charles, *The Second Curve: Thoughts on Reinventing Society* (Random House Books, 2015).

Hanh, Thich Nhat, *Being Peace* (London, 1989).

Hanusch, Frederic and Frank Biermann, 'Deep-Time Organizations: Learning Institutional Longevity from History', *The Anthropocene Review* (2019): pp. 1–23.

Harari, Yuval Noah, *Homo Deus: A Brief History of Tomorrow* (Vintage, 2017).

Harari, Yuval Noah, *21 Lessons for the 21st Century* (Jonathan Cape, 2018).

Hawken, Paul, *Blessed Unrest: How the Largest Social Movement in History is Restoring Grace, Justice and Beauty to the World* (Penguin, 2008).

Hawkes, Kristen, 'The Grandmother Effect', *Nature*, Vol. 428, No. 128 (2004): pp. 128–9.

Heilmann, Sebastian (ed.), *China's Political System* (Rowman & Littlefield, 2016).

Hershfield, Hal, 'The Self Over Time', *Current Opinion in Psychology*, Vol. 26 (2019): pp. 72–5.

Hershfield, Hal et al., 'Increasing Saving Behavior Through Age-Progressed Renders of the Future Self', *Journal of Marketing Research*, Vol. 48 (2011): pp. S23–37.

Hickel, Jason, 'The Sustainable Development Index: Measuring the Ecological Efficiency of Human Development in the Anthropocene', *Ecological Economics*, Vol. 167 (2020).

HM Treasury, *The Green Book: Central Government Guidance on Appraisal and Evaluation* (HM Treasury, UK Government, 2018).

Hobsbawm, Eric, *Nations and Nationalism Since 1780: Programme, Myth, Reality* (Cambridge University Press, 1990).

Hobsbawm, Eric, *The Age of Capital, 1848–1875* (Weidenfeld & Nicolson, 1995).

Hume, David, *A Treatise of Human Nature* (John Noon, 1739).

Hyde, Lewis, *The Gift: How the Creative Spirit Transforms the World* (Canongate, 2006).

Intergovernmental Panel on Climate Change, *Climate Change 2014: Synthesis Report* (IPCC, 2014).

IPPR, 'Prosperity and Justice: A Plan for the New Economic – The Report of the IPPR Commission on Economic Justice', Institute for Public Policy Research, London (2018).

Ivanya, Maksym and Anwar Shah, 'How Close Is Your Government to its People? Worldwide Indicators on Localization and Decentralization', Policy Research Working Paper 6138, World Bank, East Asia and Pacific Region (2012).

Jackson, Tim, *Prosperity Without Growth: Foundations for the Economy of Tomorrow* (Routledge, 2016).

Jackson, Tim and Peter Victor, 'Unraveling the Claims for (and Against) Green Growth', *Science*, Vol. 366, No. 6,468 (2019): pp. 950–1.

Jaeyun, Ryu, *5 Keys to Understanding China: A Samsung Veteran Shares How to Succeed in China* (Seoul Selection, 2016).

Jeter, Kris, 'Ancestor Worship as an Intergenerational Linkage in Perpetuity', *Marriage & Family Review*, Vol. 16, Nos 1–2 (1991): pp. 195–217.

Johnson, Steven, *Farsighted: How We Make the Decisions That Matter Most* (Riverhead, 2018).

Jungk, Robert, *Tomorrow is Already Here: Scenes from a Man-Made Word* (Rupert Hart-Davis, 1954).

Kahn, Herman, *On Thermonuclear War* (Princeton University Press, 1960).

Kasuya, Yuko and Kota Mori, 'Better Regime Cutoffs for Continuous Democracy Measures', *Users Working Paper Series 2019:25*, The Varieties of Democracy Institute, University of Gothenburg, Sweden (2019).

Kay, John, 'The Kay Review of UK Equity Markets and Long-Term Decision Making', Department for Innovation, Business and Skills, UK Government (2012).

Khanna, Parag, *Connectography: Mapping the Future of Global Civilization* (Random House, 2016).

Kotre, John, *Make It Count: How to Generate a Legacy That Gives Meaning to Your Life* (The Free Press, 1995).

Kotre, John, 'Generative Outcome', *Journal of Aging Studies*, Vol. 9, No. 1 (1995): pp. 33–41.

Kringelbach, Morten, *The Pleasure Centre: Trust Your Animal Instincts* (Oxford University Press, 2009).

Kringelbach, Morten and Helen Phillips, *Emotion: Pleasure and Pain in the Brain* (Oxford University Press, 2014).

Krznaric, Roman, 'How Change Happens: Interdisciplinary Perspectives for Human Development', an Oxfam Research Report (Oxfam, 2007).

Krznaric, Roman, 'For God's Sake, Do Something! How Religions Can Find Unexpected Unity Around Climate Change', Human Development Occasional Papers, Human Development Report Office, United Nations Development Programme (2007).

Krznaric, Roman, 'Food Coupons and Bald Mountains: What the History of Resource Scarcity Can Teach Us About Tackling Climate Change', Human Development Occasional Papers, Human Development Report Office, United Nations Development Programme (2007).

Krznaric, Roman, *Empathy: Why It Matters, and How to Get It* (Rider Books, 2015).

Krznaric, Roman, *Carpe Diem Regained: The Vanishing Art of Seizing the Day* (Unbound, 2017).

Lansing, Stephen, *Perfect Order: Recognizing Complexity in Bali* (Princeton University Press, 2006).

Le Goff, Jacques, *Time, Work, and Culture in the Middle Ages* (Chicago University Press, 1980).

Le Goff, Jacques, *Medieval Civilization 400–1500* (Folio Society, 2011).

Leicester, Graham, *Transformative Innovation: A Guide to Practice and Policy* (Triarchy Press, 2016).

Lent, Jeremy, *The Patterning Instinct: A Cultural History of Humanity's Search for Meaning* (Prometheus, 2017).

Leopold, Aldo, *A Sand County Almanac* (Oxford University Press, 1968).

Lopez, Maria Alex, *Invisible Women* (Palibrio, 2013).

Lovins, Hunger, Stewart Wallis, Anders Wijkman, John Fullerton, *A Finer Future: Creating an Economy in Service to Life* (New Society Publishers, 2018).

Macfarlane, Robert, *Underland: A Deep Time Journey* (Hamish Hamilton, 2019).

MacKenzie, Michael K., 'Institutional Design and Sources of Short-Termism', in Iñigo González-Ricoy and Axel Grosseries (eds), *Institutions for Future Generations* (Oxford University Press, 2016).

Mary Robinson Foundation – Climate Justice, 'A Case for Guardians of the Future', Mary Robinson Foundation – Climate Justice Position Paper (February 2017).

Mary Robinson Foundation – Climate Justice, 'Global Guardians: A Voice for the Future', Mary Robinson Foundation – Climate Justice Position Paper (April, 2017).

McCarthy, Natasha, *Engineering: A Beginner's Guide* (Oneworld, 2009).

McPhee, John, *Basin and Range* (Farrar, Straus and Giroux, 1980).

McQuilkin, Jamie, 'Intergenerational Solidarity, Human Values and Consideration of the Future', thesis submitted for degree of Magister Scientiarum, Faculty of Psychology, University of Iceland (2015).

McQuilkin, Jamie, 'Doing Justice to the Future: A Global Index of Intergenerational Solidarity Derived from National Statistics', *Intergenerational Justice Review*, Vol. 4, No. 1 (2018): pp. 4–21.

Meadows, Donella, *Thinking in Systems: A Primer* (Earthscan, 2009).

Meadows, Donella, Dennis Meadows, Jorgen Randers and William Behrens, *The Limits to Growth* (Universe Books, 1972).

Meadows, Donella, Jorgen Randers and Dennis Meadows, *Limits to Growth: The 30-Year Update* (Chelsea Green, 2004).

Meiksins Wood, Ellen, *The Origin of Capitalism: A Longer View* (Verso, 2017).

Mischel, Walter, Yuichi Shoda and Monica Rodriguez, 'Delay of Gratification in Children', *Science*, Vol. 244, No. 4,907 (1989): pp. 933–98.

Mitchell, Timothy, *Carbon Democracy: Political Power in the Age of Oil* (Verso, 2011).

Modis, Theodore, 'Why the Singularity Cannot Happen', in A.H. Eden et al. (eds), *The Singularity Hypotheses, The Frontiers Collection* (Springer Verlag, 2012): pp. 311–39.

Monbiot, George, *Feral: Searching for Enchantment on the Frontiers of Rewilding* (Allen Lane, 2013).

Mumford, Lewis, *The Human Prospect* (Beacon Press, 1955).

Neihardt, John G., *Black Elk Speaks* (Excelsior, 2008).

Nicholls, Margaret, 'What Motivates Intergenerational Practices in Aotearoa/New Zealand', *Journal of Intergenerational Relationships*, Vol. 1, No. 1 (2003): pp. 179–81.

Nordhaus, William, 'The Political Business Cycle', *Review of Economic Studies*, Vol. 42, No. 2 (1975): pp. 169–90.

O'Brien, Mark and Thomas Ryan, 'Rights and Representation of Future Generations in United Kingdom Policy', Centre for the Study of Existential Risk, University of Cambridge (2017).

O'Connell, Mark, *To Be a Machine: Adventures Among Cyborgs, Utopians, Hackers, and the Futurists Solving the Modest Problem of Death* (Granta, 2017).

O'Leary, Maureen et al., 'The Placental Mammal Ancestor and the Post-K-Pg Radiation of Placentals', *Science*, Vol. 339, No. 6,120 (2013): pp. 662–7.

Ord, Toby, *The Precipice: Existential Risk and the Future of Humanity* (Bloomsbury, 2020).

Ostrom, Elinor, *A Polycentric Approach for Coping with Climate Change*, World Bank Policy Research Working Paper 5095 (2009).

Owen, David and Graham Smith, 'Sortition, Rotation and Mandate: Conditions for Political Equality and Deliberative Reasoning', *Politics and Society*, Vol. 46, No. 3 (2018): pp. 419–34.

Oxford Martin Commission, 'Now for the Long-Term: The Report of the Oxford Martin Commission for Future Generations', Oxford Martin School, Oxford University (2013).

Pahl, Sabine, Stephen Sheppard, Christine Boomsma and Christopher Groves, 'Perceptions of Time in Relation to Climate Change', *WIREs Climate Change*, Vol. 5 (May/June 2014): pp. 375–88.

Parfit, Derek, *Reasons and Persons* (Clarendon Press, 1987).

Passig, David, 'Future Time-Span as a Cognitive Skill in Future Studies', *Futures Research Quarterly* (Winter 2004): pp. 27–47.

Pinker, Steven, *Enlightenment Now: The Case for Reason, Science, Humanism and Progress* (Viking, 2018).

Pope Francis, 'Laudato Si'', Encyclical Letter of the Holy Father Francis, Vatican City, Rome (2015).

Porritt, Jonathon, *The World We Made* (Phaidon, 2013).

Princen, Thomas, 'Constructing the Long Term: The Positive Case in Climate Policy and Other Long Crises', Working Paper, Frederick A. and Barbara M. Erb Institute for Global Sustainable Enterprise, University of Michigan (2007).

Princen, Thomas, 'Long-Term Decision-Making: Biological and Psychological Evidence', *Global Environmental Politics*, Vol. 9, No. 3 (2009): pp. 9–19.

Railton, Peter, 'Introduction', in Martin Seligman, Peter Railton, Roy Baumeister and Chandra Sripada, *Homo Prospectus* (Oxford University Press, 2016).

Rameka, Lesley Kay, 'Kia whakatōmuri te haere whakamua: I walk backwards into the future with my eyes fixed on my past', *Contemporary Issues in Early Childhood*, Vol. 17, No. 4 (2017): pp. 37–398.

Raskin, Paul, 'Journey to Earthland: The Great Transition to Planetary Civilization', Tellus Institute, Boston (2016).

Ratey, John, *A User's Guide to the Brain* (Abacus, 2013).

Rawls, John, *A Theory of Justice* (Belknap Press, 1971).

Rawls, John, *Political Liberalism* (Columbia University Press, 1993).

Raworth, Kate, *Doughnut Economics: Seven Ways to Think Like a 21st-Century Economist* (Random House Books, 2017).

Raworth, Kate, 'A Doughnut for the Anthropocene: Humanity's Compass in the 21st Century', *The Lancet Planetary Health*, Vol. 1, No. 2 (2017): pp. 48–9.

Read, Rupert, *Guardians of the Future: A Constitutional Case for Representing and Protecting Future People* (Green House, 2011).

Read, Rupert, 'The Philosophical and Democratic Case for a Citizens' Super-Jury to Represent and Defend Future People', *Journal of International Relations Research*, No. 3 (December 2013): pp. 5–29.

Read, Rupert and Samuel Alexander, *This Civilization Is Finished: Conversations on the End of Empire – and What Lies Beyond* (Simplicity Institute, 2019).

Rees, Martin, *On the Future: Prospects for Humanity* (Princeton University Press, 2018).

Rewilding Britain, 'Rewilding and Climate Breakdown: How Restoring Nature Can Help Decarbonise the UK', Rewilding Britain, Steyning, UK (2019).

Rifkin, Jeremy, *Time Wars: The Primary Conflict in Human History* (Touchstone, 1987).

Rifkin, Jeremy, *Biosphere Politics: A New Consciousness for a New Century* (Crown, 1991).

Rifkin, Jeremy, *The Third Industrial Revolution: How Lateral Power is Transforming Energy, the Economy and the World* (Palgrave Macmillan, 2013).

Roberts, W. A., 'Are Animals Stuck in Time?', *Psychological Bulletin*, Vol. 128, No. 3 (2002): pp. 473–89.

Saffo, Paul, 'Six Rules for Effective Forecasting', *Harvard Business Review* (July–August 2007).

Sagan, Carl, *Pale Bluet Dot: A Vision of the Human Future in Space* (Ballantine Books, 1997).

Salk, Jonas, 'Are We Being Good Ancestors?', Acceptance Speech for the Jawaharal Nehru Award for International Understanding, New Delhi, 10 January 1977. Reprinted in *World Affairs: The Journal of International Issues*, Vol. 1, No. 2 (December 1992): pp. 16–18.

Salk, Jonas, *Anatomy of Reality: Merging of Intuition and Reason* (Columbia University Press, 1983).

Salk, Jonas and Jonathan Salk, *A New Reality: Human Evolution for a Sustainable Future* (City Point Press, 2018).

Salk, Jonathan, 'Planetary Health: A New Perspective', *Challenges*, Vol. 10, No. 7 (2019): pp. 1–7.

Sanders, Michael and Sarah Smith, 'Can Simple Prompts Increase Bequest Giving? Field Evidence from a Legal Call Centre', *Journal of Economic Behaviour and Organization*, Vol. 125(C) (2016): pp. 179–91.

Sanders, Michael, Sarah Smith, Bibi Groot and David Nolan, 'Legacy Giving and Behavioural Insights', Behavioural Insights Team, University of Bristol (2016).

Schubotz, Ricarda, 'Long-Term Planning and Prediction: Visiting a Construction Site in the Human Brain', in W. Welsch et al. (eds), *Interdisciplinary Anthropology* (Springer-Verlag, 2011).

Schwartz, Peter, *The Art of the Long View: Planning the Future in an Uncertain World* (Currency, 1991).

Scott, James, *Seeing Like a State: How Certain Schemes to Improve the Human Condition Have Failed* (Yale University Press, 1998).

Scott, James, *Two Cheers for Anarchism: Six Easy Pieces on Autonomy, Dignity, and Meaningful Work and Play* (Princeton University Press, 2012).

Scranton, Roy, *Learning to Die in the Anthropocene* (City Lights Books, 2015).

Seligman, Martin, Peter Railton, Roy Baumeister and Chandra Sripada, *Homo Prospectus* (Oxford University Press, 2016).

Seuss, Dr., *The Lorax* (HarperCollins, 1997).

Shoham, Shlomo and Nira Lamay, 'Commission for Future Generations in the Knesset: Lessons Learnt', in Joerg Chet Tremmel (ed.), *Handbook of Intergenerational Justice* (Edward Elgar, 2006), pp. 244–81.

Skrimshire, Stefan, 'Deep Time and Secular Time: A Critique of the Environmental "Long View"', *Theory, Culture and Society*, Vol. 36, No. 1 (2018): pp. 63–81.

Slaughter, Richard, 'Long-Term Thinking and the Politics of Reconceptualization', *Futures*, Vol. 28, No. 1 (1996): pp. 75–86.

Smith, Graham, 'Enhancing the Legitimacy of Offices for Future Generations', *Political Studies* (2019).

Smith, Richard, 'China's Drivers and Planetary Ecological Collapse', *Real World Economics Review*, No. 82 (2017).

Solnit, Rebecca, *A Paradise Built in Hell: The Extraordinary Communities that Arise in Disasters* (Penguin, 2010).

Son, Hyeonju, 'The History of Western Futures Studies: An Exploration of the Intellectual Traditions and Three-Phase Periodization', *Futures* Vol. 66 (February 2015): pp. 120–37.

Stapledon, Olaf, *Star Maker* (Methuen, 1937). http://utenberg.net.au/ebooks06/0601841.txt

Stapledon, Olafm *Last And First Men* (Millennium, 1999).

Steffen, Will et al., 'The Anthropocene: From Global Change to Planetary Stewardship', *Ambio*, Vol. 40, No. 7 (2011): pp. 739–61.

Steffen, Will et al., 'The Trajectory of the Anthropocene: The Great Acceleration', *The Anthropocene Review*, Vol. 2, No. 1 (2015): pp. 81–98.

Steffen, Will, Johan Rockström et al, 'Trajectories of the Earth System in the Anthropocene', *PNAS*, Vol. 115, No. 33 (2019): pp. 8,252–9.

Stern, Nicholas, *The Economics of Climate Change: The Stern Review* (Cambridge University Press, 2014).

Straus, Lawrence Guy, 'Upper Paleolithic Hunting Tactics and Weapons in Western Europe', *Archeological Papers of the American Anthropological Association*, Vol. 4, No. 1 (1993): pp. 89–93.

Suzuki, David, *The Legacy: An Elder's Vision for Our Sustainable Future* (Greystone Books, 2010).

Tainter, Joseph, 'Problem Solving: Complexity, History, Sustainability', *Population and Environment: A Journal of Interdisciplinary Studies*, Vol. 22, No. 1 (2000): pp. 3–41.

Taleb, Nassim Nicholas, *The Black Swan: The Impact of the Highly Improbable* (Penguin, 2007).

Teilhard de Chardin, Pierre, *The Phenomenon of Man* (Collins, 1970).

Thompson, Dennis, 'Representing Future Generations: Political Presentism and Democratic Trusteeship', *Critical Review of International Social and Political Philosophy*, Vol. 13, No. 1 (2010): pp. 17–37.

Thompson, E.P., 'Time, Work Discipline and Industrial Capitalism', *Past & Present*, Vol. 38, No. 1 (1967): pp. 56–97.

Thorp, Jennifer, 'New College's Hall and Chapel Roofs', manuscript, New College, Oxford (2009).

Todorov, Tzvetan, *The Fragility of Goodness: Why Bulgaria's Jews Survived the Holocaust* (Weidenfeld & Nicolson, 2001).

Toffler, Alvin, *Future Shock* (Pan, 1971).

Tonn, Bruce E., 'Philosophical, Institutional, and Decision Making Frameworks for Meeting Obligations to Future Generations', *Futures*, Vol. 95 (2017): pp. 44–57.

Tonn, Bruce E., Angela Hemrick and Fred Conrad, 'Cognitive Representations of the Future: Survey Results', *Futures*, Vol. 38 (2006): pp. 810–29.

Totman, Conrad, *The Green Archipelago: Forestry in Pre-Industrial Japan* (Ohio University Press, 1989).

Totman, Conrad, *A History of Japan* (Blackwell, 2005).

Tremmel, Joerg Chet (ed.), *Handbook of Intergenerational Justice* (Edward Elgar, 2006).

United Nations Development Programme, *Human Development Report 2007/8: Fighting Climate Change – Human Solidarity in a Divided World* (UNDP, 2007).

Van der Leeuw, Sander, 'The Archaeology of Innovation: Lessons for Our Times', in Carlson Curtis and Frank Moss (eds), *Innovation: Perspectives for the 21st Century* (BBVA, 2010).

Van der Leeuw, Sander, David Lane and Dwight Read, 'The Long-Term Evolution of Social Organization', in David Lane et al. (eds), *Complexity Perspectives in Innovation and Social Change* (Springer, 2009).

Van Hensbergen, Gijs, *The Sagrada Família: Gaudí's Heaven on Earth* (Bloomsbury, 2017).

Van Schoubroeck, Frank and Harm Kool, 'The Remarkable History of Polder Systems in the Netherlands', FAO, Rome (2010).

V-Dem Institute, 'Democracy Facing Global Challenges: V-Dem Annual Democracy Report 2019', V-Dem Institute, University of Gothenburg (2019).

Venkataraman, Bina, *The Optimist's Telescope: Thinking Ahead in a Reckless Age* (Riverhead, 2019).

Von Weizsäcker, Ernst Ulrich and Anders Wijkman, *Come On! Capitalism, Short-termism, Population and the Destruction of the Planet – A Report to the Club of Rome* (Springer, 2018).

Vrousalis, Nicholas, 'Intergenerational Justice: A Primer', in Iñigo González-Ricoy and Axel Grosseries (eds), *Institutions for Future Generations* (Oxford University Press, 2016), pp. 49–64.

Wack, Pierre, 'Scenarios: Unchartered Waters Ahead', *Harvard Business Review* (September 1985): pp. 73–89.

Wack, Pierre, 'Scenarios: Shooting the Rapids', *Harvard Business Review* (November, 1985): pp. 139–50.

Wade-Benzoni, Kimberley, 'Legacy Motivations and the Psychology of Intergenerational Decisions', *Current Opinion in Psychology*, Vol. 26 (April 2019): pp. 19–22.

Wade-Benzoni, Kimberly et al, 'It's Only a Matter of Time: Death, Legacies, and Intergenerational Decisions', *Psychological Science*, Vol. 23, No. 7 (2012): pp. 704–9.

Wahl, Daniel Christian, *Designing Regenerative Cultures* (Triarchy Press, 2016).

Wallace-Wells, David, *The Unhabitable Earth: A Story of the Future* (Allen Lane, 2019).

Wells, H.G., *The Discovery of the Future* (B.W. Huebsch, 1913).

Wells, H.G., *The Conquest of Time* (Watts, 1942).

White, Lynn, 'The Historical Roots of Our Ecologic Crisis', *Science*, Vol. 155, No. 3,767 (1967): pp. 1203–7.

White, Stuart, 'Parliaments, Constitutional Conventions, and Popular Sovereignty', *British Journal of Politics and International Relations*, Vol. 19, No. 2 (2017).

Whybrow, Peter, *The Well-Tuned Brain: A Remedy for a Manic Society* (Norton, 2016).

Wilson, David Sloan, *This View of Life: Completing the Darwinian Revolution* (Pantheon, 2019).

Wright, Ronald, *A Short History of Progress* (Canongate, 2004).

Wrigley, E. A., *Energy and the English Industrial Revolution* (Cambridge University Press, 2010).

Wurster, Stefan, 'Comparing Ecological Sustainability in Autocracies and Democracies', *Contemporary Politics*, Vol. 19, No. 1 (2013).

Xu, Fei, *The Belt and Road: The Global Strategy of China High-Speed Railway* (Truth and Wisdom Press/Springer, 2018).

Zaval, Lisa, Ezra M. Markowitz and Elke U. Weber, 'How Will I Be Remembered? Conserving the Environment for the Sake of One's Legacy', *Psychological Science*, Vol. 26, No. 2 (2015): pp. 231–6.

Zeldin, Theodore, *Conversation* (Harvill Press, 1998).

Index

Page references in *italics* indicate images.

Index

Index

Index